*The QuickBooks Farm Accou...*
*Cookbook,™ Volume II:*

# Raised Farm Production Inventories, Sales, and More...

## By Mark Wilsdorf

Published by

FLAGSHIP TECHNOLOGIES, INC.
MADISON, MISSOURI, USA
www.goflagship.com

Part of the QuickBooks Cookbook™ Series...

# The QuickBooks Farm Accounting Cookbook™, Volume II: Raised Farm Production, Inventories, Sales, and More...

ISBN: 978-0-9673083-2-6

## PUBLISHER

Flagship Technologies, Inc.
14976 Monroe Road 1039
Madison, MO 65263
www.goflagship.com

## COPYRIGHT

Copyright © 2017 Flagship Technologies, Inc. All rights reserved. No part of this document may be reproduced or transmitted in any form, by any means, without prior express written permission of the publisher, except for the following provisions WHICH APPLY ONLY TO E-BOOK EDITIONS:

You MAY install an e-book edition on the number of computer devices specified at the time of purchase.

You MAY print portions of an e-book edition for personal use, subject to the page count limitations of this edition. However, you MAY NOT distribute copies of any part of this e-book or printed pages to anyone, whether for a fee or not.

These provisions are SUBJECT TO CHANGE WITHOUT NOTICE in future editions or revisions.

## TRADEMARKS

QuickBooks is a registered trademark of Intuit. ManagePLUS, FormCalc, FormCalc SST, and QuickBooks Cookbook are trademarks of Flagship Technologies, Inc. Other brand and product names used in this book may be trademarks, registered trademarks, or trade names of their respective holders.

## DISCLAIMERS

All advice and recommendations provided in this book are opinions of the author and may not be appropriate for your specific accounting and/or tax situation. Therefore you assume all risk in interpreting, applying, and using the advice and recommendations provided herein.

Seek the advice of an accounting or tax professional to review your accounting software setup and operating practices, and for answers to tax and legal questions. No part of this book should be construed as professional advice on tax or legal matters, accounting, business management, or any other endeavor.

All names and other likenesses to companies, persons, or places mentioned in this book are coincidental and not intended as an endorsement or comment of any kind about any person or business.

*Revised: 1/26/2017*

## Table of Contents

| | | |
|---|---|---|
| Chapter 1 | **Introduction** ............................................................................................ 1 | |
| | About this Book ........................................................................................... 1 | |
| | Why YOU Should be Using the Inventory Features of QuickBooks! ............. 8 | |
| | Three QuickBooks Farm Inventory Problems, and their Solutions ............. 10 | |
| | The "Ground Rules" ................................................................................. 12 | |
| Chapter 2 | **About Farm Inventories in QuickBooks** ............................................... 15 | |
| | Three Types of Cash Basis Inventory ......................................................... 15 | |
| | Accounting for Raised Inventories ............................................................ 16 | |
| | Accounting for Resale Inventories ............................................................. 23 | |
| | Accounting for Expense-Related Inventories ............................................. 26 | |
| Chapter 3 | **Overview: Working with Raised Inventories in QuickBooks** ................ 27 | |
| Chapter 4 | **Visual Inventory Examples** .................................................................. 31 | |
| | Raised Grain Example: Soybeans ............................................................ 31 | |
| | Raised Livestock Example: Beef Calves ................................................... 45 | |
| Chapter 5 | **Inventory Nuts & Bolts** ......................................................................... 59 | |
| | Accounts for Raised Inventories ............................................................... 59 | |
| | Chart of Accounts Reference .................................................................... 67 | |
| | Items for Raised Inventories ..................................................................... 68 | |
| | Getting Beginning Inventories into QuickBooks ........................................ 90 | |
| | How to Take a Physical Inventory Count .................................................. 91 | |
| | How to Make an Inventory Adjustment .................................................... 97 | |
| Chapter 6 | **Production, Sales, and Common Transactions** ................................... 111 | |
| | Sales of Raised Inventory ....................................................................... 111 | |
| | Adding Farm Production to Inventory .................................................... 123 | |
| | Adjusting for Inventory Losses (Livestock Deaths, Spoilage, etc.) ........... 129 | |
| | Adjusting for Inventory Usage (as Livestock Feed, etc.) ......................... 135 | |
| | Closing Out a Raised Inventory ............................................................. 145 | |
| Chapter 7 | **Other Inventory Adjustments and Transactions** ................................. 149 | |
| | How to Value Raised Inventories ............................................................ 149 | |

|  |  |  |
|---|---|---|
|  | Purchasing "Raised" Inventory | 155 |
|  | Transferring Raised Items to Fixed Assets | 160 |
|  | Moving Inventories from One Stage of Production to Another | 168 |
|  | Questions, Answers, and Special Situations | 171 |
| **Chapter 8** | **Depositing Payments You Have Received** | **175** |
| **Chapter 9** | **Inventory Information and Reports** | **181** |
|  | Where to Find the Information You Want | 181 |
|  | The Item List | 183 |
|  | The Inventory Center | 187 |
|  | Common Reports | 189 |
|  | Preparing Income Tax Reports | 194 |
| **Chapter 10** | **Tracking Inventory by Location** | **199** |
|  | Setting Up Subitems for Inventory Locations | 200 |
|  | Adding Production to Inventory, by Location | 204 |
|  | Entering Sales, by Location | 205 |
|  | Reports by Inventory Location | 208 |
|  | Other Activities for Location Subitems | 212 |
| **Chapter 11** | **Tracking Cash Sales Contracts** | **215** |
|  | Using Jobs to Represent Contracts | 218 |
|  | Entering a Sales Contract | 220 |
|  | Modifying or Canceling a Contract | 225 |
|  | Recording Deliveries on a Contract | 226 |
|  | Entering Progress Payments & Advances | 240 |
|  | Getting Information about Contracts and Deliveries | 243 |
|  | Contract Settlement/Payment/Closeout | 249 |
|  | More about Contract Shortages | 267 |
|  | Handling Other Contract Types | 270 |
|  | QuickBooks Pro: Using Subitems to Account for Cash Sale Contracts | 274 |
| **Chapter 12** | **Tracking Inventories for Others (Landlords, etc.)** | **285** |
|  | John Doe Farms' Business Situation | 286 |
|  | Setting up Accounts and Items | 287 |

    Adding Production to Inventory ................................................................................. 292
    Entering Sales of Landlord Inventories ....................................................................... 296
    "Settling up" with Landlords After Sales are Completed ............................................. 300
    Getting Inventory Reports and Information ................................................................ 309

**Chapter 13 Appendix** .............................................................................................. **311**
    Other Books from Flagship Technologies .................................................................... 311
    Software Products from Flagship Technologies .......................................................... 312

This page is intentionally blank.

# CHAPTER 1

# Introduction

| About this chapter | This chapter gives you an overview of the book and tells why you should consider keeping track of at least some farm inventories in QuickBooks. |
|---|---|

## About this Book

> *"This is not the kind of book you read cover to cover...*
> *it is the kind you read in bits and pieces,*
> *just to find out what you want to know."*

### This Book is About Cash Basis Accounting, not Accrual

This book is focused *exclusively* on cash basis accounting because (1) it is the most widely used accounting method on farms and ranches in the U.S., and (2) cash and accrual inventory procedures are often very different, which makes a combined discussion of both approaches complicated and confusing. (You will find some accrual accounting notes and comments throughout the book however, mostly to explain accounting concepts or the differences between the cash and accrual approaches.)

Also, this book is written with an eye toward something every farm business must do: keep records for preparing income taxes. All of the discussion and examples are built upon the idea that every accounting action you take must support the underlying goal of keeping records which will support preparing and filing U.S. Federal income taxes.

 **Do not consider anything in this book as advice on tax-related matters.** Tax laws change often and each farm business situation is unique, so use this book as a source of ideas but seek the advice of a professional tax preparer for recommendations specific to your farm business.

Finally, if your goal is to keep accrual accounting records in QuickBooks you may glean some useful ideas from this book. However, understand that most of the step-by-step procedures *are not appropriate* for the accrual inventory and accounting tasks you need to do.

 **Even cash basis recordkeepers should use *some* of QuickBooks' accrual features...**

A secondary goal of this book is to demonstrate that almost every cash basis recordkeeper should consider using some of the accrual features of QuickBooks. The Bills feature, in particular, is one which most farmers should use. And in some farming operations—especially those that need to send bills to the farm's customers—the Invoices features should be used. QuickBooks has the ability to reverse the accrual effects of these features on reports, making it easy to prepare cash basis income and expense reports.

 **In case you wonder about filing QuickBooks accrual features vs. filing income taxes on an accrual basis**

Filing Federal income taxes on an accrual basis has advantages for some farm businesses, though they are in the minority. In case you are wondering whether you could have the records needed for filing income taxes on accrual basis simply by using QuickBooks' accrual features, the answer is "No".

The IRS requires using a specific approach for calculating accrual farm income and expenses, which is related to standard accrual accounting procedures but not exactly the same. Consult a tax professional if you have questions about the recordkeeping requirements for filing income taxes on an accrual basis.

# About this Book

## This Book is Written for the Desktop Editions of QuickBooks

All of the screenshots, examples, and procedures in this book are for the desktop editions of QuickBooks: Pro, Premier, Accountant, and Enterprise.

Specifically, the book's screenshots are mostly from the QuickBooks Pro and Premier 2016 editions. However, if you use another edition you will notice few differences and should have no trouble following any of the steps for various inventory activities. Likewise, if you have a QuickBooks version which is a few years older or newer than the 2016 editions you should be able to easily follow all of the steps in this book. (The layout of QuickBooks' menus, windows, and forms usually only changes in minor ways from year to year.)

## Why not QuickBooks Online?

 **If you use QuickBooks Online most of this book *will not* be useful to you.** The inventory features in QuickBooks Online are too different from those in the desktop editions, so most of the techniques in this book do not apply to QuickBooks Online.

QuickBooks Online is Intuit's newest accounting software product. It is completely cloud based (accessible over an Internet connection, not installed on your local/desktop computer), and differs from the desktop editions in a number of ways. Here are some reasons why this book does not deal with farm inventories in QuickBooks Online:

❖ QuickBooks Online's inventory system uses FIFO (first-in, first-out) inventory method, while the desktop editions use the Average Costing method. For this reason, many inventory activities must be approached differently in QuickBooks Online.

❖ The inventory system used by the desktop editions can be easily "bent to the purpose" of cash basis farm inventories, while the FIFO system used by QuickBooks Online cannot. Most of the simple tricks and workarounds described in this book cannot be used in QuickBooks Online.

❖ As this is written, many QuickBooks Online users are still unhappy with how its inventory system works. Some of the deficiencies can be remedied by purchasing add-on software for inventory management—at additional cost—but so far, none of those inventory add-ons appear to be a good fit for typical, cash basis agricultural inventories.

Flatly stated, many of the useful and valuable things you can do with inventories in the desktop editions *simply cannot be done in QuickBooks Online*—at least not yet.

★ **Flagship Technologies, Inc. has a free ebook** comparing QuickBooks Online and the QuickBooks desktop editions, available at: 🌐 www.goflagship.com.

## Who this Book is Written "To"

This book is written to "you", with the assumption that you are someone directly responsible for keeping the accounting records of a farm business. If that is not so, I assume that you at least have an interest in farm accounting with QuickBooks. Maybe you are an Extension Service educator, a farm lender, a vocational agriculture teacher or student, or a professional accountant. The book is aimed at intermediate-level QuickBooks users, but with plenty of explanation, screenshots, and examples to let beginning users follow along with the step-by-step procedures easily.

The discussion often refers to "you" or "your" when talking about writing checks, making bank deposits, adjusting inventories, and so on. But that is just a handy, conversational way of referring to *the farm business* you are working with. You may be the owner, a partner, an employee, an advisor, or some other interested party, but the "you" actually refers to the farm business.

By the way, though this book is easy enough for beginning QuickBooks users it is not the best place to start if you are very new to QuickBooks, because it provides very little information about setting up QuickBooks for a farm business. If help with setting up QuickBooks, have a look at the first book in this series, 🌐 *The QuickBooks Farm Accounting Cookbook™, Volume I*, available at 🌐 www.goflagship.com.

Finally, I should mention that techniques and ideas in this book are meant for application to farm and ranch accounting in the U.S. They will be useful in other countries as well but in some instances may not be a good fit—especially where the accounting requirements or taxation system are very different from those in the U.S. Always consult an accounting or tax professional if you are unsure whether a particular technique described in this book is appropriate to use in your country.

## About FFSC Guidelines

The Farm Financial Standards Council (FFSC, www.ffsc.org) is made up of people with an interest in farm financial reporting and analysis, from all across agriculture. It includes representatives from agricultural lending, universities, computer software developers, and others. The FFSC works toward improvement in and standardization of accounting practices and financial reporting for agriculture.

If you are aware of the FFSC's guidelines for financial reporting you may be asking, "How does this book relate to the FFSC guidelines?" Most people who are familiar with them will tell you that few farm businesses can follow the guidelines without assistance from a professional accountant. Preparing financial statements according to the FFSC guidelines normally requires two things: a "good" (complete and accurate) set of accounting records, and an accounting professional who can make the necessary adjustments to produce FFSC-compliant reports from those records.

A primary goal of this book—and of the entire QuickBooks Cookbook™ series—is to help you get more and better management information from your bookkeeping efforts in QuickBooks. And better management information can only come from a "good" set of accounting records. The procedures and explanations in this book will help you improve the completeness and accuracy of your accounting records. Then if you ever want to prepare FFSC-compliant financial reports, your records should be better suited for getting that done.

Chapter 1 - Introduction

**"Should I be using FFSC-compliant accounting software?"**

Several good agriculture-specific accounting systems are available, and some may claim to be "FFSC compliant". What that claim is really telling you is that the accounting system uses procedures which *lead in the direction of* FFSC-compliant financial reporting. No accounting system, by itself, can produce FFSC-compliant financial reports without also applying considerable accounting expertise.

QuickBooks is not "FFSC compliant"; but then, neither is any other accounting system, really. QuickBooks has features which make the entire accounting job easier however, and in that way it encourages keeping better accounting records than most people would otherwise have.

## The "Farm vs. Ranch" thing...

I once knew a man who had eleven acres of land on the edge of a small town in the Midwest. He was a cattle buyer, and had grown up as a rancher's son—somewhere in the Oklahoma Panhandle I think. Where he grew up, there were only two kinds of people—ranchers and farmers. You were *either* a rancher or a farmer, not a combination of both (a local sentiment left over, I suppose, from the range wars of the 1880s).

But in the area around the small town where he now lived, most of the cattlemen considered themselves farmers (they had both crops and cattle). Still, he was proud to call his vast spread—all eleven acres—a ranch. He had the ranch name painted on both doors to his pickup truck and got a sort of irritated look on his face if someone mentioned his "farm".

The point of this story? Regardless of what term I might choose for talking about the business of agricultural production I will likely irritate someone, at least a little bit. A few of the choices are: farm, ranch, plantation, hacienda, truck patch, estate, homestead, greenhouse, spread, operation, and agricultural business.

I settled on "farm" partly because it is simple, quick to say, and easy to type. Wherever you see "farm" or "farm business" in this book it really means *any* business involved in agricultural production. If the word "farm" makes you cringe, just imagine your favorite alternative word in its place.

# About the QuickBooks Farm Accounting Cookbook Series

What you are reading right now is Volume II of 🌀 *The QuickBooks Farm Accounting Cookbook*™, part of the QuickBooks Cookbook™ series. The "cookbook" in the name comes from the way topics are presented: as detailed steps you can follow to complete a specific farm accounting task—similar to a recipe in a cookbook.

🌀 *The QuickBooks Farm Accounting Cookbook*™, *Volume I: QuickBooks Basics, Income & Expenses, and More...* covers a variety of topics related to using QuickBooks in farming and ranching. A large portion of the book is about setting up QuickBooks for a farm business and getting started with it, including tips and ideas about how to arrange the chart of accounts, which QuickBooks forms to use and which to avoid, and so on. The rest of the book provides "cookbook" procedures for a wide range of farm income and expense transactions.

🌀 *The QuickBooks Farm Accounting Cookbook*™, *Volume II: Raised Farm Production Inventories, Sales, and More...* (this book) focuses on sales and inventories of raised (as opposed to resale) farm production. It reveals the benefits of keeping inventories in QuickBooks for at least some of the farm's production, and shows how to get production into QuickBooks simply and easily; track inventory quantities, storage locations, forward contracts and deliveries on contracts, grain inventories for multiple landlords; handle spoilage, thefts, livestock deaths, and other inventory losses; and much more.

For information on new releases or to purchase other books in the series visit 🌀 www.goflagship.com.

## Print and ebook editions

Most books in the QuickBooks Cookbook™ series are available in both print and ebook editions. Ebook editions are readable on Microsoft Windows and Apple Macintosh computers as well as Android and Apple mobile devices (Android phones and tablets, iPhone, iPad, etc.).

Chapter 1 - Introduction

# Why YOU Should be Using the Inventory Features of QuickBooks!

Your farm business could most likely benefit from using some of the inventory *features* of QuickBooks even if you don't actually want to "keep inventories". Using some of those features even part of the time—for even just one or two things your farm produces—can provide a lot of management information and other benefits for a very small investment of your time.

 **A central goal of the entire QuickBooks Cookbook™ series** is to show how to get the biggest management benefits from using QuickBooks, with the smallest investment of time and effort.

## But I Don't Want to Keep an Inventory of Anything!

### Are you sure about that?

The beauty of using QuickBooks in a cash basis business is that you *do not* have to do a full-blown job of "keeping inventories for everything" to get worthwhile management benefits from using QuickBooks' inventory features—even if you only use a couple of them, and use them in a simple way. Here is an example:

❖ Let's assume the two major products of your farm are corn and soybeans.

❖ You set up two inventory Items in QuickBooks to track inventories for them—one named Corn and the other named Soybeans.

❖ After harvest you adjust the Corn and Soybeans Items' inventory quantities to match your estimate of the bushels of each you have on hand (in grain bins, in commercial storage, etc.).

❖ As the year progresses you enter corn and soybean sales in QuickBooks using the Corn and Soybeans Items. Each time you enter a sale, QuickBooks automatically updates the inventory quantity for the Item you sold.

### Why YOU Should be Using the Inventory Features of QuickBooks!

- ❖ Throughout the marketing year you can get reports at any time, showing total bushels sold as well as the remaining bushels of corn and soybeans in inventory—available to sell or to contract for sale.

- ❖ When you prepare a balance sheet, the value of your corn and soybean inventories will be included in it automatically, as current assets. (If market prices have changed much you might want to update the value of your remaining inventories first, by making an inventory adjustment 97. It is simple and easy to do.)

- ❖ At income tax time, the sales you recorded with the Corn and Soybeans Items will be included in totals of farm income, as you might expect. But because you recorded those sales using Items, you will also have a record of the bushels of each commodity that were sold.

Compared to just entering sales (using non-inventory Items), this minimal use of QuickBooks' inventory features makes it possible to know how much of any commodity you have sold over any period of time, and how much you have on hand at any point time. And how much extra effort was required? Only an inventory adjustment to record the quantities on hand after harvest.

## Benefits You Should Know About…

No one wants to invest time and effort in learning something without an expectation that investment will pay off. As for the subject of inventories of raised farm production, you need reasons that will make you want to continue reading! Here are some of the benefits you can gain from using the inventory features of QuickBooks. They can…

- ❖ Give you a close estimate of the quantity of grain or other inventories in storage at any time, without climbing or measuring a bin or taking a physical count, even if you have made numerous sales over a period of weeks or months. (*Common Reports* 189)

- ❖ Tell you the quantity of hay, bushels of grain, or head of market livestock in different locations—in bins and commercial storage;

**9**

farrowing, nursery, and finishing units; pastures, pens, or lots; etc. (*Tracking Inventory by Location* 199)

❖ Tell you the total bushels (or head, or pounds, or tons, etc.) you have contracted for sale, how much has been delivered on each contract, and how much remains to be delivered to fulfill each contract. (*Tracking Cash Sales Contracts* 215)

❖ Make it easier to prepare balance sheet reports at any time, even if you only keep inventories for the major products you raise. (*Updating Inventory Values for Preparing a Balance Sheet* 153)

❖ Help you keep track of resale items—resale livestock, produce, or other resale items—properly, for income tax purposes, automatically as you enter purchases and sales of those items. At year's end you can have totals for sales of resale items and for their purchase cost, with almost *no* additional effort. *(A book about resale inventories is planned as the next volume to be released in the QuickBooks Cookbook™ series.)*

This is not an exhaustive list of the possible benefits, but hopefully it raises your interest in learning more about the inventory possibilities for your farm business. The bottom line is that *you* decide which items you want to inventory in QuickBooks and how much effort you want to devote to "keeping inventory". The job can be as simple or as detailed as you want.

 **The big secret** is that tracking inventories in QuickBooks *requires much less effort than you might think.* You just need to know some shortcuts and workarounds to make it easy, and that's what this book is about.

# Three QuickBooks Farm Inventory Problems, and their Solutions

Despite many changes over the years, three problems remain in accounting for farm business inventories with QuickBooks. Here are descriptions of the three problems, plus descriptions of how this book will help you overcome them.

1. **Inventory feature confusion.** The easy capabilities QuickBooks has for managing farm and ranch inventories seem buried under

layers of menus, small business accounting jargon, and reports with unfamiliar names. To track cash contracts for grain sales, for instance, you have to know that they should be entered on the Sales Orders form; to see how many bushels of grain were sold so far this year you need the Sales by Item Detail report; and so on. Knowing "where to go" in QuickBooks to do a certain job or to get the information you want is often unclear.

**This book** helps you connect the farm inventory jobs you want to do, with the QuickBooks features you need for getting them done. You will find out exactly "where to go, and what to do" to accomplish a wide variety of farm inventory tasks.

2. **Lack of manufacturing inventory features.** Farms and ranches are similar to manufacturers: they buy raw materials, supplies, and labor, and make (raise or produce) things. But QuickBooks' inventory system was designed for retail businesses—businesses that purchase merchandise at wholesale, then sell it at retail.

So the basic design of QuickBooks assumes all inventory is purchased, and does not provide an automated way to get farm production (harvested grain, raised livestock) into inventory. And traditional manufacturing inventory approaches (Work In Process and Finished Goods inventories) are not workable solutions in a typical farm business using cash basis accounting.

**This book** provides simple, easily repeated steps you can use to manage farm inventories, including procedures for many of the unusual or non-typical situations you may encounter.

3. **QuickBooks makes automatic inventory postings which are wrong for cash accounting.** QuickBooks simplifies inventory transactions by posting some amounts automatically "behind the scenes" when an inventory transaction is entered. But QuickBooks was designed for accrual accounting, and those automatic postings—which are meant to simplify *accrual* accounting for inventories—produce incorrect results for cash basis accounting.

**This book** provides simple workarounds you can use to "trick" QuickBooks into handling inventory transactions properly, so the automatic postings it makes are appropriate for cash basis accounting.

Chapter 1 - Introduction

# The "Ground Rules"

The following text styles and symbols are used throughout this book to convey special meaning:

| | |
|---|---|
| Vendors > Pay Bills | Indicates a series of menu selections needed to reach a particular command. This example means to select the Vendors from the main menu, then select Pay Bills from its submenu. (The ">" character separates the individual menu selections.) |
| *Ctrl-R* | Indicates a key or keys to be pressed. This example means to press the "R" key while holding down the "Ctrl" (Control) key. |
| Show hints | This type style is used when describing text in a window or dialog in QuickBooks or another program. |
| 🌐 goflagship.com | Links to Web pages outside of this publication are preceded by a small "earth" graphic. In ebook editions, clicking any of those links will open a page in your Web browser. |
| 7 | Print versions of this book display references to other pages as a small page symbol containing a page number. This example is referring to page 7. |
| ① | Numbers like this identify features in screenshots. The number corresponds to a number in the discussion following the screenshot. |
| ★ | Informational note. |
| 🔧 | Technical note; usually about QuickBooks settings, etc. |
| ▲ | Warning or cautionary note. |
| 📝 | General notes and comments. |

The "Ground Rules"

 Hints, tips, and ideas.

 Discussions of accounting theory or special accounting topics.

## Licensed items

Some graphic images in this publication are used under licenses obtained through Shutterstock.com or IconFinder.com.

We also gratefully acknowledge use of the following licensed items which require specific attribution, in compliance with the authors' or owners' licenses.

 **Kwrite notepad icon**, modified from original, ( www.iconfinder.com/icons/1409/kwrite_notepad_icon). By David Vignoni ( www.icon-king.com). Licensed under LGPL ( www.gnu.org/licenses/lgpl-3.0.en.html).

This page is intentionally blank.

**CHAPTER 2**

# About Farm Inventories in QuickBooks

| About this chapter | Inventories of the things you buy and sell can be divided into three types for cash basis accounting. This chapter describes the three inventory types and the basics of how they can be handled in QuickBooks. |
|---|---|

## Three Types of Cash Basis Inventory

From a cash basis accounting perspective, farm inventories are either *sales related* or *expense related* and can be broken down into the three types.

### Sales-related inventories

**Raised inventories** are the farm business equivalent of manufactured inventories in a manufacturing business. They include anything your raise or produce to sell, such as grain crops, vegetables or other produce, and market livestock born on the farm (but not purchased market livestock—those are resale inventories). Raised inventories also include unfinished production such as growing crops, as well as things you produce to use as an input for producing something else, such as corn you raise to feed livestock.

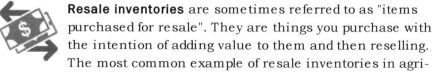

**Resale inventories** are sometimes referred to as "items purchased for resale". They are things you purchase with the intention of adding value to them and then reselling. The most common example of resale inventories in agriculture is resale livestock (feeder pigs, feeder calves, feeder lambs,

15

etc.) but there are many kinds of resale inventories, as you will see later.

### Expense-related inventories

**Expense-related inventories** includes things like feed, seed, fertilizer, and fuel—farm inputs and supplies that are consumed by the farm business. In cash basis accounting these items are normally expensed at the time of purchase. If you write a check for seed corn for instance, you probably enter it in QuickBooks as an expense, not as an addition to seed inventory (which is what would happen in accrual accounting).

## Accounting for Raised Inventories

**Raised farm inventories are <u>the main focus of this book</u>,** and this section describes the workarounds necessary for handling them properly in QuickBooks, for cash basis accounting.

*The discussion is a bit heavy on accounting theory,* so if you have a limited amount of accounting experience you may not fully understand everything described here. But that's OK: you *do not* need to understand all of accounting details. The step-by-step procedures found in later chapters will show you "how" to get the results you want, regardless of whether you fully understand the "why".

### Capitalized Inventory, Part I: Assigning Asset Value to Inventories

Inventories are assets of the farm business, to be included on the farm balance sheet just as land, machinery, and buildings are. But how do inventories get assigned an asset value? Let's explore that a bit...

In accrual accounting, things get into an inventory system—and an asset value gets assigned to them—in one of two ways: (1) via purchase transactions (an inventory's purchase cost becomes its asset value) or (2) by making/raising/producing something, then adding

## Accounting for Raised Inventories

up the raw materials, labor, and other costs of producing the item and assigning the total to the item as its asset value.

What about in cash basis accounting? *Purchased* inventories which you plan to resell (i.e., resale inventories) [23] are handled the same as in accrual accounting: cattle bought for resale or a truckload of pumpkins bought to resell at a roadside produce stand usually valued at their purchase cost. However *raised inventories* like grain, fruit or other produce crops, or market livestock born on the farm must be handled differently.

Why? Because in cash basis accounting the cash costs of producing a crop of wheat or a load of market lambs have already been expensed. The cost of farm inputs (fertilizer, seed, feed, veterinary services, fuel, etc.) were not accumulated in an asset account as they would have been in accrual accounting; instead, they were written off as expense when they were purchased. Unlike accrual accounting, in cash accounting there is no accumulated balance of production costs sitting in an account somewhere, available to assign as the asset value of an inventory which you have produced.

> ★ **In cash basis accounting** raised inventories are often simply assigned a value by making an inventory adjustment [98], which you will learn about in Chapter 5 - Inventory Nuts & Bolts [59].

QuickBooks is a double-entry accounting system, which means that every transaction posts a dollar amount at least two accounts. You cannot assign a value to one account—say, an asset account representing the value of grain you have in storage—without also affecting the balance in some other account, called the *offsetting account* of the transaction. But suppose you *only* want to assign a value to the asset account representing the grain—you don't want to change the balance in some other account which might affect your financial reports—so what should you do?

The solution is to use an equity account as the offsetting account. Because of how balance sheets work, that will essentially discard or "throw away" the offsetting part of the transaction. In later chapters you will see how to set up an equity account named Capitalized Inventory [59] and select it as the offsetting account when making inventory adjustments, like this:

## Chapter 2 - About Farm Inventories in QuickBooks

### More about offsetting accounts in QuickBooks

Though QuickBooks is a double-entry accounting system, the second or offsetting account of a transaction is not always apparent. When you enter a check or a bank deposit for instance, QuickBooks automatically selects the offsetting account for you. But for some transaction types, like inventory adjustments, you have to manually select an offsetting account to use.

### Accounting 101: Capitalized Inventory and Capitalized Costs

To *capitalize* a cost means to carry it on the books as an asset rather than deducting ("expensing") it immediately. When you depreciate a piece of machinery that is what you are doing—you carry it on the books as an asset, and only deduct a portion of its cost as expense each year over the life of the machine.

In accrual accounting, inputs associated with producing crops, livestock, and so on are not expensed when they are purchased. Instead, they are expensed when the item is sold (known as Cost of Goods Sold; see below) 19. Until then, the cost of the inputs is *capitalized:* kept on the books as balances in asset accounts with names like Growing Crops, Soybean Inventory, Growing Market Livestock, etc. (When income taxes are filed on an accrual basis the calculation is handled differently, but this describes the general idea of how accrual accounting works.)

In cash basis accounting, production expenses are deducted when they are paid. When you assign a value to an asset like Growing Crops or Soybean Inventory you are *not* capitalizing production expenses, because they have already been deducted or expensed. However, you are doing something similar: by assigning a value to inventories you are treating them as capital (assets) on the books until they are sold. Using an equity account as the offsetting account when adjusting the value of raised inventories lets you capitalize them (assign an asset value to them) without considering the production costs invested in producing them—a necessity for maintaining cash basis inventories in QuickBooks.

## Capitalized Inventory, Part II: Cost of Goods Sold

Related to the discussion above, is a workaround which is necessary because of how the Inventory Part Item type works. (Inventory Part is the Item type used for inventories in QuickBooks.) When you use an Inventory Part Item in a transaction QuickBooks does some things automatically behind the scenes, meant to simplify accounting for inventories. Unfortunately, some of those "automatic things" do not fit with cash basis accounting. But that's not a big problem, because you can set up Inventory Part Items in a slightly nonstandard way to "trick" QuickBooks into handling inventories properly for cash basis accounting.

When Inventory Part Items are set up in the standard way for *accrual* accounting, here is what happens when you enter a sale of an inventory Item:

1. Income is **increased** by the dollar amount of the sale.
2. Cash (the checking account balance usually) is **increased** by the same amount.
3. The Item's inventory (asset) account balance is **decreased** by the *value* of the Item—its purchase cost or production cost, not its selling price.
4. Cost of Goods Sold (COGS) expense is **increased** by the same amount as in (3).

   ★ **The Accounting 101** 21 **topic below** provides details on the Cost of Goods Sold account.

In QuickBooks, the Inventory Part Item type automatically accomplishes all four of these things when you use it in a sales transaction. That's great if you are doing accrual accounting but not great for cash basis accounting.

Here's the problem. Letting QuickBooks post the Item's asset value to Cost of Goods Sold (COGS) expense would essentially *double count* the costs of producing the Item. Why? Because in cash accounting, the costs associated with making/raising/producing the Item *have already been deducted as expense*. Transferring the Item's asset value to expense (COGS)—necessary in accrual accounting—is just plain wrong in cash basis accounting.

The solution is simple though. When you set up Inventory Part Items for raised inventory, select an equity account in place of a Cost of Goods Sold (COGS) account. That will cause amounts which would have been posted to COGS to be discarded—"thrown away"—thus avoiding the double counting problem.

 **This idea only applies to *raised* inventory Items.** Resale inventory Items are set up differently and <u>do</u> post to COGS or a similar account.

Chapter 5 shows how to set up an equity account named Capitalized Inventory 59 which you can use for this purpose. (Yes, this is the same equity account described above, in the prior topic.) 16
 Amounts posted to an equity account rearrange balances within the equity section of the balance sheet but do not materially distort the balance sheet or affect net equity.

Here's where the Capitalized Inventory account is used when setting up an Inventory Part Item for raised inventory:

# Accounting for Raised Inventories

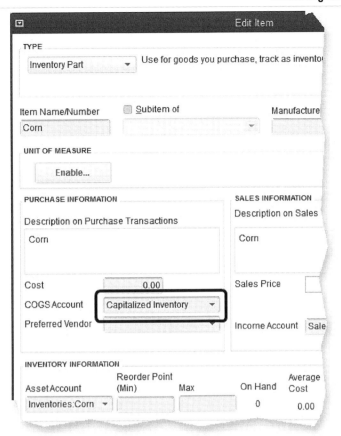

### Accounting 101: Cost of Goods Sold (COGS)

In cash basis accounting, expenses are deducted or expensed in the accounting period when the expenses were paid.

In accrual accounting, expenses associated with producing, growing, or manufacturing an item are not deducted until the item is sold. Until then, the expenses are accumulated and held as a balance in an asset account. When an inventory item is sold, the accumulated expenses get transferred from the asset account to a Cost of Goods Sold (COGS) account. Amounts posted to COGS appear on profit and loss reports as an expense (or more correctly as a deduction from gross income, but the idea is still the same). This is how accrual accounting delays the deduction of production expenses until the accounting period when an item is sold.

> Here's an example: suppose you plant a winter wheat crop in October, then harvest and sell the wheat in July of the next year. The accrual approach would be to accumulate wheat expenses in an asset account as inputs like seed, fuel, and fertilizer are purchased—maybe in September and October, the wheat is being planted. Then in July when the crop is sold, the balance in the asset account would be transferred to COGS. Profit and loss reports for July would show income from the sale of the wheat and also a deduction for the wheat's production expenses as COGS.
>
>  **This explanation is meant to describe, in general, how accrual accounting works.** Preparation of income taxes on an accrual basis is done a bit differently, but based on the same overall idea.

## More Things to Know

### Be sure to generate *cash basis* tax reports

If you are a cash basis tax filer—as is assumed throughout this book—be careful to generate *cash basis* reports for tax preparation. Whether you use one of QuickBooks' specialized tax reports 194 or a profit and loss report, if you fail to prepare it on a cash basis some income or expense may be reported in the wrong tax year.

Here's how to select the *Cash* option for a report:

1. **Click the Customize Report button** at the top of the report.

    The Modify Report window will open.

2. **Click on the Display tab** at the top of the Modify Report window.

3. **Select the** *Cash* **option** in the Report Basis section of the Display tab.

# Accounting for Raised Inventories

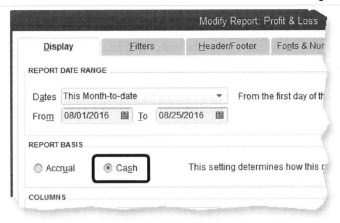

4. **Click the OK button** to save the settings and update the report.

# Accounting for Resale Inventories

**This book is _not_ about resale inventories.** This section just provides an overview of working with them in QuickBooks. As with the raised inventories discussion in the prior section 16, don't be concerned if you do not understand all of the accounting theory discussed here. That is not necessary for gaining a basic idea of how QuickBooks handles resale inventories.

## What is "Resale Inventory"?

*Resale inventories* are inventories of things purchased for resale. The most common examples in agriculture are resale livestock: feeder pigs, feeder calves, stocker cattle, feeder lambs, etc., purchased to feed and grow to a larger size or weight, then resell. But here are a few more examples:

❖ Hanging-basket plants bought from a neighbor to sell at a farmer's market booth.

❖ A truckload of pumpkins bought to resell at a roadside produce stand.

❖ Horse feed, tack, grooming supplies, and other horse care products purchased to retail from a corner showroom in your hay barn, to expand sales by making your horse hay business a "one stop shop" for customers.

- ❖ Miscellaneous grain handling equipment (augers, grain vac's, etc.) which you sell as part of the farm's business rather than setting up a separate dealership business.

## Accounting for Resale Items

If your farm business involves resale items you probably already know how to keep records for them. When you sell a resale item you enter the income from the sale in QuickBooks. Then at tax time, you also have to be able to find the item's original purchase cost, because it is not deductible until the year when the item is sold. If you buy calves in October and sell them the following April, you need to have their purchase cost available from October's records, so that it can be deducted as expense.

Whether you realize it or not, when you delay deducting the cost of an item until it is sold *you are doing a form of accrual accounting*, at least in a minor way. (Yes, this is true even if you only intend to keep cash basis records.) Because QuickBooks was designed for accrual accounting, it makes the job of accounting for resale items easy. In fact, using the Inventory Part Item type for resale Items keeps track of both the purchase cost and the sales income for an item almost automatically, when you enter purchase and sale transactions in QuickBooks using the Item.

To understand how the Inventory Part Item type works for resale items, let's consider the financial effects of both a purchase and a sale.

## Purchase the Item for $1,000

If you enter a check for the purchase, this is what happens:

1. The balance of the asset account associated with the Item is **increased** by $1,000 (the cost of the item).

2. The balance in the checking account is **decreased** by $1,000.

# Accounting for Resale Inventories

That's all there is to it. Entering the purchase of a resale inventory item just stores the item's cost in an inventory asset account.

## Sell the Item for $1,350

Entering a sales transaction for an Inventory Part Item causes these things to happen:

1. Sales income is **increased** by $1,350.
2. The checking account balance is **increased** by $1,350.

   *Technically speaking, in QuickBooks a bit more goes on behind the scenes.* The sale amount usually gets posted first to an account called Undeposited Funds—a sort of "holding tank" for received payments. It only makes its way into the checking account later, when you include amounts from Undeposited Funds in a bank deposit.

3. The balance in the Item's asset account is **decreased** by $1,000 (the cost of the item).
4. Cost of Goods Sold expense is also **increased** by $1,000.

## So how does QuickBooks track the cost of resale items?

As mentioned before, the cost of a resale item is not deductible as expense until the item is sold. Steps **3** and **4** in the example above cause the $1,000 cost of the item to be moved into an expense account called Cost of Sold  or COGS. In fact, *every* sale of a resale item adds to Cost of Goods Sold expense. At year's end, Cost of Goods Sold contains the accumulated cost of all resale items sold during the year.

*Cost of Goods Sold is the standard accounting term* for an account used for deducting the purchase cost of resale items when the items are sold. However, in agriculture you might name the account differently—maybe "Cost of livestock and other resale items" (similar to the wording on IRS Form 1040 Schedule F) or something else entirely.

The fact that QuickBooks transfers the cost of resale items to COGS automatically when you enter a sale is what makes accounting for resale items easy. Profit and loss reports then show the total income from resale items sold during the year, and also their total purchase cost. Both numbers can be used directly when preparing income taxes.

 **A book about farm resale inventories in QuickBooks** is planned as the next volume in the QuickBooks Cookbook™ series.

# Accounting for Expense-Related Inventories

 **This book is _not_ about expense-related inventories.** However, this section provides a brief overview of the problems and opportunities for working with them in QuickBooks.

❖ **Expense-related inventories** includes things like feed, seed, fertilizer, and fuel—any of the farm inputs and supplies consumed in the farm business. In cash basis accounting these items are normally expensed at the time of purchase. If you write a check for seed corn for instance, you would normally enter it in QuickBooks as an expense, not as an addition to inventory (though that is what would happen if you were tracking seed inventories in accrual accounting).

❖ **In QuickBooks, the accounting techniques for expense-related inventories are different** from those for raised inventories 16 and resale inventories 23, and are generally more complicated.

❖ **In most cases,** tracking expense-related inventories in QuickBooks is not worth the accounting effort it requires. However, tracking certain kinds of expense-related inventories can provide worthwhile management and accounting benefits. The discussion of those situations and techniques is beyond the scope of this book but may appear in a future addition to the QuickBooks Cookbook™ series.

**CHAPTER 3**

# Overview: Working with Raised Inventories in QuickBooks

| About this chapter | Here are the steps for getting started with raised inventories in QuickBooks, and for working with them as part of your day-to-day accounting activities. |
|---|---|

## Getting Started with Inventories

Keeping inventories can be as simple or as complicated as you want. You can start at any time of year—there's no need to wait until the beginning of a new accounting year. Also, you can start by inventorying just one or a few items at first, to gain experience with how inventories work in QuickBooks. Many farm businesses eventually only keep inventories for one or two items.

Here are the general steps to take for getting started with inventories in QuickBooks. The details of each step are described in Chapter 5 [59].

**Set up accounts** [59] **you will need**
for keeping inventories.

**Set up some Inventory Part Items** [68]
for the things you want to inventory.
(Or you can set them up later as needed).

**Take a physical inventory count** [91] of
the things you want to inventory, and
**assign a value** [149] **to each of them.**
Just count the items you want to
begin tracking as inventories now.
You can add more later, at any time.

Use an inventory adjustment [97] to **get
beginning inventories into QuickBooks**
for the items you have counted.

## Day-to-Day Inventory Activities

Once you have beginning inventories established, QuickBooks will maintain correct inventory quantities automatically as you enter sales transactions for grain, livestock, or other raised farm items—all you need to do is the the Inventory Part Items you have set up when entering sales of the inventories they represent. The exception, is that you will need to update inventories from time to time to add farm production to inventory—after harvest, after calving season, etc.—and also when inventory losses occur. Here are typical inventory activities you will do, in no particular order:

**Use the inventory Items** [80] **you created
when entering sales in QuickBooks**
for the items you inventory.

**Update inventories for farm production,** [149]
**and also for inventory losses** [129] when
they occur.

**Get inventory reports** [181] whenever you
want information about remaining
inventories, sales, etc.

**Update inventory values** [149] **before preparing balance sheet reports,** so inventories will be accurately represented as farm assets.

## Special Inventory Activities

Many special recordkeeping activities are also possible, including things like:

❖ **Tracking quantities in different storage locations** [199].

❖ **Managing sales contracts** [215]—quantities contracted, delivered, remaining to deliver, contract settlement, etc.

❖ **Tracking inventories for multiple landlords** [285], along with the inventories for your farm business.

This page is intentionally blank.

# CHAPTER 4
# Visual Inventory Examples

| About this chapter | This chapter introduces you to raised inventory activities in a visual way, with screenshots of typical transactions for a crop (soybeans) and a livestock enterprise (raised beef calves). It provides a visual roadmap to typical inventory activities for a production season or year, leaving detailed explanations to later chapters. |
|---|---|

## Raised Grain Example: Soybeans

Here are examples of typical inventory transactions for a crop of soybeans. The examples are pretty basic—they do not include advanced activities like tracking inventories in different storage bins/locations 199, tracking cash contracts 215, or managing inventories for multiple landlords 285. However, they do show how to calculate total soybean production from QuickBooks inventory records.

For simplicity, the examples are based on fewer transactions than would be typical in an actual farm business.

### Setting up the necessary Items

See: *Setting Up Raised Inventory Items* 80

 **Before you can set up Items, the necessary accounts must be in place.** See: *Accounts for Raised Inventories* 59.

To set up a new Item, open the Item list (Lists > Item List), then select Item > New from the button bar menu at the bottom of the window, to open the New Item (or Edit Item) window. There, you can set up an Inventory Part Item to represent soybean inventories:

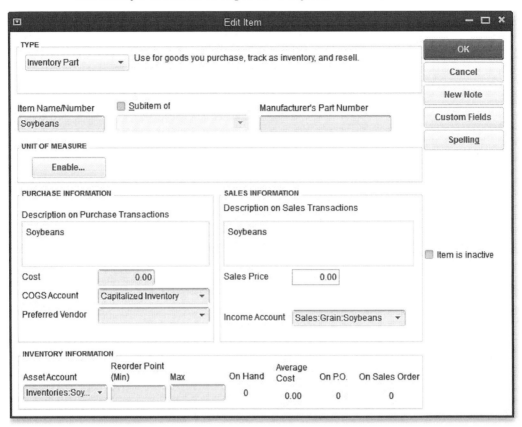

Besides an inventory Item like the Soybeans Item above, you may also need other Items (not necessarily of the Inventory Part type) for entering related charges or other details in soybean transactions. You can add those Items at any time—either beforehand, or when they are needed (while entering a transaction).

## Raised Grain Example: Soybeans

Here is an example, an Item for recording soybean checkoff deductions when entering soybean sales:

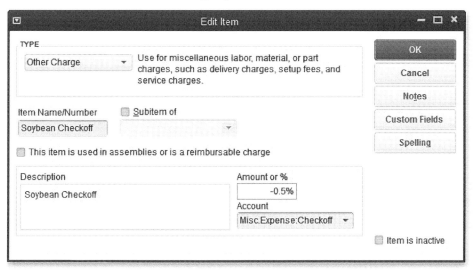

## Entering a beginning inventory

See: *How to Take a Physical Inventory Count* [91], *Getting Beginning Inventories into QuickBooks* [90]

If you have soybeans on hand when you begin keeping track of soybean inventories in QuickBooks, that beginning inventory needs to be entered in QuickBooks. Open the Item List (Lists > Item List), then select Activities > Adjust Quantity/Value On Hand from the button bar menu at the bottom of the window. Then enter a Quantity and Total Value adjustment, to provide a beginning quantity and value for the Soybeans Item:

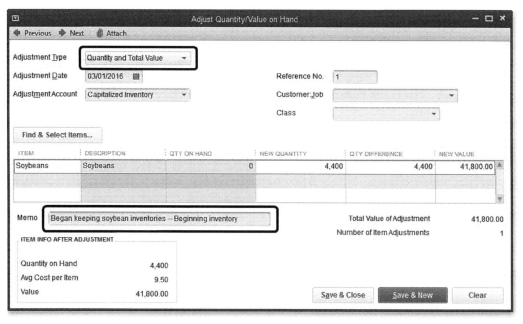

## Entering soybean sales

See: *Sales of Raised Inventory* 111

To enter a cash sale of soybeans, use the Soybeans Item on the Sales Receipts form (Customers > Enter Sales Receipts). For credit sales (where the customer will pay you sometime in the future), or especially if you may want to send a bill to the customer, enter the sale on the Invoices form (Customers > Create Invoices).

Here is a soybean sale entered on the Sales Receipts form:

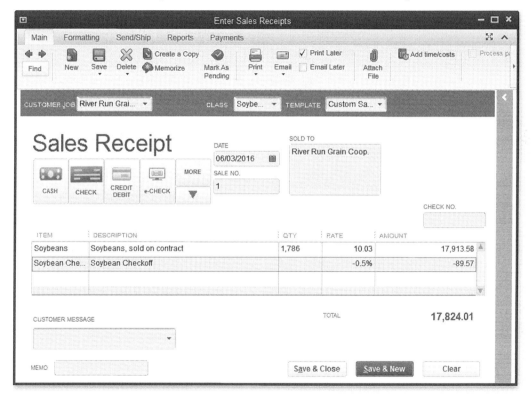

Chapter 4 - Visual Inventory Examples

## Getting information about inventories, and sales

See: *Common Reports* 189

❖ **Current inventory quantity.** You can get information about current inventories at any time, from several different places in Quick-Books. Both an Item QuickReport 189 and a Stock Status by Item report 189 (Reports > Inventory > Stock Status by Item) are good sources of current inventory information for an Item or a group of Items.

Here is a QuickReport for the Soybeans Item, showing the current inventory quantity:

❖ **Inventory asset value.** You can also get summary or detail reports which include the value (asset value) of the current inventory. (In cash basis accounting, raised inventories are assigned a value by making an inventory adjustment 97.)

Here is an Inventory Valuation Detail report 190 (Reports > Inventory > Inventory Valuation Detail), with soybean inventories valued at $9.50 per bushel. If a balance sheet were prepared as of the same date as this report, it would include an asset value of $7005.25 for the soybean inventories:

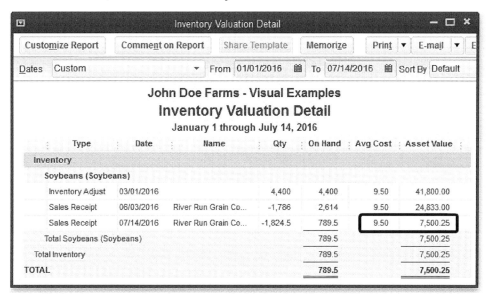

- ❖ **Sales.** To see the quantity and dollar amount of soybean sales for any period of time, you can get either a Sales by Item Summary 📖 (Reports > Sales > Sales by Item Summary) or Sales by Item Detail 📖 (Reports > Sales > Sales by Item Detail) report:

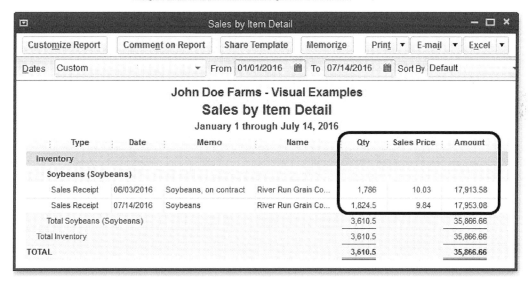

Chapter 4 - Visual Inventory Examples

## Correcting inventories before harvest

See: *How to Take a Physical Inventory Count* 91, *How to Make an Inventory Adjustment* 97

Before new crop soybeans are harvested take a physical count of soybeans on hand and, if necessary, make an inventory adjustment like the one below to correct the quantity in QuickBooks. This step is optional, but recommended if you might later want to estimate the year's total soybean production 41 from your inventory records.

To make the adjustment, open the Item List (Lists > Item List), then select Activities > Adjust Quantity/Value On Hand from the button bar menu at the bottom of the window. Then enter a Quantity adjustment to update the inventory quantity:

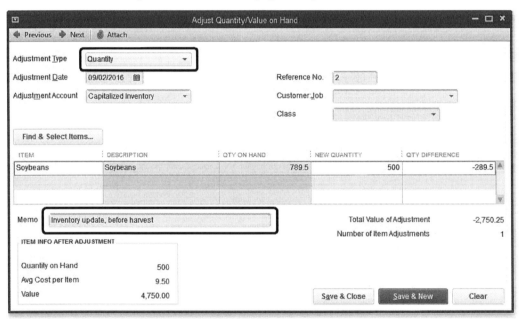

## Entering sales during harvest

See: *Sales of Raised Inventory* 111

This example is here just to make the point that sales made during harvest are *entered the same as any other sales.* If you begin harvest with little or no soybean inventory on hand, and you don't update inventories as harvest progresses (most people don't), sales you enter during harvest likely may cause the inventory quantity in QuickBooks to go negative. But there is no need for concern if that happens. You can correct QuickBooks' inventories later, typically after harvest, when you have a good estimate of the actual inventory of soybeans on hand.

Here is a cash sale made during harvest, entered on the Sales Receipts form (**Customers > Enter Sales Receipts**).

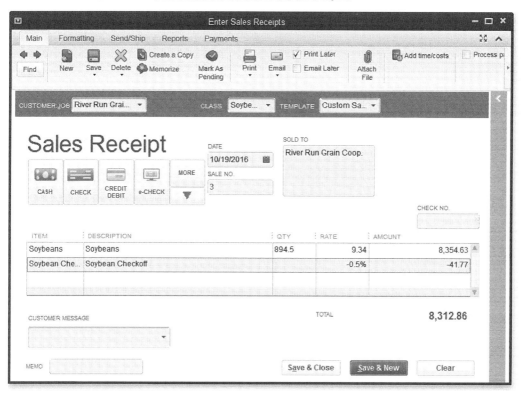

## Adjusting inventory after harvest

See: *Adding Farm Production to Inventory* 123

Waiting until harvest is completed to adjust inventories just once is easiest. It requires less accounting effort than making several adjustments during harvest. However, you are free to update inventories at any time—something you might want to do if, for instance, you need to prepare a balance sheet sometime during harvest and want up-to-date inventories included on it. You can use any approach you want for counting or estimating the physical quantity currently on hand:

- Use any combination of bin measurements, eyeball estimates, and weighed production. Do not include prior sales, such as sales made during harvest—they are irrelevant to the current quantity you have on hand.

- If all of your soybean production was weighed at harvest, you have another option. You can easily (and with good accuracy) estimate the current inventory by (1) subtracting sales made during harvest from the total bushels harvested, then (2) adding any inventory which was on hand when harvest began. For example, if 28,904 bushels were harvested, 3,380 bushels were sold during harvest, and the pre-harvest inventory was 500 bushels, the current inventory should be 28,904 - 3,380 + 500 = 26,024 bushels.

You can adjust just the inventory quantity, or both the quantity and value. Here is a Quantity adjustment:

### Raised Grain Example: Soybeans

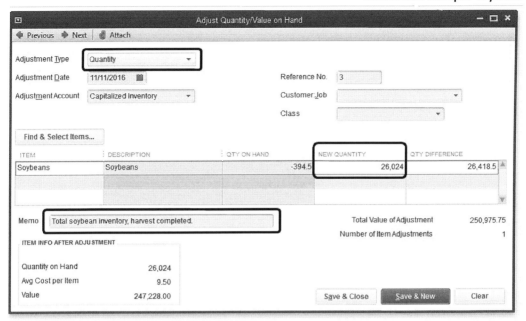

## Estimating production from inventory records

You can use inventory information to calculate total production for a particular period of time. The formula for doing that is:

**Ending Inventory + Sales − Beginning Inventory = Production**

where "beginning inventory" and "ending inventory" mean the inventory on hand as of the first and last dates of the time period you are considering. To calculate production for this soybean example:

❖ **Ending Inventory** is the quantity on hand at the completion of harvest—the 26,024 bushels [40] entered on November 11th.

❖ **Beginning Inventory** is the quantity on hand when harvest began, estimated to be 500 bushels [38] on September 2nd.

> ★ **Taking a physical count before harvest is not absolutely necessary** for calculating production. If you believe your QuickBooks inventories were reasonably accurate when harvest began, you could simply pick any date prior to harvest as a beginning inventory date, and get an inventory report for that date to find out the beginning inventory quantity. Just be

## Chapter 4 - Visual Inventory Examples

sure to use this same date as the beginning date for the sales report described below.

❖ **Sales** is the quantity sold between the beginning and ending inventory dates, or from September 2nd through November 11th in this example.

You can get total sales for the period from either a Sales by Item Summary 192 (Reports > Sales > Sales by Item Summary) or Sales by Item Detail 192 (Reports > Sales > Sales by Item Detail) report, filtered to include only sales made between the beginning and ending dates. (The report will—and should!—include *all sales* made between these two dates, regardless of whether they were sales of old crop or new crop soybeans, or whether they were sales from storage or hauled directly from the field to a buyer.)

Here is an example, showing that total soybean sales from September 2nd through November 11th were 3,244.5 bushels:

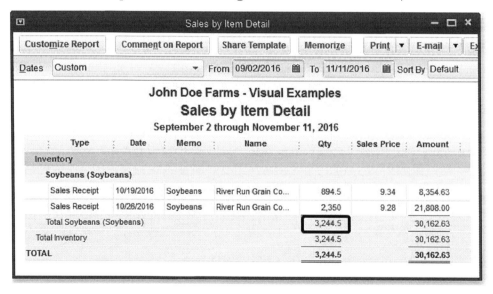

Using this information, total production can be estimated as:

**26,024 + 3,224.5 - 500 = 28,748.5 bushels**

If this production was harvested from 584 acres of soybeans, the average yield would be:

**28,748.5 bushels / 584 acres = 49.2 bushels per acre**

# Updating inventory values for preparing a market value balance sheet

See: *How to Value Raised Inventories* 149, *How to Make an Inventory Adjustment* 97

Before preparing a market value balance sheet you may need to update the value of your inventories to reflect their current *net market value* (market price, less transportation and other selling costs).

To adjust the inventory value for the Soybeans Item open the Item List (Lists > Item List), then select Activities > Adjust Quantity/Value On Hand from the button bar menu at the bottom of the window. Select *Total Value* as the Adjustment Type, and enter a new total value for Soybeans. In the example below, the inventory's value is being reduced from $9.50 to $9.25 per bushel.

 **QuickBooks will not let you simply enter a new per-bushel price.** You must calculate a total value for the inventory (23,674 bushels * $9.25 = $218,984.50), and enter that in the New Value column.

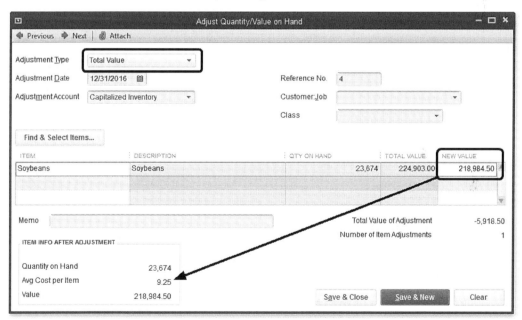

## Closing out the inventory

See: *Closing Out a Raised Inventory* 145

If you store soybeans in your own storage facilities, and you completely sell out of soybeans before the next harvest season, you will almost certainly need to adjust inventories to zero after selling the last load of soybeans. Why? Because inventory quantities in QuickBooks are *always just an estimate* of what you actually have on hand. Shrinkage, storage losses, and inaccurate quantity estimates usually mean that inventory quantities in QuickBooks cannot exactly match the quantity you sold. After your bins have been emptied and all sales have been entered, QuickBooks will usually show a small positive or negative quantity on hand and will need to be adjusted to zero.

To make the adjustment, open the Item List (**Lists > Item List**), then select **Activities > Adjust Quantity/Value On Hand** from the button bar menu at the bottom of the window. Then make a Quantity adjustment to zero out the inventory for Soybeans:

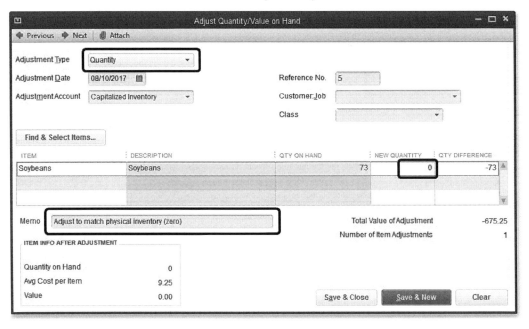

# Raised Livestock Example: Beef Calves

This section provides examples of a full cycle of QuickBooks inventory transactions for spring-born raised calves, including adding new calves (births) to inventory, entering sales, moving calves to a different stage of production, and so on. For simplicity, the examples are based on fewer transactions than may be typical for an actual farm business.

 **These examples are for *raised* calves, not calves bought for *resale*.** Accounting for resale livestock is handled differently and will be discussed in the next book in the QuickBooks Cookbook™ series.

**Calves...Stockers...Feeders...*Huh?***

These terms may be confusing if you are unfamiliar with beef cattle terminology in the U.S. Though each term can have a slightly different meaning depending on the context in which it is used, here are some basic definitions which apply to the discussion and examples below:

- **Calves** refers to calves from birth until the time they are weaned (taken away from the mother cow), which usually happens when they are six to eight months old.

- **Stockers (or "stocker calves" or "stocker cattle")** are weaned cattle, usually under a year of age, being fed to grow at a moderate rate of gain until they are big enough to go to a feedlot for feeding to market weights.

- **Feeders (or "feeder calves" or "feeder cattle")** are cattle being fed a high-energy diet (usually) of grain until they reach market weight for harvest as beef.

- **Steers** are male cattle which have been castrated.

- **Heifers** are female cattle up to the time of the birth to their first calf, when they may then be called cows. (Sometimes, even young females up to about the time of their second calf are called heifers. In that context, "heifers" is a generic term for young female cattle.)

## Setting up Items

See: *Setting Up Raised Inventory Items* 80

 **Before you can set up Items, the necessary accounts must be in place.** See: Accounts for Raised Inventories 59.

QuickBooks Items for calves and stocker cattle are needed for the examples below. To set up a new Item, open the Item list (Lists > Item List), then select Item > New from the button bar menu at the bottom of the window.

Here is the Item for inventories of calves:

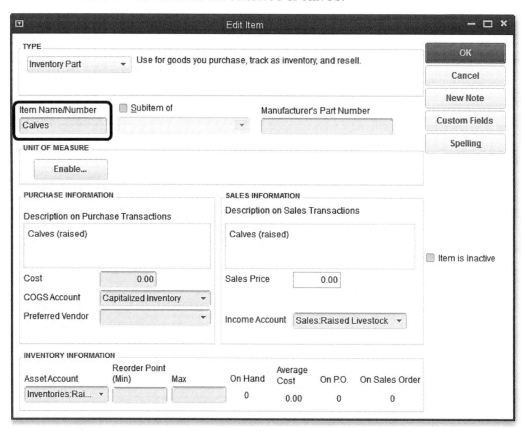

The Item for stocker cattle inventories is set up the same way, but with a different Item name:

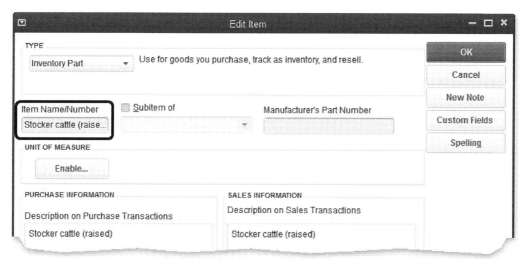

## Entering a beginning inventory

See: *How to Take a Physical Inventory Count* 91, *Getting Beginning Inventories into QuickBooks* 90

When you start keeping inventories for something, take a physical count or estimate the quantity on hand and enter a beginning inventory quantity and value for it. This example is for a beginning inventory of calves as of January 1st, but it could have been for any date during the year—whenever you begin keeping inventories for an item.

To enter beginning inventories, open the Item List (Lists > Item List), then select Activities > Adjust Quantity/Value On Hand from the button bar menu at the bottom of the window. Then enter a Quantity and Total Value adjustment, to provide a beginning quantity and value for the Item:

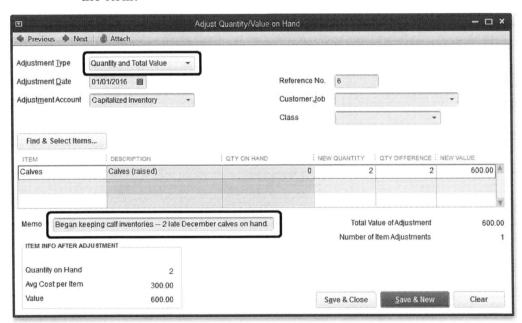

## Adjusting inventory after calving (adding production to inventory)

See: *Adding Farm Production to Inventory* 123

You can add calves to the inventory count in QuickBooks as often as you like, but updating inventories too often usually requires more accounting effort than it is worth. The practical approach is to wait until calving season is completed to take a physical count or estimate of the inventory of new calves, and update the quantity in QuickBooks then.

However, there are exceptions. If you need to prepare a balance sheet sometime during calving season—maybe for a meeting with your lender, for instance—then it makes sense to update Quick-Books' inventory count of live calves at that time so they will be included as assets on the balance sheet report.

To make an inventory adjustment, open the Item List (Lists > Item List), then select Activities > Adjust Quantity/Value On Hand from the button bar menu at the bottom of the window. You can make either a Quantity adjustment, or a Quantity and Total Value adjustment to update both the quantity of calves and their current value:

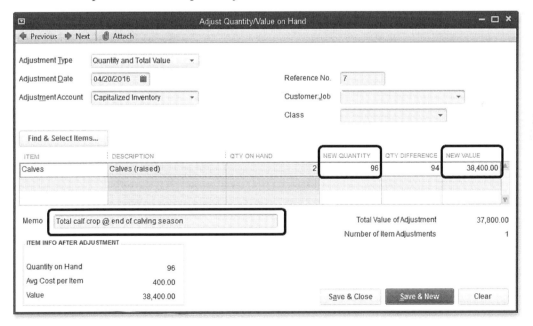

## Moving calves from one production stage to another

See: *Moving Raised Inventories from One Stage of Production to Another* [168]

Most kinds of growing livestock move among two or more stages of production as they are being raised. Calves may move to a weaning or stocker cattle stage, then later to a feeder cattle stage. Pigs may move from farrowing, to a nursery stage, and on to one or more growing/finishing stages. Other kinds of raised livestock typically follow a similar path among production stages.

Having a separate Item to represent inventories at each stage is best. It is especially useful when you need to assign a value to your inventories, as when preparing a balance sheet, because having separate Items makes it easier to assign an appropriate value to the inventory at each stage of production.

So, whether or not you need to move inventory among Items as you move livestock among different stages of production will depend on whether you have a separate Item for each stage. Also, it's worth noting that some producers have separate Items to represent different production stages but only update inventory quantities and values for them when necessary, such as when preparing a balance sheet. The choice of when (and whether) to update inventories is always up to you.

# Raised Livestock Example: Beef Calves

You can move animals from one production stage to another by making an inventory adjustment like the one below, involving Items for the two different stages. Open the Item List (Lists > Item List), then select Activities > Adjust Quantity/Value On Hand from the button bar menu at the bottom of the window. Then make either a Quantity or Quantity and Total Value adjustment:

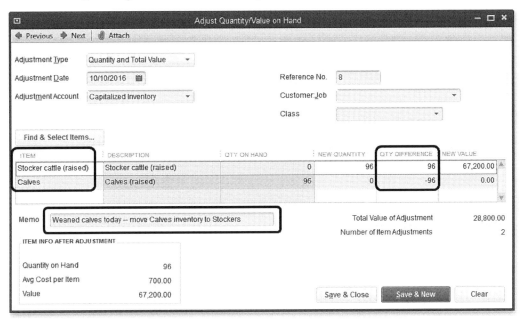

## Adjusting for death loss (or other losses)

See: *Adjusting for Raised Inventory Losses (Livestock Deaths, Spoilage, etc.)* 129

Deaths, thefts, or other losses can occur at any stage of production of course. When they occur, adjust inventories to reflect the loss.

Actually, there are a couple ways to handle this. One is to make an inventory adjustment whenever you have a loss. This keeps inventories current in QuickBooks but involves more accounting effort. The other way is to simply update the inventory count from time to time—like when livestock are moved from one stage of production to another (at weaning maybe), or ahead of preparing a balance sheet.

## Chapter 4 - Visual Inventory Examples

For raised inventories, all adjustments for losses are handled the same way: as a simple decrease in the quantity and value of the inventory Item. Unlike resale livestock, because the costs of producing raised livestock have all been expensed along the way, there is no value or cost which needs to be deducted when raised livestock die or are stolen, etc.

To make an inventory adjustment, open the Item List (Lists > Item List), then select Activities > Adjust Quantity/Value On Hand from the button bar menu at the bottom of the window. This adjustment records the death loss of two stocker calves from respiratory disease:

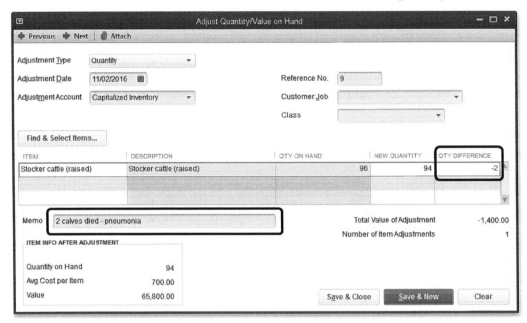

# Raised Livestock Example: Beef Calves

## Entering sales of raised livestock

See: *Sales of Raised Inventory* 111

When you receive payment at the time of a sale, enter it on the Sales Receipts form (Customers > Enter Sales Receipts). Otherwise, if selling livestock which you won't be paid for until later, or if you might need to send a bill to the purchaser, it may be preferable to enter the sale on the Invoices form (Customers > Create Invoices).

This example records the sale of part of a group of stocker cattle. Steers and heifers are listed on separate lines so the sales receipt can serve as a record of weights and prices received (not required, but useful information).

> ★ **Another alternative is to have separate inventory Items for steers and for heifers.** That makes it possible to have separate price and quantity information for each, on QuickBooks reports.

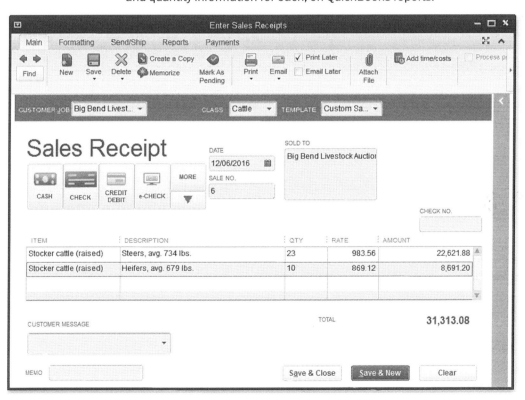

## Chapter 4 - Visual Inventory Examples

### Getting information about inventories, and sales

See: *Common Reports* 189

❖ **Current inventory quantity.** You can get information about current inventories at any time, from several different places in Quick-Books. Both an Item QuickReport 189 and a Stock Status by Item report 189 (Reports > Inventory > Stock Status by Item) are good sources of current inventory information for an Item or a group of Items. Here is a QuickReport for the Stocker cattle Item:

❖ **Inventory asset value.** You can also get summary or detail reports which include the value (asset value) of the current inventory. (In cash basis accounting, raised inventories are assigned a value by making an inventory adjustment 97.) Here is an Inventory Valuation Detail report 190 (Reports > Inventory > Inventory Valuation Detail), showing inventory quantities and value for the Calves and Stocker cattle Items:

# Raised Livestock Example: Beef Calves

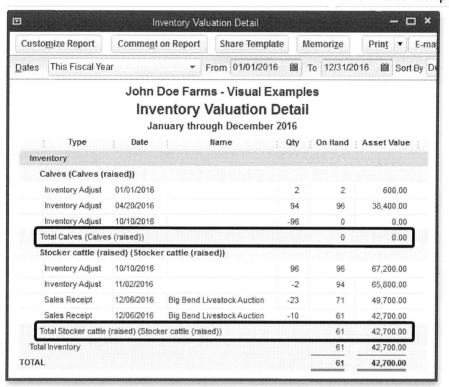

❖ **Sales.** To see the quantity and dollar amount of sales for any period of time, you can get either a Sales by Item Summary [192] (Reports > Sales > Sales by Item Summary) or Sales by Item Detail [192] (Reports > Sales > Sales by Item Detail) report.

## Chapter 4 - Visual Inventory Examples

Here is a Sales by Item Detail report:

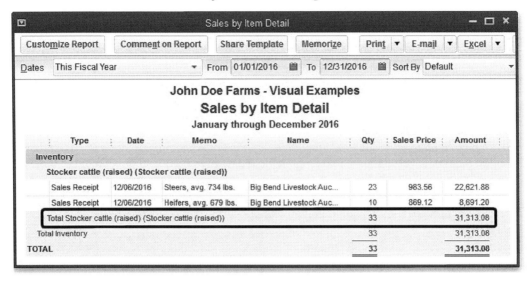

## Updating inventory values for preparing a market value balance sheet

See: *How to Value Raised Inventories* [149], *How to Make an Inventory Adjustment* [97]

Before preparing a market value balance sheet you may need to update the value of your inventories to reflect their current *net market value* (market price, less transportation and other selling costs).

To adjust the inventory value for the Stocker calves Item open the Item List (Lists > Item List), then select Activities > Adjust Quantity/Value On Hand from the button bar menu at the bottom of the window. Select *Total Value* as the Adjustment Type, and enter a new total value for Stocker calves (or any number of inventory Items) as shown below:

# Raised Livestock Example: Beef Calves

 **QuickBooks will not let you simply enter a new per-head or per-pound price.** You must calculate a total value for the inventory (61 head * $777.45 per head = $47,425.00), and enter that in the New Value column.

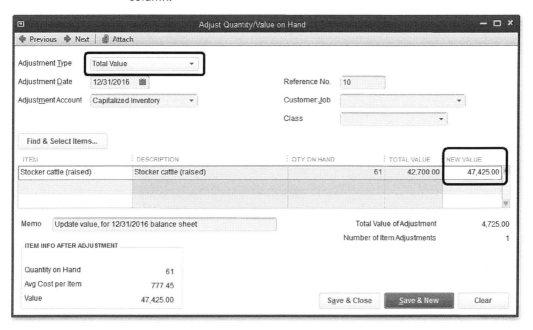

This page is intentionally blank.

**CHAPTER 5**

# Inventory Nuts & Bolts

| About this chapter | This chapter is partly informational, partly reference. It shows how to set up accounts and Items for tracking inventories, how to take a physical inventory count, how to make inventory adjustments, and how to enter beginning inventories. |
|---|---|

### What you NEED TO KNOW about this chapter...

Because it is partly a reference for inventory-related activities, this chapter is chock-full of details...and not all of them are exciting! If you mostly want to *get started with inventories right now*—there's no need to dampen your enthusiasm by taking time to read the entire chapter now.

Instead, consider reading the sections about accounts and inventory Items, and just skim the rest of the chapter. Then later when you need details about a particular inventory activity, come back here to read the section or two which contains the details you need.

## Accounts for Raised Inventories

### Income Accounts

If you are already using QuickBooks you probably have some income accounts which you use for recording sales of grain, livestock, produce, etc. Those accounts will work just fine for recording sales of inventory items, too—you probably won't need to set up any additional income accounts.

59

# Chapter 5 - Inventory Nuts & Bolts

Most people like to arrange their income accounts to provide the detail they want to see on profit and loss reports. Generally this means having a separate income account for each of the farm's major income-generating activities, for example:

> **Grain sales**
>     Corn
>     Soybeans
>     Wheat
> **Raised Livestock Sales**
>     Calves
>     Feeder Cattle
> **Resale Livestock Sales**
>     Cost of Resale Livestock
> **Custom Work Income**
>     Custom Combining
>     Trucking

## To add an income account:

1. **Open the Chart of Accounts window** (Lists > Chart of Accounts) and **select** Account > New from the button menu at the bottom of the window.

    The Add New Account: Choose Account Type window will open.

2. **Select Income** as the account type, **then click the Continue button.**

## Accounts for Raised Inventories

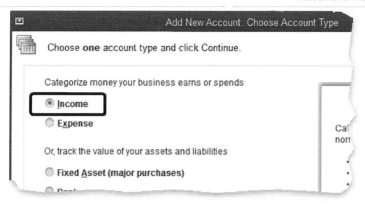

The Add New Account window will open.

3. **Fill in details for the new account,** as shown below.

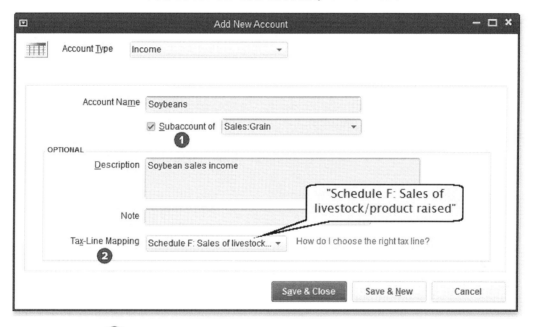

- ❶ **Subaccount of.** *Optional.* If the new account is to be a subaccount of another account, checkmark the Subaccount box and select a parent account in the box to the right.

- ❷ **Tax-Line Mapping.** *Optional.* Assigning a tax line to income and expense accounts allows QuickBooks to print an Income Tax Report 194 at year's end, with income and expenses grouped in the same categories as a U.S. Federal income tax form such as form 1040 Schedule F.

4. **Click the Save & Close button** to save the new account and close the window.

## Expense Accounts

Inventories have no relationship to expense accounts. You will not need additional expense accounts for working with inventories.

## Asset Accounts

You need one or more asset accounts for representing the value of your inventories on balance sheet reports. If you are using Quick-Books to prepare balance sheets you may already have asset accounts set up for inventories. If not, you will need to add them.

Keep in mind that for any asset account representing inventories, the account balance is only an *estimate* of what the inventories are worth (either in terms of market value or book value). For that reason, having a zillion different inventory asset accounts is a bit absurd: it implies more precision than is actually possible. Besides that, having more accounts than you really need clutters up the balance sheet, making it more difficult to read and understand. It is best to keep things simple and have no more than a few asset accounts for inventories—one for each major inventory category, at most.

The following are general examples of some inventory asset accounts. The individual accounts have all been made subaccounts of a parent account called Inventories. Though not required, this makes for better balance sheet organization because it groups inventory assets together on reports, and causes reports to have a subtotal for each subaccount as well as a grand total for the parent account, Inventories.

# Accounts for Raised Inventories

        **Inventories**
            **Corn**
            **Soybeans**
            **Calves (pre-weaning)**
            **Calves (weaned)**

Or even simpler:

        **Inventories**
            **Grains**
            **Market Livestock**

Or simplest:

        **Inventories**

If you are concerned that your balance sheets won't show enough detail, adding more asset accounts is not the answer. Instead, consider including one of QuickBooks' Item reports[189] as a supporting document along with the balance sheet. An Item report can provide details like bushels of grain in storage, value per bushel, market livestock numbers on hand, and so on, while allowing the balance sheet to remain uncluttered.

## To set up an asset account:

1. **Open the Chart of Accounts window** (Lists > Chart of Accounts) and **select** Account > New from the button menu at the bottom.

    The Add New Account: Choose Account Type window will open.

2. **Select Other Account Types** then click the dropdown arrow to its right and **select Other Current Asset** as the account type, **then click the Continue button.**

## Chapter 5 - Inventory Nuts & Bolts

🔧 **Most inventories are current assets, but not all.** A *current asset* is anything you would normally expect to sell or use up within a year. Inventories you expect to have on hand for longer than a year are *long term assets;* for those, you can use the Other Asset account type.

The Add New Account window will open.

3. **Fill in the account details** in the The Add New Account window.

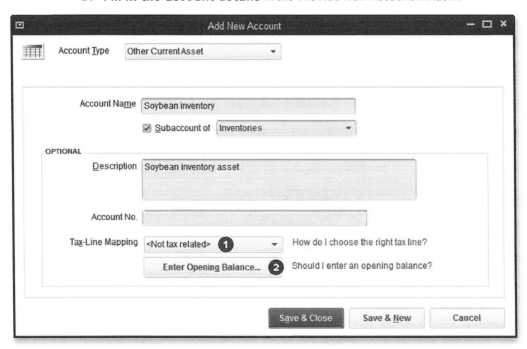

① **Tax-Line Mapping.** Select *<Not tax related>*. Tax-line mapping is mostly appropriate for income and expense accounts, not as-

# Accounts for Raised Inventories

set, liability, or equity accounts.

❷ **Enter Opening Balance.** *Do not* enter an opening balance for inventory asset accounts. Their balances (asset values) will be established when you enter beginning inventories⌐90⌐.

4. **Click the Save & Close button** to save the new account and close the window.

## Liability Accounts

Inventories have no relationship to liability accounts. You will not need additional liability accounts for working with inventories.

## Equity Accounts

*This topic applies only to raised inventories.*

You need to set up an equity account to use for activities like entering beginning inventories⌐97⌐ and making inventory adjustments⌐149⌐. You can also use it in place of a Cost of Goods Sold account when setting up raised inventory Items⌐80⌐.

⭐ **For details on why you need an equity account** to work with raised inventories, see Accounting for Raised Inventories⌐16⌐ in Chapter 2.

### Setting up an Equity account: *Capitalized Inventory*

1. **Open the Chart of Accounts window** (Lists > Chart of Accounts) and **select** Account > New from the button menu at the bottom of the window.

## Chapter 5 - Inventory Nuts & Bolts

The Add New Account: Choose Account Type window will open.

2. **Select Equity** as the account type, **then click the Continue button.**

The Add New Account window will open.

3. **Fill in account details** in the The Add New Account window.

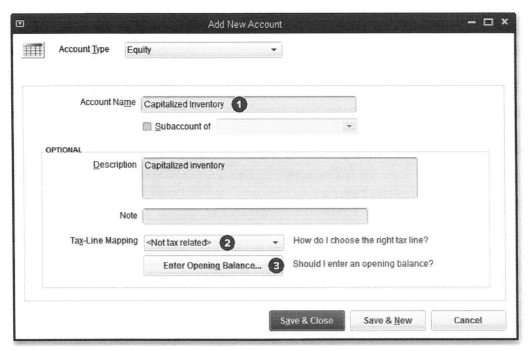

① **Account Name.** You may use any name you want, but Capitalized Inventory is a good choice because it implies specific meaning to accountants. Other choices might be Inventory Capitalization, Inventory Adjustment Offsets, or Inventory Offsets.

Accounts for Raised Inventories

> ★ *Capitalized Inventory* is the name of the equity account used throughout this book for raised inventory adjustments.

**②  Tax-Line Mapping.** Select *<Not tax related>*. Tax-line mapping is mostly appropriate for income and expense accounts, not asset, liability, or equity accounts.

**③  Enter Opening Balance.** There is no need to assign an opening balance. The account's balance will be determined by inventory transactions and adjustments.

4. **Click the Save & Close button** to save the new account and close the window.

# Chart of Accounts Reference

Here is a list of accounts referred in various chapters of this book.

| Account Name | Type | Comment |
|---|---|---|
| Farm Checking | Bank | |
| Accounts Receivable | Accounts Receivable | Amounts owed to the farm business |
| Undeposited Funds | Other Current Asset | |
| Inventories<br>　　Corn<br>　　Soybeans<br>　　Grain sorghum<br>　　Hay<br>　　Raised livestock | | Raised inventories |
| Resale Inventories | | Resale inventories |
| Fixed Assets<br>　　Breeding Livestock<br>　　Machinery & equipment<br>　　Land | Fixed Asset | |
| Accounts Payable | Accounts Payable | Amounts owed by the farm business to others |

Chapter 5 - Inventory Nuts & Bolts

| Account Name | Type | Comment |
|---|---|---|
| Capitalized Inventory | Equity | Capitalized value of raised inventories |
| Sales<br>    Grain<br>        Wheat<br>        Corn<br>        Grain sorghum<br>        Soybeans<br>    Hay<br>    Produce<br>    Raised Livestock<br>    Resale Grain<br>    Resale Livestock | Income | |
| Cost of Resale Items | Cost of Goods Sold | Cost or basis of livestock and other items purchased for resale |
| Misc. Expense<br>    Checkoff<br>Feed<br>    Grain Purchased<br>Storage & Warehousing | Expense | Commodity checkoff deductions<br><br>Grain purchased for feed |
| Sales of Fixed Assets<br>Gain/Loss on Fx Asset sales | Other Income | |

# Items for Raised Inventories

## About QuickBooks Items

### What are Items?

An *Item* is an identifier for things you buy and sell. Items are found in QuickBooks' Item List (Lists > Item List):

# Items for Raised Inventories

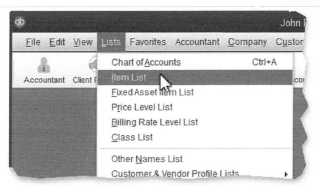

Setting up a new Item involves selecting an Item type—QuickBooks has several Item types, which will be described later—choosing a name for the Item, and associating it with an account. Having an account associated with the Item allows QuickBooks to post income or expense to the appropriate account when you use the Item in a transaction.

For instance, you might have an Item named Alfalfa Hay associated with the Sales:Hay account. When you enter a sale using the Alfalfa Hay Item, QuickBooks will post income to the Sales:Hay account. Any number of Items can be associated with the same account. You might have other Items named Orchardgrass Hay, Mixed Grass Hay, and Red Clover Hay, all of which would post income to the Sales:Hay account.

You can set up a lot of Items all at once—which you might do when getting started with QuickBooks—or you can simply set up new Items as you need them. Either way, once you have most of the Items set up that you use frequently, they give you a quick and easy way to enter transaction details without much typing. All you need to do is select the appropriate Item to describe what was bought or sold.

## Why Items? Why Not Just Use Accounts?

What's the point of having all those different Items (Alfalfa Hay, Orchardgrass Hay, Mixed Grass Hay, and Red Clover Hay) if they all post income to the same account? Why not just use the Sales:Hay account directly when you enter a hay sale? Here are reasons why Items are preferable to using accounts:

## Chapter 5 - Inventory Nuts & Bolts

- ❖ **Items add descriptive detail** to a transaction without any typing. Simply selecting an Item from a list describes exactly what was bought or sold—Alfalfa Hay or Red Clover Hay—as opposed to just "hay".

- ❖ **Using Items lets you enter quantities** for the things you buy and sell. If you want to keep track of bushels, pounds, head, tons, etc. for the things you buy or sell, you can do that *only* if you use Items when entering a transaction. And the quantity information you enter this way is available on reports.

  > ★ **When you enter income or expense using accounts instead of Items** the only way to enter quantities is by putting them in the transaction's Memo or Description field. However, QuickBooks cannot extract quantity information from those fields to provide quantity totals on reports.

- ❖ **Using Items lets you have more detail about sales and purchases** without cluttering up the Chart of Accounts. An alternative to Items is adding more subaccount levels in the Chart of Accounts. Instead of just a Sales:Hay you could have accounts like Sales:Hay:Alfalfa, Sales:Hay:Orchardgrass, and so on. But the more subaccounts you add, the more cluttered your income and expense reports and the Chart of Accounts become.

- ❖ **Some QuickBooks features depend heavily on Items, or require them.** If you want to use QuickBooks' inventory features, for instance, you *must* use Items. And if you use the Jobs feature (also called Customer:Jobs) you will soon learn that most Job-related reports will be limited if you have not used Items in transactions involving Jobs.

*I've always just used accounts. Why should I switch to using Items?*

Back in the "early days" of QuickBooks, most farmers used accounts for recording income and expenses; only a few used Items, for two reasons:

1. When people switched to QuickBooks from paper recordkeeping systems, many simply continued the bookkeeping habits they had learned on the paper system: the ledger columns in a loose-leaf paper recordkeeping system are comparable to accounts in QuickBooks.

# Items for Raised Inventories

2. Early on, QuickBooks did not have a lot of features or reports built around using Items, so it did not provide a lot of opportunity for doing much with them. Consequently, Items were used more for tracking retail business inventories than for anything else.

QuickBooks' Item-related features have improved and expanded significantly over the years; so much in fact, that most QuickBooks professionals now recommend *always* using Items whenever possible. (Most QuickBooks transaction types support using Items; only a few do not.)

If you have mostly used accounts in the past, switching to using Items requires changing a few habits. For instance, many farmers are accustomed to recording income directly in the Deposits window (Banking > Make Deposits). But the Deposits Window does not support using Items, so you will need to learn to enter sales on a Sales Receipt or Invoice first, then include the payment in a Deposit [175] as a separate step. The good news is that this is simpler and more automatic than it sounds, once you have developed the new habit of entering transactions that way.

### Should I use Items for "everything"?

Entering quantities is not important for expense categories which have no common unit of measure. Supplies expense, for example, might include purchases of fence posts, duct tape, welding rod, and paint remover. Consequently, a quantity total for Supplies expense would not provide much useful information.

If entering quantities for things like Supplies, Veterinary Expense, Liability Insurance, and so on is not important, is there still any reason to use Items for them? Using Items for such things may not matter from an accounting standpoint, it *does* matter from the standpoint of developing regular, repeatable data entry habits. Using Items whenever possible develops the habit of entering transactions the same way most of the time, reducing the potential for confusion and errors.

So it's not a bad idea to set up a Supplies Item and use it when entering purchases of fence posts, duct tape, welding rod, or paint remover. And the ability to enter a quantity in transactions *may* come in handy sometimes—like recording *how many* fence posts were bought—even though a quantity total for the Supplies Item may be a meaningless number on reports.

## About QuickBooks Item Types

When setting up a new Item in QuickBooks you must choose an *Item type* for it. In farm businesses, the most commonly used types are Inventory Part, Non-inventory Part, Service, and Other Charge. Each of these types supports entering quantities (bushels, pounds, head, etc.) in transactions and getting quantity information on reports.

- **Inventory Part** Items are the only Item type you can use for tracking inventories. When an Inventory Part Item is used in a transaction, QuickBooks updates the inventory quantity and value associated with the Item, as well as recording income or expense.

     You *must* use the Inventory Part type when setting up an Item for keeping inventories.

- **Non-inventory Part** Items are for things you buy and sell but do not care to inventory. Using a Non-inventory Part Item in a transaction normally just records income or expense. The quantities you enter for Non-inventory Part Items appear on purchase and sale reports but have no connection with inventories.

- **Service** Items are mostly the same as Non-inventory Part Items but are meant for services you purchase or services you provide, such as custom application or custom harvesting.

- **Other Charge** Items are for miscellaneous charges such as grain storage charges or commodity checkoff deductions.

- **Other QuickBooks Item types** are available for specific uses, but the four types described above are the main ones you will use to identify the things you buy and sell.

### Which Item type should I use?

In some situations you may wonder whether you should use an Inventory Part or a Non-inventory Part Item. Here are some thoughts on that...

**One view** suggests using the Non-inventory Part type for anything you raise or produce which is sold immediately after it is harvested. The idea is that the production never was held as an inventory; or if it was, that it was held only briefly. Using the Non-inventory Part type for such Items allows entering quantities in transactions but avoids the need to update inventories for harvested production or similar inventory activities [123].

For example, if you operate a fresh strawberry and blackberry enterprise you might never have a physical inventory of berries in storage (or at most, rarely longer than overnight). In that case you could use the Non-inventory Part type when setting up Items for strawberry and blackberry sales.

**The competing view** is that there are good reasons for using Inventory Part Items for *all* farm production. The main reason is that someday you may want to include the value of your growing (unharvested) strawberry and blackberry crops in the farm balance sheet. That will be easy to do if the strawberries and blackberries are represented as Inventory Part Items, because then you can simply use an inventory adjustment [98] to assign an asset value to each crop.

## Can I change an Item's type?

QuickBooks allows changing *some* Items to another type:

- **Inventory Part** Items can be changed to the Inventory Assembly type but not to any other type.
- **Non-inventory Part** Items can be changed to the Inventory Part, Non-inventory Part, or Service types.
- **Service** Items *cannot* be changed to any other type.
- **Other Charge** Items can be changed to Inventory Part, Non-inventory Part, or Service types.

Note that QuickBooks *will* let you change Non-inventory Part and Other Charge Items to the Inventory Part type, but *will not* let you change Inventory Part Items to a non-inventory type.

## Can I just use the Items I already have? Or do I need to set up new ones to work with inventories?

### Non-inventory Part and Other Charge Items

If you someday decide to keep inventories for the things represented by Non-inventory Part or Other Charge Items, you can switch those Items to the Inventory Part type.

*Example:* You have been entering corn sales using a Non-inventory Part Item named Corn, but now you want to start keeping track of corn inventories.

1. **Edit the Corn Item** by going to the Item List (Lists > Item List), right-clicking the Corn item, then selecting *Edit Item* from the popup menu.

   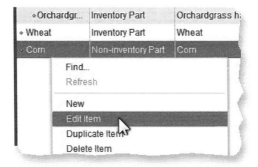

   The Edit Item window will open.

2. **Change the Type to Inventory Part.**

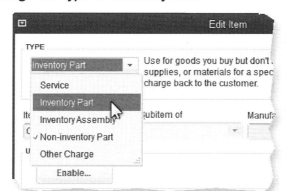

3. **Click OK** to confirm the change, when QuickBooks notifies you that switching to the Inventory Part type is not reversible.

   The Edit Item window will be redisplayed, to show the Inventory Part type's additional fields.

4. **Select accounts** in the COGS Account and Asset Account fields, as described in *Setting Up Raised Inventory Items* 80 later in this chapter.

5. **Click OK** to save the changes and close the Edit Item window.

   After this, you can use the Corn Item for tracking corn inventories.

## Service Items

You cannot change the type of a Service Item. A workaround is to rename the existing Item, then add a new Item of the desired type, using the old Item's name.

*Example:* You have been entering soybean sales using a Service Item named Soybeans, but now you want to begin tracking soybean inventories. You need an Inventory Part Item for soybeans but want to continue using the name "Soybeans" for the new Item. Here's a way to do that:

1. **Edit the existing Soybeans Item** by going to the Item List (Lists > Item List), right-clicking the Soybean item, then selecting *Edit Item* from the popup menu.

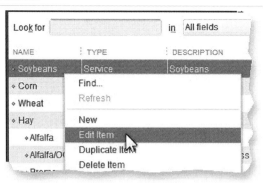

The Edit Item window will open for the Soybeans Item.

2. **Change the Item's Name** to something like Soybeans_OLD, and **checkmark the** *Item is inactive* **box.**

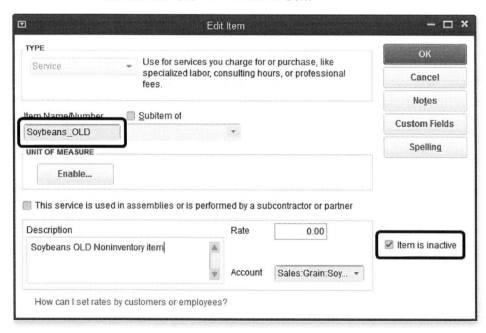

Having "_OLD" in the name will remind you not to use the Item in new transactions. Marking it inactive will keep it from showing in the Item List.

3. **Click OK** to save the changes and close the Edit Item window.

With the existing Item renamed to Soybeans_OLD you are free to add a new Inventory Part Item named Soybeans, to use for tracking inventories.

4. **Add a new Inventory Part Item named Soybeans** as shown in *Setting Up Raised Inventory Items* later in this chapter.

## Organizing the Item List

Having specific information goals will make it easier to organize the Item list in a way that will help produce the kinds of inventory information you want, and can even make the list easier to use for transaction entry.

QuickBooks lets you have up to five Item levels—i.e., Items with up to four levels of subitems. Think of subitems as subcategories of the parent Item, just as subaccounts are subcategories of an account. One difference however, is that dollar amounts posted to subaccounts are included in the balance of their parent account, while transactions involving subitems do not contribute to the parent Item's inventory quantity or value. In other words, an Item's inventory quantity and value are completely separate from those of its subitems.

The main reason to use subitems is to control how Items are grouped in the Items List and on reports:

❖ Having Item groups (each parent Item along with its subitems makes up a group) makes finding and selecting Items easier when entering transactions.

❖ More importantly, Item groups control how quantities and dollar amounts are subtotaled on reports. That can provide a lot more information than you would get by just using single-level Items with no subitems.

Here is a Corn Item with subitems added for specialty types of corn:

    **Corn**
        **High Lysine**
        **Organic**

## Chapter 5 - Inventory Nuts & Bolts

And here is an Inventory Stock Status by Item report[189] filtered to show only inventories for Corn and its subitems. The report demonstrates how using subitems provides report detail for subcategories of a parent Item, while still getting a total for the parent Item.

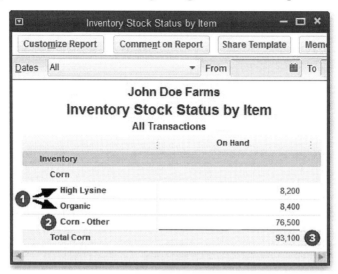

**① High Lysine** and **Organic** are subitems of the Corn parent Item. They identify inventories of special types of corn.

**② Corn - Other** represents inventories for the Corn parent Item.

> **In QuickBooks reports,** any name with "- Other" added to it identifies amounts for the parent Item, parent account, parent Class, etc.

**③ Total Corn.** Though the report shows a separate quantity for each subitem, it also provides a total for Corn and all of its subitems, combined.

The important point is that how you organize Items and subitems gives you control over how information is arranged on reports, which can lead to getting exactly the information you want. In fact, some techniques such as tracking inventories by location[199] are based entirely on structuring the Item list in a specific way.

Here is the same Corn Item as above, but with subitems added to represent storage locations. Bins 1 and 2 may contain regular yellow corn. Bins 3, 4, and 5 may be used for storing either High Lysine or Organic corn:

Corn
    Bin 1
    Bin 2
    High Lysine
        Bin 3
        Bin 4
        Bin 5
    Organic
        Bin 3
        Bin 4
        Bin 5

And here is an inventory report for Corn, prepared like the report above. It shows how much of each type of corn is stored at different locations.

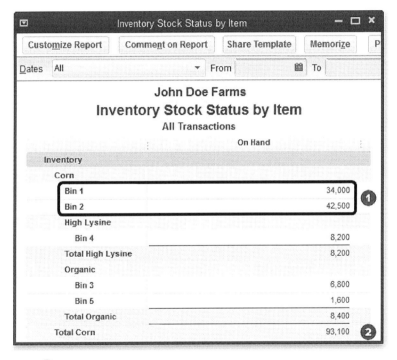

**① Bin 1** and **Bin 2**. The inventories that were lumped together as Corn - Other in the prior report above, a total of 76,500 bushels, are now split between two storage locations subitems, Bin 1 and Bin 2.

**Total Corn** is the same quantity as in the prior report, just divided among more subitems.

**Don't waste time trying for the "perfect" Item list setup.**

A common mistake of new QuickBooks users is trying to set up everything perfectly from the start. The truth is, that creating the most useful arrangement of Items (or accounts, or Classes, or any other QuickBooks list) happens over time as you gain experience with QuickBooks.

So it's best to just "take the plunge" and get started—go ahead and add some Items now, even if you are not sure how the Item List should be arranged. QuickBooks offers a lot of flexibility for reorganizing lists any time you want. You can rename Items, move parent-level Items to become subitems of other Items, attach a subitem to a different parent Item, and so on.

## Setting Up Raised Inventory Items

***Problem*** I need to set up some inventory Items in QuickBooks. How should I do that?

***Solution*** See the steps shown below.

***Discussion*** QuickBooks only tracks inventories for Inventory Part Items, so you must set up Inventory Part Items for things you want to inventory.

🔧 **If you have been using QuickBooks for a while** you may already be using other Item types for things you sell which you now want to inventory. If so, you will need to switch to using Inventory Part Items. If you want to continue using the same Item names as you have been, you can do that. For details, see the discussion in *About QuickBooks Items* .

## How to Set Up Inventory Part Items for Raised Inventories

 **The steps shown below are for adding Items prior to entering transactions,** but you can also define new Items "on the fly" as you need them. If you type a name for the new Item in the Item field of a transaction you are entering, and QuickBooks does not find an existing Item with that name, it will ask if you would like to set up a new Item. Click Yes, then follow the same setup steps as shown below.

1. **Open the Item List window** (Lists > Item List), then **select** Item > New from the button menu at the bottom of the window.

   The New Item window will open.

2. **Fill in details for the new Item:**

## Chapter 5 - Inventory Nuts & Bolts

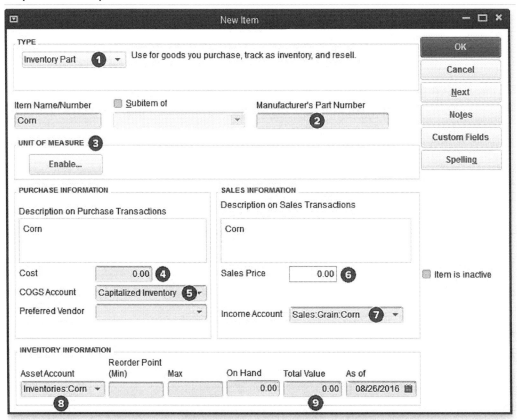

① **Type.** You must select the Inventory Part type for Items you will use for tracking inventories.

② **Manufacturer's Part Number.** *Optional.* This field is available for any short note or other information you might want to include about the Item and have displayed on (some) reports.

③ **Unit of Measure.** *(Not available in all QuickBooks versions).* The Unit of Measure feature lets you sell an Item in any of several different units (such as pounds, hundredweights, and tons) yet keep inventories in a single common unit of measure (such as pounds). It is a somewhat advanced feature of higher-end QuickBooks editions and is not discussed in this book.

④ **Cost.** Normally you should leave 0.00 in this field. (It is used for suggesting a price when you purchase the Item; that is,

# Items for Raised Inventories

when you select it on a purchase form such as a Check or Bill.)

**⑤ COGS Account.** In accrual accounting you would select a Cost of Goods Sold (COGS) account here. However in cash basis accounting you must select an equity account, such as the Capitalized Inventory [59] account described earlier. Selecting an equity account here will cause QuickBooks to discard the unwanted financial effects of the posting it would normally make to a COGS account when an Item is sold.

> ⚠ **This advice is for *raised* inventory Items, <u>not</u> *resale* Items!** For resale items you *should* select either a Cost of Goods Sold account or a contra-income account.

**⑥ Sales Price.** Generally you should leave 0.00 in this field. (It is used for suggesting a "retail price" when you sell the Item; that is, when you select it on a sales form such as Sales Receipt or Invoice.)

**⑦ Income Account.** Select the account where you want the income to be posted when the Item is sold (when it is used on a sales form such as a Sales Receipt or Invoice). For example, you might want income for a Corn Item posted to an income account called Sales:Grain or Sales:Grain:Corn.

**⑧ Asset Account.** Select the account you want to use for representing the Item's value on balance sheet reports. For inventories this should normally be a current asset account [62].

**⑨ On Hand, Total Value, As of.** These fields are for specifying a beginning inventory quantity and value for the Item, as of the date you began keeping inventories for the Item. *Generally you should not enter anything in these fields*—see the gray note below [84].

3. **Click the OK button** to save the new Item and close the window, **or the Next button** to set up another Item.

Chapter 5 - Inventory Nuts & Bolts

**When is it OK to enter an *On Hand* quantity and a *Total Value*?**

Assigning a beginning *On Hand* quantity and *Total Value* when setting up an Item may seem like something you should do, but usually it is not. Avoid entering anything for either of them except when: (A) you are setting up QuickBooks and have not yet begun entering transactions, or (B) you are careful to supply an *As of* date which is *earlier than* the first date of any inventory transactions.

When you supply a beginning *On Hand* quantity and *Total Value* for an Item, (1) the Item's inventory quantity gets adjusted as of the *As of* date, and (2) the *Total Value* amount gets posted to the Item's asset account, and offset to the Opening Balance Equity account as of that same date. If you happen to use an *As of* date *later than* the date of some of your inventory transactions, strange problems will result. For instance, balance sheets dated later than the *As of* date will show a higher balance for Opening Balance Equity than on earlier-dated balance sheets. Quantity reports for the Item may be similarly affected.

If you are past the initial setup phase for QuickBooks (i.e., if you are actively entering transactions) it is best <u>not</u> to supply an *On Hand* quantity and *Total Value* when setting up a new Item. Instead, create the Item, then use an inventory adjustment to establish a beginning quantity and value for it. Just be sure to date the inventory adjustment earlier than the first date when the Item is used in a transaction.

This approach keeps the value of newly added inventories from being included in Opening Balance Equity, which should be reserved for equity contributed by the owners when the farm business was started.

## Setting Up a Capitalized Inventory Item

Occasionally the Capitalized Inventory [65] account needs to be used on a QuickBooks form which does not allow accounts to be used. Sales Receipts and Credit Memos, for example, only let you select Items, not accounts. The solution is to set up an Item to represent the Capitalized Inventory account, and use it in those situations.

> ★ **See the raised inventories** [16] **discussion in Chapter 2** if you need details about why an equity account is necessary for working with inventories in cash basis accounting.

# Items for Raised Inventories

## How to Set Up a Capitalized Inventory Item

1. **Open the Item List window** (Lists > Item List), **then select** Item > New from the button menu at the bottom.

The New Item window will open.

2. **Fill in details for the new Item** as shown below.

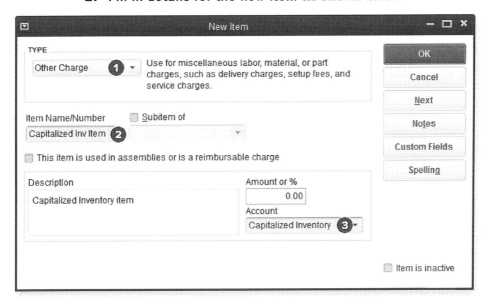

① **Type.** Other Charge is selected here, but the Service and Non-inventory Part types would work just as well.

② **Item Name/Number.** The Item name should remind you that the Item represents the Capitalized Inventory [65] account (or whatever equity account you have set up for working with raised inventories). Though you *may* use the same name for both the Item and the account it represents, that probably is not a good idea. Using slightly different names may prevent confusion later. In this example the Item is named "Capitalized Inv Item" to make it different from the account name, Capitalized Inventory.

③ **Account.** Select Capitalized Inventory [65] here (or whatever equity account you have set up for raised inventory adjustments).

3. **Click OK** to save the new Item and close the window.

## Miscellaneous Items Reference

The setup details for most Items are shown in the chapters where those Items are used in examples. However, a few Items are not specific to any particular chapter, so their setup windows are provided below, in alphabetical order by Item name.

## DamageDiscnt

Used for recording grain damage discounts, usually as a deduction (a negative amount) on sales forms (Sales Receipts, Invoices).

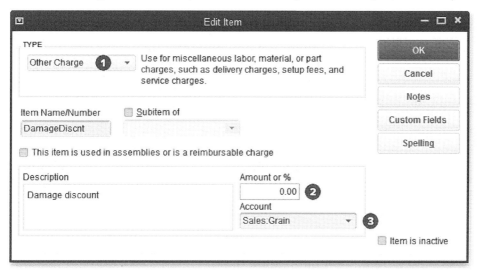

① **Type.** Other Charge is an appropriate type for this Item, though the Service or Non-inventory Part types could also be used.

② **Amount or %.** The Amount is left as 0.00 because the amount will vary.

③ **Account.** Sales:Grain is an income account. Because this Item will normally be used to enter a negative amount on sales forms, it will normally subtract from grain income.

## Corn Checkoff

Used for recording corn checkoff expense, usually as a deduction (a negative amount) on sales forms (Sales Receipts, Invoices).

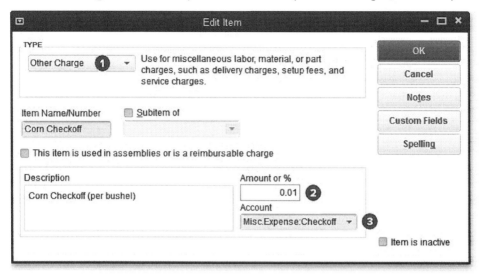

> **❶ Type.** Other Charge is an appropriate type for this Item, though the Service or Non-inventory Part types could also be used.
>
> **❷ Amount or %.** The Amount is entered as 0.01 (1 cent) in this example, to represent 1 cent per bushel. (Commodity checkoff rates may differ in each state, so your rate may be different.)
>
> **❸ Account.** Misc.Expense:Checkoff is an expense account (assumed to already be set up).

# Items for Raised Inventories

## Storage Fees

Used for recording grain storage fees, usually as a deduction (negative amount) on sales forms (Sales Receipts, Invoices).

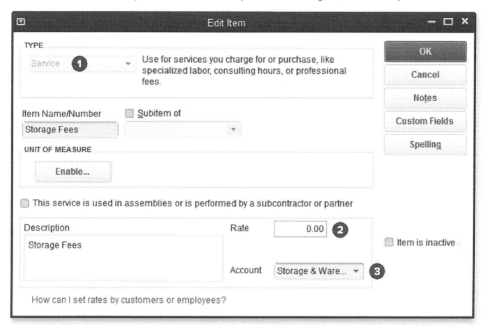

**① Type.** This example is set up as a Service Item but the Other Charge type would also be appropriate.

**② Rate (price).** The Rate is left as 0.00 because the price of the Item will vary.

**③ Account.** The Storage & Warehousing is an expense account (assumed to already be set up). Using this Item may be used a deduction amount on sales forms (Sales Receipts, Invoices) or as a positive amount on purchase forms (Checks, Bills) will post expense to the Storage & Warehousing account.

# Getting Beginning Inventories into QuickBooks

Here are typical steps for getting beginning inventories established in QuickBooks:

**Set up accounts** [59] **you will need**
for keeping inventories.

**Set up some Inventory Part Items** [68]
for the things you want to inventory.
(Or you can set them up later as needed).

**Take a physical inventory count** [91] of
the things you want to inventory, and
**assign a value** [149] **to each of them.**
Just count the items you want to
begin tracking as inventories now.
You can add more later, at any time.

Use an inventory adjustment [97] to **get
beginning inventories into QuickBooks**
for the items you have counted.

You may include beginning inventories for any number of Items in the same inventory adjustment [97] entry; however, here is an example adjustment for a single Item, Soybeans, from the *Raised Grain Example: Soybeans* [31] section of Chapter 4:

## Getting Beginning Inventories into QuickBooks

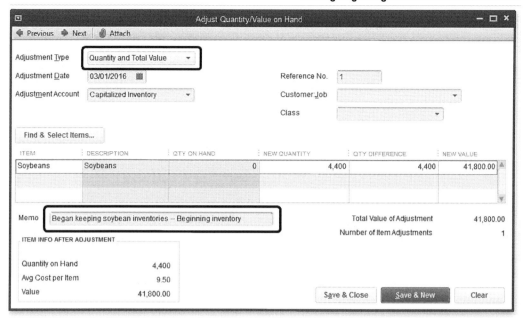

Each of the steps listed above is described in detail in other sections of this chapter.

## How to Take a Physical Inventory Count

The reason to take a physical inventory count is to know how much of something you actually have on hand, before updating inventories in QuickBooks.

 A *physical inventory count* means counting the items you actually have on hand, as opposed to the inventory quantity maintained by an accounting system—which is always just an estimate (though hopefully a close estimate) of your actual inventories.

QuickBooks can track inventory changes as you enter sales and purchases, but reports and other information will be useless unless QuickBooks *begins* with correct inventory quantities. Also, the inventory quantities in QuickBooks (or any accounting system) will eventually disagree with the actual quantities on hand due to accounting errors, miscounting, and inventory losses like spoilage, theft, or death loss. Taking a physical count from time to time—even if just once a year—is necessary for bringing the inventory quantities in QuickBooks back in line with what you actually have on hand.

*Taking a physical count is not difficult;* nor does it need to take a lot of time. It can be as simple or as detailed as you want—it can even be just an estimate if you prefer. And if you only want to track inventories for a few items, you only need to count those items.

> **Accounting 101: Perpetual vs. periodic inventories**
>
> Basically, there are two kinds of inventory systems.
>
> With **periodic inventories** the accounting system *does not* track inventory changes as you enter transactions. Rather, the inventory quantity is updated manually by taking a physical count once a month, quarter, or year—the frequency depends on how current you want your inventory records to be. If you prepare a balance sheet once or twice a year and do it entirely outside of QuickBooks (maybe in a spreadsheet), then you are essentially using a periodic inventory system: you have to count or estimate inventories on hand every time you prepare a balance sheet.
>
> Most accounting software, including QuickBooks, supports the other kind of inventory system: **perpetual inventories**. With perpetual inventories, the accounting program maintains a record of inventory quantities and inventory value continuously ("perpetually") as a normal part of day-to-day activities, such as entering purchases and sales of inventory items.
>
> A problem all perpetual inventory systems face is that sooner or later the accounting system's quantities will be incorrect; that is, they won't match the actual physical quantity of items on hand. Accounting errors, inventory losses, theft, and so on eventually cause the accounting system's quantities to be out of sync with actual, physical inventories. Taking a physical count from time to time is necessary to adjust (correct) the accounting system's quantities.

# What Should You Count?

Sales-related inventories [15] are the kinds of inventory most often tracked in a farm business. They include things like grain, livestock, or other farm production, plus items purchased for resale. If you only want to keep inventories for one or a few items—maybe just the grain you have in storage—then you only need to take a count or estimate the inventory of those items.

## "Gotchas" to look out for...

Due to timing differences in depositing payments you have received versus when inventories are delivered or picked up, under- or overcounting inventories is easy to do. Here are a couple examples to illustrate the kinds of situations to watch out for:

- **A neighbor delivered 40 head of calves to you, worth about $28,000,** but she agreed to let you pay for them next month when you have money from selling other cattle.

    The neighbor's calves are your property now, even though you have not paid for them. From an accounting standpoint, the correct approach would be to count them as inventory but also enter a Bill (Vendors > Enter Bills) to record the amount you owe for them. Counting the calves as inventory (assets) without recording the fact that you still owe for them (a liability) would overstate your assets by about $28,000.

- **You have 5,000 bales of bromegrass hay in storage** but one of your hay customers has paid you in advance for 1,000 bales, and you have entered the $4,250 payment in QuickBooks as a hay sale.

    Because you have entered the payment it will show up as an asset on the farm balance sheet (probably in either Undeposited Funds 176 or the checking account balance). If you also include the 1,000 paid-for bales as part of your inventory, you will be double-counting assets by roughly $4,250. Really only 4,000 bales should be counted as inventory if you want the balance sheet to be correct.

# When Should You Take an Inventory Count or Estimate?

If you are just getting started with inventories in QuickBooks you need to take a physical count of the things you want to inventory, and establish beginning inventories for them. Beyond that, also consider taking a physical count or estimate at these times:

Chapter 5 - Inventory Nuts & Bolts

- ❖ **When production has been added to inventory.** If you plan to use QuickBooks as a source of *current* information about your inventories, such as quantities on hand, or contracted quantities and contract deliveries⌐215¬, you need to update quantities in QuickBooks whenever farm production has been added⌐123¬, such as after completing harvest of a crop, at the end of a calving season, or after moving a group of pigs from farrowing to a nursery unit.

- ❖ **When inventory losses have occurred** such as livestock deaths, theft, or grain lost to spoilage. Usually you will know approximately how much was lost and can use that information to make an inventory adjustment for the loss⌐129¬. But if not, you may need to take a physical count before making the adjustment.

- ❖ **When preparing a balance sheet** your inventories need to be current; otherwise the balance sheet report may not be as accurate as it should be. If you aren't sure whether the inventory quantities in QuickBooks are correct, it would be a good idea to take a physical count or estimate and update them before preparing the balance sheet.

- ❖ **Once a year, at least.** There is no value in having inventory records if they are inaccurate. So take a physical count—or for some inventories, an estimate—and update the inventory quantities in QuickBooks at least once a year. A good time to do that is just ahead of preparing an end-of-year balance sheet.

 **Don't be concerned if you do not have time right now** for counting all of the things you want to inventory. Get started by counting just one or two items which are important to you, then count and add other items later as time allows.

## How to Take a Physical Inventory Count

If you don't have inventory Items set up in QuickBooks yet—which is likely the first time you take an inventory count—then the best approach may be to just grab a notebook and pencil (or your smartphone or tablet computer) and "walk around", taking counts or making quantity estimates of the things you want to inventory.

If you *do* have inventory Items set up in QuickBooks, another option is to print a Physical Inventory Worksheet. It lists all of your inventory Items and their quantities, and has blanks for writing in a count for each Item.

## How to print a Physical Inventory Worksheet

1. **Open a Physical Inventory Worksheet** window (Reports > Inventory > Physical Inventory Worksheet).

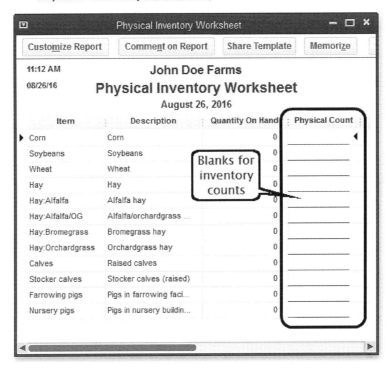

2. *Optional.* **Customize the worksheet** to show just the columns you want.

   To do that, click the Customize Report button at the top of the window, then select the columns you want in the worksheet.

3. **Click the Print button** at the top of the window to print the worksheet.

## How accurate does the count need to be?

The answer to this question can vary a lot from one farm business to the next, and mostly boils down to answering this question: *How do you plan to use the inventory information you keep in QuickBooks?*

Having accurate inventories in QuickBooks is most important if you plan to make management decisions based on them, such as knowing how much of something you have available to sell or to contract for sale. For example, if QuickBooks shows that you have 3,750 bushels of soybeans on hand, can you trust that number well enough to be comfortable with contracting 3,500 bushels for sale? You can probably trust it only if you took an accurate physical count after harvest and been diligent about entering soybean sales in QuickBooks.

## Assigning values to inventories

You cannot really separate the job of taking an inventory count from the job of assigning values to inventories. While counting things, observe their condition, size, and other attributes which might affect their value, and take notes. For instance:

- ❖ Does the corn in one of yours bins have a quality or condition problem which would reduce its selling price?

- ❖ Are there weevils in the stored wheat? Is the test weight good, or low enough to cause the selling price to be docked?

- ❖ What do the calves weigh? What quality are they—No. 1s or No. 2s? What is the proportion of steers to heifers? (Heifers normally sell for less than steers of the same age, weight, and condition.)

Having some details written down will make it easier to assign values which more closely represent what the items are worth.

# How to Take a Physical Inventory Count

### Goals for valuing raised inventories

How you assign values to inventories, which are farm assets, will depend on your goals for using asset information. For instance, do you want assets to be valued at market value or a book value of some kind when you prepare balance sheets?

In agriculture, raised inventories are often valued at *net market value*: market value less selling costs (hauling, commissions, etc.) To estimate a net market value for stored grain for instance, you could use its current price at a particular market, less the cost of loading out the grain and and hauling it to market. (*At-the-farm price* is another term which essentially means the same thing as net market value.)

See also: *How to Value Raised Inventories* 149 for a more detailed discussion.

## Using the Physical Count to Update Inventories in QuickBooks

Once you have a physical count, update inventory quantities and values in QuickBooks by making an inventory adjustment as described next in this chapter.

# How to Make an Inventory Adjustment

You will make inventory adjustments from time to time, for a variety of reasons. The steps are basically the same whether the adjustment is for:

- ❖ **Establishing beginning inventories**
- ❖ **Updating inventories for production**—harvested grain, livestock births, etc.
- ❖ **Adjusting for inventory losses:** spoilage, theft, death loss, etc.
- ❖ **Correcting errors** such as accounting errors or mistakes made in counting physical inventories

Chapter 5 - Inventory Nuts & Bolts

❖ **Updating the value of inventories** for preparing a balance sheet

## Steps for Making an Inventory Adjustment

Here are detailed instructions for adjusting the quantity or value of *raised* inventories.

 **Do not adjust the value of *resale* inventories** (items purchased for resale), except to correct accounting errors, or for death loss, etc. Resale items should remain valued at their purchase cost (basis), plus freight if any, for income tax accounting purposes.

1. **Open the Adjust Quantity/Value on Hand window.**

    There are several ways to open the window:

    ❖ **From the main menu,** select Vendors > Inventory Activities > Adjust Quantity/Value on Hand.

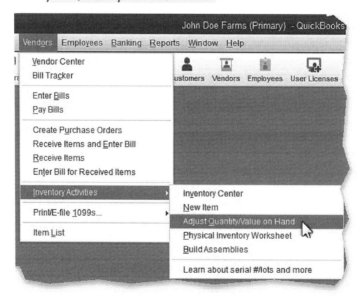

    ❖ **From the Item List** (Lists > Item List), click on the Activities button at the bottom of the window, then select *Adjust Quantity/Value on Hand* from its popup menu.

# How to Make an Inventory Adjustment

- ❖ **From the Inventory Center** (Vendors > Inventory Activities > Inventory Center; *available in QuickBooks Premier and higher editions*), right-click anywhere in the left pane, then select Adjust Quantity/Value on Hand from the popup menu.

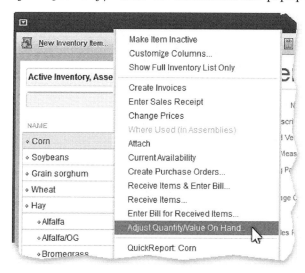

The Adjust Quantity/Value on Hand window will open:

1. **Header area** where you select the adjustment type, date, and account.

2. **Find & Select Items button** lets you select a number Items at once, useful when you need to enter adjustments for multiple Items.

3. **Detail area** where Item quantities and values are adjusted.

2. **Fill in the header fields** as appropriate.

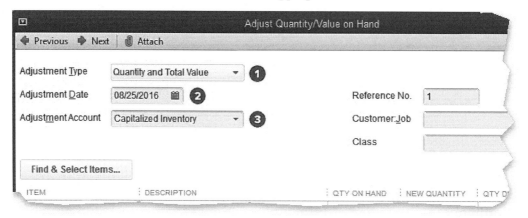

## How to Make an Inventory Adjustment

**① Adjustment Type.** The choices are to adjust the Quantity, Total Value, or Quantity and Total Value of Items you select for adjustment. (You may adjust Item quantities or values, or both.)

> ★ **QuickBooks uses the term *Total Value* to avoid confusion.** It means the value of an Item's entire inventory quantity. If you have 10 of an Item and each is worth $200, its total value would be $2,000.

**② Adjustment Date.** Usually this should be the date an inventory count or estimate was made, but not always.

For example, suppose today is January 2nd and you are preparing a balance sheet as of December 31st (of last year). If you didn't get to make an inventory count until today, January 2nd, you might want the adjustment dated December 31st so inventory (asset) values will be up to date for the December 31st balance sheet.

**③ Adjustment Account.** An account named Capitalized Inventory [65] is used throughout this book as the offsetting account for raised inventory adjustments. (You may use a different account for this purpose but *it must be an an equity account* and should be reserved for offsetting the unwanted financial effects of raised inventory adjustments.)

**Adjustment Account: the offsetting account for this transaction**

"Under the hood" QuickBooks is a double-entry accounting system: a second or *offsetting* account is involved in every transaction. Most of the time—like when you enter a check or a bank deposit—QuickBooks automatically selects the offsetting account for you, so you may not even realize that one is involved. In some kinds of transactions though, you must select the offsetting account.

3. **Select the Items you want to adjust,** in the form's detail area.

   If the Items are already set up [68] you can simply select them; if not, you will need to add the new Item(s) you need.

   ### How to select existing Items

   To select Items which already exist you can:

101

## Chapter 5 - Inventory Nuts & Bolts

❖ **Begin typing an Item name in the Item column, or select an Item from the list of Items.**

You can click in the Item column on a blank row, then begin typing. QuickBooks will display a list of Items matching what you have typed, and you can select one.

Or you can click on the down arrow in the Item column, and QuickBooks will display a drop-down list of all Items. Scroll through the list, then select an Item by clicking on it.

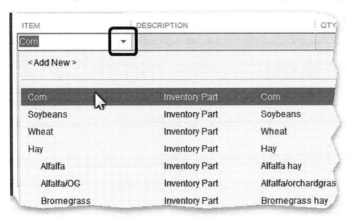

❖ **Select several Items at one time, using t**he Find & Select Items button.

Clicking the button opens a window which lets you select Items by checkmarking them:

## How to Make an Inventory Adjustment

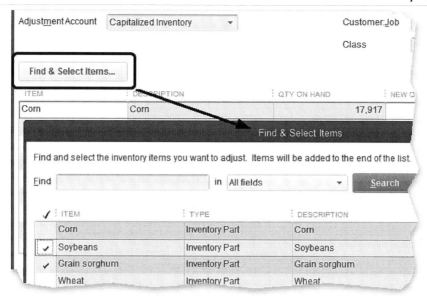

When you are done selecting Items click the Add Selected Items button (at the bottom of the window), and the check-marked Items will be added to the Adjust Quantity/Value on Hand window.

### How to add new Items

If you have things you want to inventory but do not yet have Items set up for them you can add new Items a couple different ways. You can:

❖ **Go to the Item list and add new Items there** 81, then come back to the Adjust Quantity/Value on Hand window and select the new Items.

❖ **Add new Items "on the fly" as you need them.** Here's how:

  a. **Type a new Item name** in the Item column of the Adjust Quantity/Value on Hand window, **then press the Tab key** or click elsewhere in the window.

  QuickBooks will notify you that the Item name was not found and will give you an opportunity to add it:

Chapter 5 - Inventory Nuts & Bolts

b. **Click Yes** to add the new Item.

QuickBooks will open the New Item window, with the name you typed pre-entered in the Item Name/Number field:

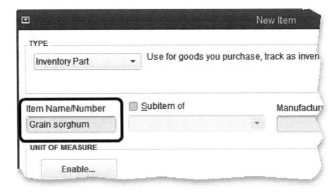

c. **Complete the Item's setup** by selecting accounts and filling in other information in the New Item window.

For details see *Setting Up Raised Inventory Items* 80.

# How to Make an Inventory Adjustment

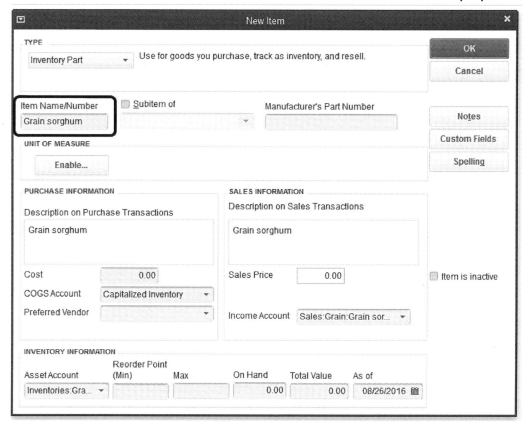

d. **Click the OK button** to add the new Item and close the window.

You will be returned to the Adjust Quantity/Value on Hand window, with the newly-added Item listed there:

**105**

## Chapter 5 - Inventory Nuts & Bolts

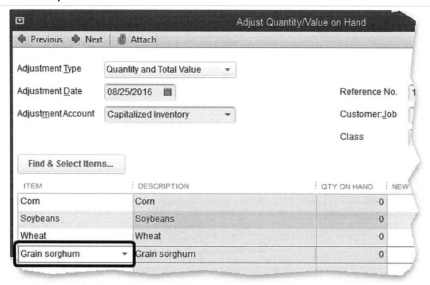

4. Enter a New Quantity and New Value for each Item.

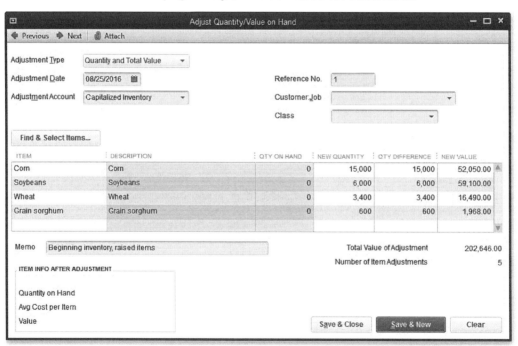

## How to Make an Inventory Adjustment

### If you are entering beginning inventories

For each Item, the New Quantity should be the quantity from an inventory count 91 or estimate, and the New Value should be the *total value* for the Item, not a per-unit value. For instance, if you have 1,000 bushels of wheat worth $4.00 per bushel, enter a New Value of $4,000.

For details on valuing inventories see *How to Value Raised Inventories* 149.

**New Values and the QuickBooks calculator**

If you entered 6,000 as the New Quantity for Soybeans and want to value them at $9.85 per bushel:

i. **Click in the New Value column** on the Soybeans Item line.

ii. **Type the following:**

        6000*9.85=

That is, type "6000", an asterisk "*" (the calculator's multiplication sign), "9.85", and finally an equal sign "=". When you are done, the calculator window should look like the one at right.

iii. **Press Enter** to accept the calculated result in the New Value column.

| NEW QUANTITY | QTY DIFFERENCE | NEW VALUE |
|---|---|---|
| 15,000 | 15,000 | 52,050.00 |
| 6,000 | 6,000 | 59,100.00 |
| 3,400 | 3,400 | 16,490.00 |
| 600 | 600 | 1,968.00 |

### If you are adjusting existing inventories

When adjusting quantities you have the option of entering an inventory change as a Quantity Difference instead of a New Quantity.

For instance, if you have 84 calves in inventory and 3 drown when they fall through thin ice on a pond, you could enter a Quantity Difference of -3. QuickBooks will automatically calcu-

**107**

late the New Quantity as 81. (Or, you could directly enter the New Quantity as 81—you can do it either way.)

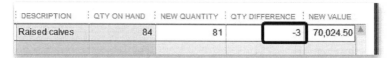

5. *Optional:* **Type a note in the Memo field** to remind you of the adjustment's purpose—useful information if you later need to review or edit old/prior adjustments:

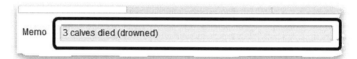

Some examples:

- *Beginning inventory, raised*
- *Update soybean inventory before harvest*
- *Inventory @ end of harvest*
- *Calving season completed*
- *Death loss, week of 5 Dec. 2016*

6. **Click the Save & Close button** to save your beginning inventories (or inventory adjustments) and close the window.

**Save often!**

When entering a large number of inventory adjustment lines you risk losing what have typed if you happen to accidentally press the *Escape* key, which will close the Adjust Quantity/Value on Hand window.

To minimize chances of losing what you have typed, you can save what you have entered after every few lines: click the Save & New button, then the Previous button (at the top of the window). That will save what's on the form, then return to it to let you add more rows.

## Inventory Adjustment Questions & Answers

### *I have a lot of adjustments to make. Should I put them all in one entry or split them up among several?*

Here are some general tips:

- **When you have a lot of adjustments to make, group related adjustments in separate adjustment entries** even if the Adjustment Date is the same on all of them. Grouping adjustments makes their purpose more clear, and lets you include more specific comments in the Memo field of each one.

    *Example:* Suppose you need to update corn, soybean, and grain sorghum inventories after completing harvest, but you also need to reduce the inventory of feeder calves due to death loss. The death loss should be in a separate entry from the one for harvested grains. And if your grain adjustments involve multiple grain storage locations 199 or other complications—like separate adjustments for Corn, White Corn, and Popcorn—then it may make sense to use a separate adjustment entry for each grain.

- **Usually, you shouldn't make adjustment entries that have a large number of lines.** Having a lot of Item lines in a single entry can lead to errors or confusion if you need to review or edit the adjustment later. Splitting adjustments among several separate entries is preferable.

    *Example:* Suppose you are getting ready to prepare a balance sheet and need to adjust values for several dozen inventory Items: grains, cattle, sheep, fertilizer and other crop supplies, feedstuffs, and general supplies like diesel fuel. Splitting those adjustments among several entries would be preferable to lumping them together in one big entry.

- **Use the Memo field to label each adjustment.** Giving a specific reason for the adjustment can be useful information later if you need to review adjustments you made in the past.

Chapter 5 - Inventory Nuts & Bolts

## *How can I delete an inventory adjustment?*

1. **Open the inventory adjustment window** (Vendors > Inventory Activities > Adjust Quantity/Value on Hand).

2. **Use the Previous and Next buttons** at the top of the window to position to the adjustment you want to delete.

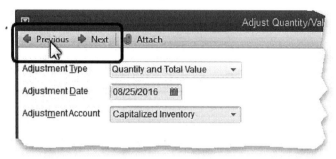

3. **Select** Edit > Delete Inventory Adjust to delete the entire adjustment.

     **If you only want to delete a specific line** and not the entire adjustment entry, click on the line you want to delete, then select Edit > Delete line.

**CHAPTER 6**

# Production, Sales, and Common Transactions

| About this chapter | This chapter describes basic, common transactions for raised inventories 15. |

## Sales of Raised Inventory

### Cash Sales of Raised Inventory (Sales Receipt)

***Problem*** Last week I sold 2,000 bushels of corn that we had in storage at a local elevator. I received a check in today's mail for the corn. How should I enter the sale?

***Solution*** This is a cash sale, so enter it on the Sales Receipts form.

***Discussion*** Purely from an accounting standpoint, a *cash sale* means selling or delivering something and being paid immediately, and a *credit sale* means selling or delivering something but not expecting payment until later—even if "later" is only a few days later.

Cash sales are entered as a single transaction, on the Sales Receipts form. Credit sales are entered in two steps: (1) you enter the sale as an invoice (on the Invoices form) when you deliver goods or they are picked up by the buyer, then (2) when the buyer pays, you receive payment 263 on the invoice to "close" it (to cancel out the amount the buyer owes on the invoice).

From a practical standpoint though, things usually work a bit differently. You may not be paid for days or weeks after delivering grain to an elevator, selling livestock at auction, or letting your neighbor pick up a couple big round bales of straw from you to use for livestock bedding. So technically, these are credit sales. But if you are like most farm recordkeepers, you don't typically enter an invoice for such sales. More likely, you just wait until payment is received—i.e., the check arrives from the grain elevator or livestock auction, or your neighbor stops by to pay for the straw—then make a single entry for the sale, on the Sales Receipts form.

This is why the corn sale in this example is entered as a sales receipt rather than as an invoice.

## How to Enter a Cash Sale of Inventory

1. **Open the Sales Receipts form** (Customers > Enter Sales Receipts).

2. **Fill in the form** as shown below.

# Sales of Raised Inventory

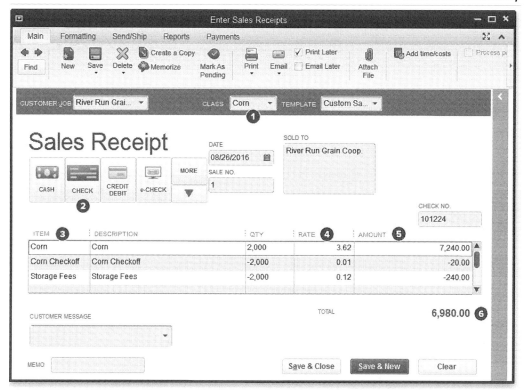

1. **Class.** *Optional.* The Corn Class selected here indicates that the sale represents income to the farm's corn enterprise. Using Classes allows getting separate profit and loss reports for specific enterprises or "departments" of the farm business. However, the discussion of Classes is beyond the scope of this book.

2. **Payment Type.** Select a payment type by clicking the appropriate button. *Check* is selected here.

3. **Item**

    ❖ **Corn** is an Inventory Part Item, so the Corn line of this transaction will reduce Corn inventories by 2,000 bushels and will post income to the account associated with the Corn Item [81].

    ❖ **Corn Checkoff** is an assessment on corn sales for market development and promotion. QuickBooks multiplies the negative quantity (-2000) on this line by the per-bushel charge (0.01) to calculate the Amount. Because the Amount is negative it will deduct from the sales receipt's total, and will post expense to Misc.Expense:Checkoff, the account associated with the Corn Checkoff Item 88.

❖ **Storage Fees** records the elevator's charge for storing the crop. QuickBooks multiplies the negative quantity (-2000) on this line by the per-bushel charge (0.12) to calculate the Amount. Because the Amount is negative it will deduct from the sales receipt's total, and will post expense to Storage & Warehousing, the account associated with the Storage Fees Item 89.

④ **Rate (Price).** Often it is preferable to enter the Qty (quantity) and Amount, and let QuickBooks calculate the Rate. For inventory and financial accounting purposes the quantity and Amount need to be accurate, but the Rate is mostly informational and can sometimes be an odd decimal amount.

⑤ **Amount.** QuickBooks will calculate the Amount automatically by multiplying the Qty (quantity) by the Rate. However, as mentioned above, if you enter the Qty and the Amount, QuickBooks will calculate the Rate instead.

⑥ **Total.** The total must match the amount of the check you received. If not, most likely you have entered an incorrect Amount for one of the Items.

3. **Click the Save & Close button** to save the transaction and close the form, **or Save & New** to save the transaction and keep the Sales Receipts form open for entering another sale.

### But do I really need to enter selling fees on separate Item lines?

In the example above, Corn Checkoff and Storage fees are deducted on Item lines separate from the Corn Item. The alternative would be to enter the entire payment on one line as corn income. Which way is best? Entering net proceeds of the sale on a single line is OK to do but may not provide the information you need for management or income tax purposes.

## Sales of Raised Inventory

**Management information.** Storage fees can be a significant expense. If you don't make a separate entry for them you will not know how much you have spent for storage during the year. The same can be true for commissions and selling fees; inspection fees; dockage and other quality discounts; yardage, feed, and veterinary charges when selling livestock through an auction; and so on. If you set up separate Items for such expenses you can get reports showing the total amounts spent on those items over a period of time.

You don't need to have a separate Item for *every* fee and deduction. For instance, you might set up an Item named Livestock Selling Fees and use it for deducting the combined total of commissions, yardage, inspection, veterinary fees, and feed charges associated with selling livestock at auction. Just decide which expenses you want details on, and set up Items accordingly.

**Income tax records.** If you sell grain or other products to a cooperative, at the end of the year you may receive an IRS form 1099-PATR from them showing the gross dollar amount of those products which you sold to them. Called *per-unit retains,* cooperatives get to deduct those amounts from their taxable income if they report them to you on a 1099-PATR, to disclose that you are responsible for paying the income taxes on them.

How does this relate to the way you enter sales in QuickBooks? On the 1099-PATR, cooperatives report the *gross dollar amount* of sales you made to them. If you enter sales in QuickBooks as *net dollar amounts* (without separating out selling fees and other discounts) then the 1099-PATR won't match the corn sales reported by QuickBooks, and you will have to figure out why they are different. Most likely, you will have to reduce corn sales income and increase expenses to make your Federal income tax filing conform to the amounts on the 1099-PATR.

## What happens (in QuickBooks) when you enter a sale of raised inventory?

Selling an inventory Item affects inventory quantities and several account balances. Here are short descriptions of changes resulting from the corn sale shown above. (Reviewing how the Corn Item 81 is set up may help with understanding these changes.)

❖ **Corn inventory.** QuickBooks keeps track of the quantity on hand for Inventory Part Items. The sale will decrease the Corn Item's inventory quantity by 2,000 bushels.

- **Income.** The sale will add $7,240 to the Sales:Grain:Corn income account, which will be included on profit and loss reports and income tax reports.

- **Asset value.** The balance in the Inventory:Corn asset account will be reduced, *but not by the amount of the sale!* The reduction in asset value is based on the Corn Item's *Average cost per Item,* which is not visible in the Sales Receipts form but is available in the Corn Item's setup window 86, in some Item reports 189, and also in the Inventory Center 187.

    If Corn's *Average cost per Item* is currently $3.47, then the Inventory:Corn account's balance would be reduced by: 2,000 * $3,47 = $6,940.

- **Capitalized Inventory (an equity account).** QuickBooks is a double-entry accounting system, so the $6,940 decrease in asset value described above must be offset by also posting $6,940 to some other account. In accrual accounting this amount would be posted to a Cost of Goods Sold (COGS) account. But the Corn Item is set up for cash basis accounting, so the offsetting amount is posted to an equity account named Capitalized Inventory 65.

- **Undeposited Funds.** The amount of the payment (check) received was $6,980, and that amount will be posted to the Undeposited Funds account 176, discussed in the next topic below.

## What about depositing the check?

Sales Receipts record income from a sale but they also record the *proceeds* from the sale—the check, cash, etc. which was received as payment. Normally, QuickBooks automatically posts sale proceeds to the Undeposited Funds 176 account—a sort of temporary "holding tank" for received payments, where they will stay until you choose to include them in a bank deposit 175.

However, you have the option of showing a *Deposit To* field on the Sales Receipts form, to allow choosing the account where you want sale proceeds to be posted. To show the *Deposit To* field, remove the checkmark from the Preferences setting at: Edit > Preferences > Payments > Company Preferences [tab] > Use Undeposited Funds as a default deposit to account. It will appear in the form's header area:

## Sales of Raised Inventory

⭐ **Most QuickBooks users should leave the *Deposit To* field disabled,** so received payments will always be posted to Undeposited Funds. See Chapter 8 - Depositing Payments You Have Received  to learn more.

## Raised Inventory Sales Questions & Answers

### Is it OK to enter sales if they will cause the inventory quantity to be negative in QuickBooks?

Yes. A negative inventory quantity only means that QuickBooks *says* you have sold more of an Item than you actually had available. That may or may not be true depending on how up-to-date your inventories are in QuickBooks.

In a typical farming operation, a negative inventory more often means that you have entered some sales before having an opportunity to update inventories for production (livestock births, harvested grain or forages, etc.). If you enter grain sales in QuickBooks during harvest but don't adjust inventories for harvested production until later, your inventories will be negative for a while simply because QuickBooks didn't "know about" the harvested grain.

In a retail business, negative inventory quantities can signal supply problems. They often mean that more of something has been promised to customers than is actually available. This can happen when sales are entered in QuickBooks (invoiced) before merchandise is actually delivered or picked up by customers. Maybe more of the Item needs to be ordered, or maybe more has been ordered but the shipment has not arrived yet. However, a negative inventory can also be caused by making an error when entering a transaction (entering the wrong quantity) or an error in counting items when taking a physical inventory.

The bottom line is that negative inventory quantities are not a problem so long as you know *why* they are negative.

Chapter 6 - Production, Sales, and Common Transactions

### How to turn off "*You don't have sufficient quantity on hand to sell item XYZ.*" warnings

If you try to enter a sale for a greater quantity than you have in inventory, QuickBooks may display a message like this:

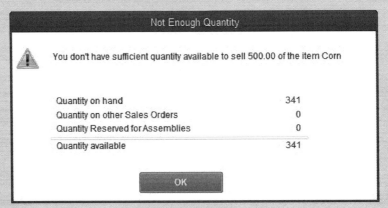

That's OK if you *want* to be warned when attempting to sell more of something than QuickBooks says you have on hand. But if you don't care that the inventory quantity will be negative, seeing this message every time you use the Item in a transaction may be annoying.

You can stop this warning message easily though, by changing the Preferences setting at **Edit > Preferences > Items & Inventory > Company Preferences [tab] > Warn if not enough inventory to sell**:

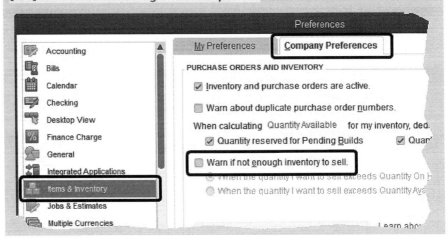

## *I sold part of the crop direct from the field at harvest—it was never put into storage. Do I have to add the crop to inventory in QuickBooks before I can enter those sales?*

No, you can enter sales at any time regardless of the inventory quantity in QuickBooks, without causing any problems. (See the question above 117, about negative inventories.) The reason this does not cause problems is that you are free to make an inventory adjustment 97 at any time. Prior sales and purchases can be completely ignored when updating QuickBooks' inventories to match what you currently have on hand.

Here is an example, beginning with a sales receipt for a corn sale made early during harvest, in September:

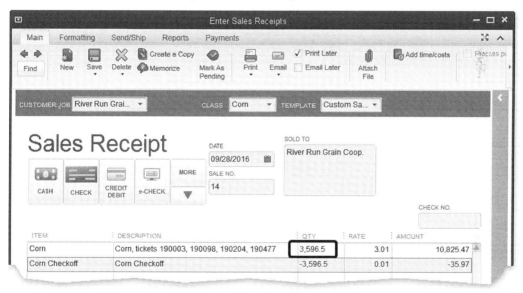

Assuming the corn inventory was zero when harvest began, the October 1st inventory would be negative by the quantity sold in September:

After harvest, the corn inventory can be adjusted to match the actual quantity on hand at that time, without regard to the sales made in September:

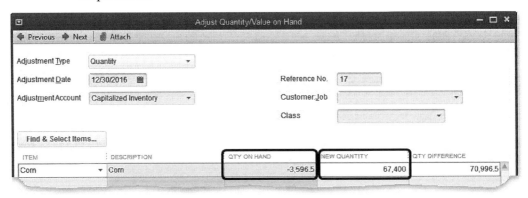

## Don't forget inventory quantities that are "in limbo"

Inventory adjustments should reflect the quantity you own, *which is not necessarily the same as the quantity you have on hand.* For example, you may have delivered grain or livestock to a buyer but not yet been paid for it.

Technically, items you have transferred to a buyer are no longer "your" inventories. You have traded one asset (the items you delivered) for another (accounts receivable—the amount the buyer owes you for the items). In accrual accounting, you would enter an invoice when items are transferred to a buyer, and it would record

## Sales of Raised Inventory

the decrease inventories, as well as the amount the buyer owes the farm business (accounts receivable).

In traditional cash basis accounting, such items are "in limbo": the physical inventory is gone but no accounting entry is made to record the inventory decrease. Nor is there any accounting entry to record the fact that buyer of the items now owes the farm business for them. If a balance sheet were prepared, it would include the asset value of inventories which the farm business no longer owns, and would fail to include the accounts receivable amount. (Accounts receivable are an asset of the business.)

Fortunately, QuickBooks makes it possible for cash basis recordkeepers to use invoices too. (QuickBooks can produce cash basis reports even if you use some of its accrual features, like invoices.) So if you are willing to use invoices you can prevent the problem of "in limbo" inventories. But most people don't want to bother with entering invoices for items when they expect to receive payment within a few days. An alternative then, is to include not-yet-paid-for items as if they were still inventories owned by the farm business.

Here is an example. Suppose you have harvested 23,000 bushels of soybeans, sold 3,000 bushels directly from the field, and put the remaining 20,000 bushels in storage. If you adjust soybean inventories in QuickBooks, what inventory quantity should you use?

That depends. Have you entered the 3,000 bushel sale yet? If not, and if you don't want to enter an invoice for it, the 3,000 bushels should be included in your inventory. The quantity for inventory adjustment should be 23,000 bushels, not 20,000 bushels. That way, your soybean inventories will still be correct later when you enter the 3,000 bushel sale: the sale will reduce the 23,000 bushel inventory to 20,000 bushels—the same as your actual physical inventory of soybeans.

If you forget to include "in limbo" quantities when adjusting inventories the fix is easy: just make another inventory adjustment (or edit the original one) to update the inventory quantity.

### Accounting 101: Using invoices to keep track of outstanding sales

Farming and ranching operations have traditionally used cash basis accounting, so most of us still rely on "cash basis habits" to get things done—habits about the way we enter transactions and do other activities, which make for simple, efficient bookkeeping. Unfortunately, those habits prevent many people from taking advantage of some accrual features of QuickBooks which could lead to better accounting.

Invoices are one of those features. Whenever you sell (or deliver) something but are not paid immediately, entering an invoice would provide a couple of benefits: (1) it would reduce inventory quantities for the items on the invoice, keeping your QuickBooks inventories current, and (2) it would record the amount the buyer owes you for the items. You can use invoices yet still get cash based income and expense reports for preparing income taxes, measuring profits, etc. (QuickBooks can reverse the accrual income recorded by invoices which are not yet paid, to produce cash basis reports.)

How much you should use invoices in cash basis accounting is sort of a balancing act, and a matter of personal preference. If you delivered three loads of grain today and expect to receive a check within a couple days, *usually* there would not be much benefit in entering an invoice for the grain. You can just wait until you receive a check from the buyer, then enter the sale in QuickBooks using the Sales Receipts form.

But suppose "today" is December 31st and you want to prepare an end-of-year balance sheet. In that case, entering an invoice for the three loads of grain would be a good idea. It would cause your balance sheet to present a more accurate picture of the farm business' assets, by showing reduced grain inventories but an increased accounts receivable amount.

Often you may not know the exact dollar amount to enter on an invoice—for a grain sale, you won't know the payment amount until you receive the buyer's settlement sheet, complete with all dockage and other deductions. In that case, enter the invoice for an approximate amount, then correct it later when you know the actual payment amount.

# Adding Farm Production to Inventory

***Problem*** I've just finished corn harvest and have about 28,000 bushels in storage. How do I adjust inventories in QuickBooks to show this quantity of corn on hand?

***Solution*** Make an inventory adjustment to update the Corn Item's quantity and value.

***Discussion*** In cash basis accounting, inventories of raised farm production just "magically appear" on the day you enter them into the accounting system. The example in this section is for corn inventories, but you would use the same steps for adding any kind of raised farm production—harvested grain or produce, livestock births, etc.—to your QuickBooks inventories.

> ⚠ **This section applies to raised inventories *but not to resale inventories*.** Raised items get into QuickBooks through inventory adjustments. Resale items become inventories when you enter a purchase transaction for them.

## When should you add production to inventory?

You could add corn to inventory each day of corn harvest, or you could add new calves to inventory as each calf is born…but neither would be very practical!

Choosing when to update inventories is a personal decision, but the most efficient approach is usually to wait until harvest is finished, or calving/lambing/kidding season is over, or a group of sows has completed farrowing, etc. If you enter some sales before adding production to your inventories—making grain sales during harvest, for instance—QuickBooks may warn that you are selling more inventory than you have on hand. But putting up with those warnings for a while (you can also turn them off ) is easier than trying to keep inventories updated during busy times.

123

## How to Adjust Inventories for Raised Farm Production

1. **Have a current physical count or estimate available** for Items you need to update. In this example, the current inventory of corn has increased to 28,000 bushels.

2. **Open the Adjust Quantity/Value on Hand window** (Vendors > Inventory Activities > Adjust Quantity/Value on Hand).

3. **Fill in the header fields,** as appropriate.

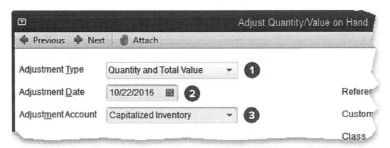

① **Adjustment Type.** Choose either *Quantity*, or *Quantity and Total Value*. *Quantity* lets you update inventory quantities only. *Quantity and Total Value* lets you also update inventory values—something you may want to do, especially, when preparing a balance sheet.

② **Adjustment Date.** This should be the date of the most recent known inventory quantity, such as the date a physical count was taken or estimated, or was known by other means such as weight tickets.

③ **Adjustment Account.** Use Capitalized Inventory [65] or another equity account you have reserved for raised inventory adjustments.

4. **Select the inventory Items you want to adjust.**

   You can adjust quantities and/or values for any number of Items, but in this example we will only adjust one, the Corn Item [86].

   As you select Items, QuickBooks will display their current quantity on hand:

# Adding Farm Production to Inventory

5. **Enter a New Quantity** for Corn, then press the Tab key.

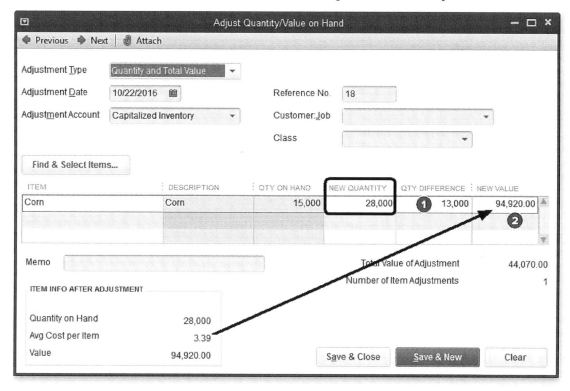

1. **Qty Difference.** When you enter a New Quantity QuickBooks subtracts the Qty on Hand from it to calculate the Qty Difference.

2. **New Value.** When you change the quantity QuickBooks calculates a New Value for the inventory based on the Item's existing Avg Cost per Item: 28,000 bushels * $3.39 per bushel = $94,920.00.

> **Where does the average cost come from?** It is simply the Item's total cost or total value divided by the quantity on hand. *For raised inventories, "average value" would be a more accurate term.*

6. **Enter a New Value** for Corn, then press the Tab key.

Assuming you want value inventories based on market values, if corn's net market value  (market price less transportation and other selling costs) is currently about $3.24 per bushel, the New Value would be $90,720. (See also: *How to Value Raised Inventories* 149).

🔧 **You must enter the *total value* of the inventory, not its per-unit value.** In this case the total is: 28,000 bushels * $3.24 per bushel = $90,720. Updating inventories would be easier if QuickBooks let you simply enter a new per-unit value, but it doesn't.

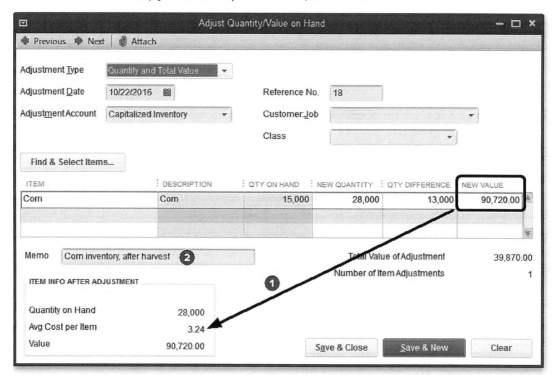

① **Avg Cost per Item.** After entering a New Value, if you click on the Corn Item's row again, you will see that QuickBooks has recalculated the Avg Cost per Item as $3.24. (It was $3.39 before.)

② **Memo.** Entering a reason for the adjustment is important. It can provide useful information later when reviewing adjustments, by reminding you of its purpose.

# Adding Farm Production to Inventory

**Using the QuickBooks calculator**

When making inventory adjustments, the calculator feature is handy for computing New Values. Here's how it would be used for the New Value entry above:

1. **Click in the New Value column** on the Corn Item's line.

2. **Type the following:**

    28000*3.24=

    That is, type "28000", an asterisk "*" (the calculator's multiplication sign), "3.24", and then an equal sign "=". When you are done, the calculator window should look like the one at right. (The calculator window opens when you type a math symbol, like the "*" for multiplication.)

    |   |           |
    |---|-----------|
    |   | 28,000.00 |
    | * | 3.24      |
    | = | 90,720.00 |
    |   | 90,720.00 |

3. **Press Enter** to accept the calculated result, 90,720.00, as the New Value entry.

7. **Click the Save & Close button** to save the inventory adjustment and close the window, **or Save & New** to save the adjustment and keep the window open for entering another.

## Understanding the Effects of an Inventory Adjustment

Let's explore the effects of the inventory adjustment above, for the Corn Item:

❖ **Quantity on Hand.** QuickBooks' inventory quantity for the Corn Item was updated. It is now 28,000 bushels.

❖ **Asset value of the corn inventory.** Every inventory Item has an asset account associated with it [83], which represents the Item's value on balance sheets. QuickBooks posted the $90,720 value of the Corn Item [86] to its asset account, Inventories:Corn. QuickBooks did that automatically, behind the scenes.

❖ **Adjustment Account.** Because QuickBooks is a double-entry accounting system, the $90,720 posted to Inventories:Corn must be offset by posting an equivalent amount to some other account. In this case Capitalized Inventory [65] was the offsetting account (selected as the Adjustment Account in the form's header area), so

127

it received the offsetting amount. Again, QuickBooks did this posting automatically, behind the scenes.

If you remember that Assets = Liabilities + Equity (the basic balance sheet formula, also known as the *accounting equation*), the offsetting post to Capitalized Inventory makes intuitive sense: assets (Inventories:Corn) have increased but liabilities have not, so equity (Capitalized Inventory) must be increased to keep the equation in balance. Or looked at differently, when the farm business produces something (creates an asset), the value of the owner's equity in the business has increased.

### Accounting 101: Double-entry accounting and inventory adjustments

QuickBooks is a double-entry accounting system, which means that every transaction affects at least two accounts, *even if you are not always aware that it does.*

For instance, if you use the Write Checks form (Banking > Write Checks) to enter a check for fuel, the amount of the check will be posted to Fuel Expense but also to the checking account—as a decrease in the bank balance; the second or "offsetting" part of the double entry.

Inventory adjustments likewise involve at least two accounts. Entering a new value for an inventory Item changes the balance of the inventory asset account associated with the Item. The second or offsetting part of the entry gets posted to the Adjustment Account you selected in the top part of the inventory adjustment window.

 **Want to see for yourself?** The next time you make an inventory adjustment, first open a Register window for the asset account associated with one of the Items you will be adjusting. And also, open a Register window for the Adjustment Account (i.e., Capitalized Inventory). Then enter the inventory adjustment. Afterward, look at the Register windows: you will see that a new transaction line has been added in each of them.

 **To open a Register window:** Open the Chart of Accounts window (Lists > Chart of Accounts), then click on the account you are interested in, to select it. Then type *Ctrl-R*. (or right-click on the account to show its pop-up menu, then select *Use Register* from the pop-up menu). Register windows are only available for balance sheet accounts: assets, liabilities, and equity.

# Adjusting for Inventory Losses (Livestock Deaths, Spoilage, etc.)

*Inventory shrinkage* is the accounting term for reductions in inventory value due to loss, theft, damage, or declines in quality. In a farm business it includes things like death loss of market livestock, spoilage of grain or produce, or storm damage to a growing crop.

 **In accrual accounting,** inventory losses are deductible as an expense.

**In cash basis accounting,** raised inventory losses *are not* deductible. Why? Because in cash basis accounting, production expenses associated with the raised items which have died or were spoiled or lost, *have already been deducted* as expense. Taking an expense deduction for inventory losses after already having deducted the costs of producing it (for seed, fertilizer, fuel, feed, etc.) would basically amount to double counting expenses. So when a loss occurs, only inventory quantities are adjusted.

 **Items purchased for resale are an exception.** When items like resale livestock die or are lost, their purchase cost *is* deductible as expense.

To keep inventories current you need to adjust them whenever you have an inventory loss. If you depend on QuickBooks for management information such as knowing how many bushels of grain or head of livestock you have available to sell, adjust inventories as soon as possible after a loss. Otherwise, consider waiting until a convenient time for taking a physical inventory count [91] and adjust inventories then, or ahead of preparing a balance sheet.

## Quantity Loss: A Livestock Death Loss Example

***Problem*** Two of our calves died. How do I adjust inventories for that? ...or... We lost about 500 bushels of corn to spoilage due to a grain bin roof leak. How do I adjust inventories for the loss?

***Solution*** Make an inventory adjustment to reduce the inventory quantity in QuickBooks.

*Discussion* When have a loss from inventory but the remaining Items are unaffected—they have not been damaged or lost any value—you can use a *Quantity* adjustment as a quick way to adjust for the loss.

Livestock deaths are a common example of this situation. If one animal dies due to disease or injury, the value of the remaining animals usually has not been affected. The example below adjusts inventory of the Calves Item for the loss of two calves.

1. **Open the Adjust Quantity/Value On Hand window** (Vendors > Inventory Activities > Adjust Quantity/Value on Hand).

2. **Fill in the header fields,** as appropriate.

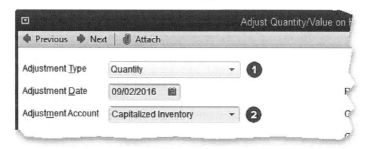

① **Adjustment Type.** Choose *Quantity* when only the inventory quantity needs to be adjusted. A Quantity adjustment lets you update the Item's quantity while keeping leaving per-unit value unchanged.

② **Adjustment Account.** Use Capitalized Inventory 65 or another equity account you have reserved for raised inventory adjustments.

3. **Select the Item you want to adjust;** Calves in this example.

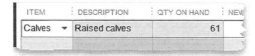

4. **Adjust the Item's inventory** by typing -2 in the Quantity Difference column, **then press the Tab key.**

You can either enter a New Quantity, or enter a Quantity Difference and let QuickBooks calculate the New Quantity. Because

## Adjusting for Inventory Losses (Livestock Deaths, Spoilage, etc.)

two calves died, entering a Quantity Difference of -2 is easy and makes intuitive sense:

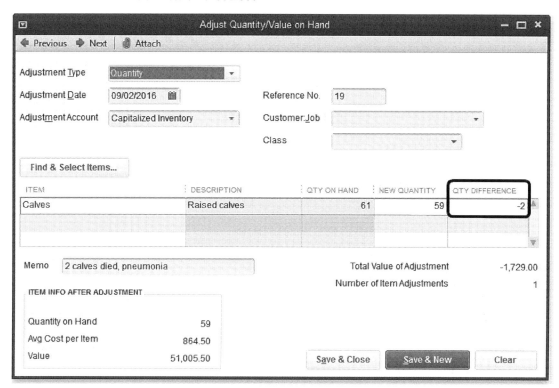

5. **Click the Save & Close button** to save the inventory adjustment and close the window.

## Quantity *and* Value Loss: A Grain Sorghum Example

***Problem*** Moisture migrated into the top part of a bin of not-quite-dry-enough grain sorghum and formed a moldy layer of grain at the surface. We removed 400 bushels of the top layer with a grain vac and dumped in a pile outside, to be spread on fields later—a complete loss. With other pockets of mold in the bin plus the beginnings of a weevil infestation, the remaining grain is probably worth 25 cents per bushel less than before. How should I adjust my grain sorghum inventory?

***Solution*** Make an inventory adjustment using the Quantity and Total Value adjustment type, to change both the quantity and the value of the inventory.

***Discussion*** The grain sorghum inventory needs to be adjusted for the decreased quantity (the 400 bushel loss), but also for the 25-cent decline in value of the remaining bushels. Correcting the inventory quantity can be important for management purposes—to know how many bushels are left, available to sell or to use as feed. And adjusting the value is important, especially, when preparing a balance sheet.

This example assumes the bin contains the entire inventory of grain sorghum, but the same ideas would apply if the inventory were spread among several storage locations.

1. **Open the Adjust Quantity/Value On Hand window** (Vendors > Inventory Activities > Adjust Quantity/Value on Hand).

2. **Fill in the header fields,** as appropriate.

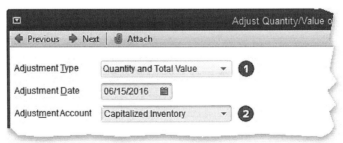

## Adjusting for Inventory Losses (Livestock Deaths, Spoilage, etc.)

**❶ Adjustment Type.** Select *Quantity and Total Value*.

**❷ Adjustment Account.** Use Capitalized Inventory [65] or another equity account you have reserved for raised inventory adjustments.

3. **Select the Item you want to adjust;** Grain Sorghum for this example.

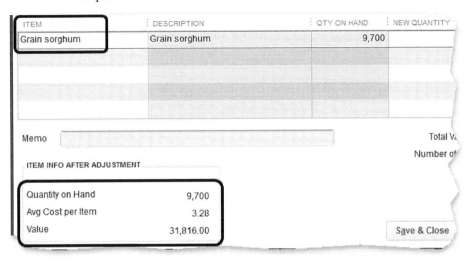

4. **Update the Item's quantity** by either entering a New Quantity or a Quantity Difference, **then press the Tab key.**

    Because 400 bushels were lost, the easy way to make the adjustment is by entering -400 in the Quantity Difference column and letting QuickBooks calculate the New Quantity:

5. **Update the Item's value** by entering a value in the New Value column, **then press the Tab key.**

    You must enter the *total value* of the inventory (which will now be 9,300 bushels). It would be simpler if you could just enter a per-bushel price and have QuickBooks calculate the New Value, but it doesn't work that way—you have to do the calculation yourself.

## Chapter 6 - Production, Sales, and Common Transactions

The average value for the grain sorghum Item currently is $3.28 per bushel (see the screenshot in step 3 above). Reducing the value by 25 cents would result in a new value of $3.28 - $0.25 = $3.03 per bushel. So the New Value would be calculated as: 9,300 bushels * $3.03 per bushel = $28,179, and entered this way:

### Using the QuickBooks calculator

The calculator feature in QuickBooks can make the New Value calculation easy:

1. **Click in the New Value column** on the Grain Sorghum line.

2. **Type the following:**

    3.28-.25*9300=

   That is, type "3.28", then a minus sign "-", then ".25", then an asterisk "*" (the calculator's multiplication symbol), then "9300", and finally an equal sign "=". The calculator window, which opens when you type a math symbol like the minus sign, should look like the one at right.

3. **Press Enter** to accept the calculated result, 28,179.

6. **If you click on the Grain Sorghum line** to return to that line of the form, you can see how the adjustment will affect both the quantity and value for the Grain Sorghum Item, in the Item Info box toward the lower left part of the window:

7. **Click the Save & Close button** to save the inventory adjustment and close the window.

# Adjusting for Inventory Usage (as Livestock Feed, etc.)

## Corn Inventory Used as Livestock Feed

**Problem**   We fed about 550 bushels of corn to calves in our backgrounding (post-weaning) lots this month. How should we adjust corn inventories for the amount used for feed?

**Solution**   Make an inventory adjustment to reduce the Corn Item's inventory quantity by the number of bushels fed.

**Discussion**   To keep QuickBooks inventories current for quantities consumed within the farm business, all you need to do is make a quantity adjustment. Decreasing the quantity on hand will automatically decrease the inventory value by a proportional dollar amount.

1. **Open the Adjust Quantity/Value On Hand window** (Vendors > Inventory Activities > Adjust Quantity/Value on Hand).

2. **Make an inventory adjustment for feed usage,** like the following:

Chapter 6 - Production, Sales, and Common Transactions

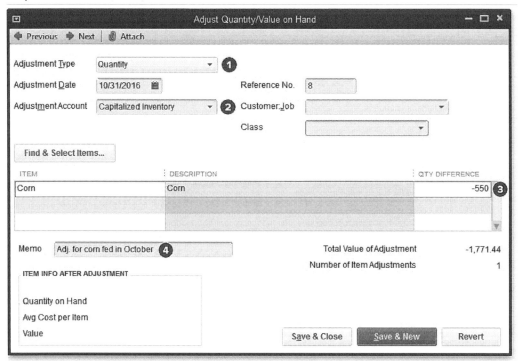

① **Adjustment Type.** Choose the *Quantity* adjustment type.

② **Adjustment Account.** Use Capitalized Inventory [65] or another equity account you have reserved for raised inventory adjustments.

③ **Qty Difference.** You can update the inventory quantity by entering either a New Quantity or a Quantity Difference. The estimated usage was 550 bushels, so the easy approach is to enter a Quantity Difference of -550 (that's *negative* 550).

④ **Memo.** Include a comment in the Memo field as a reminder of the reason for the adjustment.

3. **Click the Save & Close button** to save the inventory adjustment and close the window.

# Adjusting for Inventory Usage (as Livestock Feed, etc.)

**Keeping a record of inventory usage, between adjustments**

When grain or forage is used for feed, common practice is to adjust their inventories periodically—maybe every couple weeks, or monthly. Between those times you need a simple way to keep inventory usage/consumption.

Your system could be as uncomplicated as a clipboard hanging on the wall of your feed processing center, where you write down ingredient quantities for each feed batch. Or it might be notepad in the pickup truck you use for hauling hay out to cows, or a note-taking or voice recording app on a smartphone. Or you might use a smartphone to send text messages to your email address, to have an electronic record of feed usage. These are just a few examples of ways to keep a physical record of inventory use.

More sophisticated recordkeeping systems may be called for in some situations, especially when multiple employees or family members are involved. A paper or computerized system of feed tickets or scale weight tickets might produce a ticket or electronic record for each batch of feed, showing pounds of each ingredient used as well as the destination pen or group of livestock to which it was delivered.

Often the simplest solution is the best. Instead of keeping daily records of usage you might just count, measure, or eyeball the remaining inventory quantity—take a "mini" inventory count—when the time comes to make an inventory adjustment.

## Tracking Inventory Used for Specific Purposes

***Problem*** I have been adjusting corn inventories for feed usage as shown in the example above, and I'd like to get a report showing just the total quantity used for feed, separate from corn sales and other inventory adjustments. But in the reports I have tried, the feed usage is all jumbled together with other transactions—sales, purchases, and so on. How can I get a report that shows only the feed usage?

***Solution*** Add a Class or a Customer:Job name to the inventory adjustments you make for feed usage. Then you will be able to filter reports for that Class or Customer:Job name, so they include only feed usage adjustments.

## Discussion

Without something like a Class or a Customer:Job name, there is nothing in an inventory adjustment which can identify it with a particular category of adjustments, for reporting purposes.

Here is a report fragment demonstrating the problem. Arrows indicate the adjustments for corn used for feed, mingled with other transactions for the Corn Item:

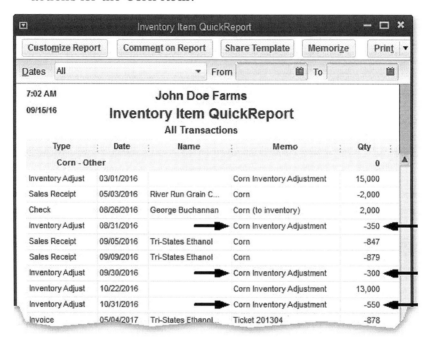

This section shows how to set up a Class name, use it in inventory adjustments, and filter reports to include only the feed usage adjustments.

 **Customer:Jobs are an alternative to using Classes,** as described at the end of this section 144.

## Setting up a Class

If you are already using the Classes feature of QuickBooks, you may have an existing Class you can use on inventory adjustments. For example, you might have a Cattle Class which you could apply to inventory adjustments when corn has been used as cattle feed. Other-

## Adjusting for Inventory Usage (as Livestock Feed, etc.)

wise, you will need to set up a Class for that purpose—or more than one Class if corn is fed to different types of livestock, for example.

**Don't see Classes mentioned in QuickBooks menus or forms?**

If not, you need to enable the Classes feature:

1. **Select** Edit > Preferences > Accounting > Company Preferences [tab] > Use class tracking for transactions.

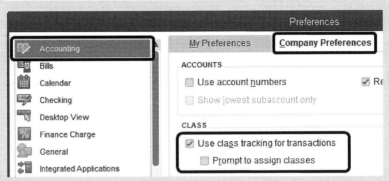

2. *Optional.* **Checkmark** *Prompt to assign classes.*

   When *Prompt to assign classes* is enabled, QuickBooks reminds you to select a Class if you fail to select one when entering a transaction.

3. **Click on the OK button** to save your changes and close the Preferences window.

 *Class fields do not automatically appear on all QuickBooks forms.* Some forms must be customized to include the Class field. On most forms, select Formatting > Customize Data Layout from the ribbon bar at the top of the form:

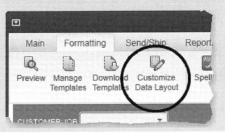

**139**

## How to add a new Class

1. **Open the Class list window** (Lists > Class List).

2. **Select** Class > New from the button menu at the bottom of the window.

   The New Class window will open.

3. **Type a name for the new Class:**

   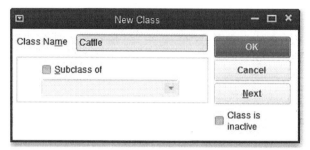

    **Classes are not limited to single-level names.** You may often see Class names like Cattle:Backgrounding, Corn:White, or Corn:Popcorn. In these examples, the name in front of the colon (e.g., Corn) is the parent Class, and the name following the colon (e.g., White, or Popcorn) is a subclass of the parent. If you have more than just a few Classes, arranging them in this way makes the Class list easier to use, and groups related information together on Class reports.

4. **Click the OK button** to add the new Class.

## Using the Class on an inventory adjustment

Here is the same inventory adjustment shown earlier, but with a Class selected in the Class field.

### Adjusting for Inventory Usage (as Livestock Feed, etc.)

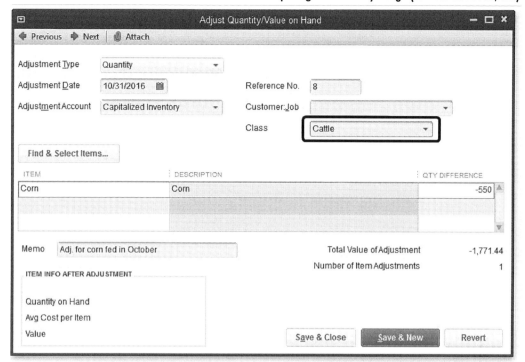

🔧 **You can only assign one Class to an inventory adjustment.** If you need to assign several different Classes to inventory adjustments, you can do that by making separate adjustment entries.

## Getting an inventory report filtered by Class

Let's get a QuickReport for the Corn Item again, but this time filtered by the Cattle Class so it will only show inventory adjustments for feed usage.

1. **Open the Item List** (Lists > Item List).

2. **Click on the Item for which you want to report on,** to select it; Corn in this example.

3. **Select** Reports > QuickReport from the button menu at the bottom of the window.

141

## Chapter 6 - Production, Sales, and Common Transactions

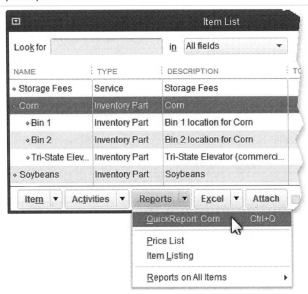

A QuickReport window will open for the Corn Item—the same as shown earlier, with feed usage mixed in with other transactions:

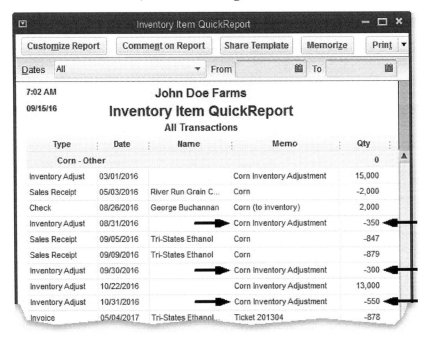

4. **Click the Customize Report button** near the top of the report window.

# Adjusting for Inventory Usage (as Livestock Feed, etc.)

The Modify Report window will open.

5. On the Filters tab, **select Class** in the Filter panel, **then select the Cattle Class in the dropdown list** in the center of the window.

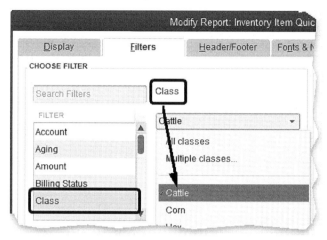

6. **Click the OK button** to close the Modify Report window.

The report will be redisplayed, showing only transactions tagged with the Cattle Class. Here, an approximately 1,200 bushels of corn were fed to cattle from August through October:

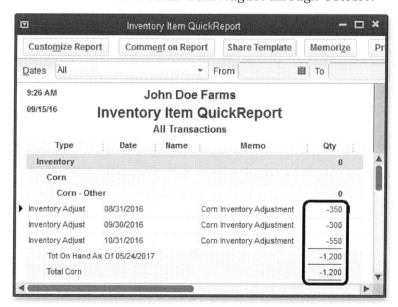

143

Chapter 6 - Production, Sales, and Common Transactions

### What about using *Customer:Job* names instead of *Classes*?

Many QuickBooks users assume the purpose of the Customer:Jobs list is only to identify customers and keep track of their names and addresses, but its uses are much more wide ranging. Think of the Customer:Jobs list as a list of Customer names plus a list of activities (Jobs) related to those names, which you can use for identifying transactions.

For in-house transactions (internal to your farm business) it may be helpful to have a customer named House, or something similar. Then, instead of using a Class to keep track of corn inventory usage as was shown above, you might set up a Job named House:Cattle, and use it on inventory adjustments.

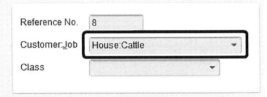

Like Classes, you can filter reports for specific Customer:Jobs, to limit them to specific types or groups of transactions.

### Cost accounting for inventory consumed within the farm business

Some farm businesses use the Classes feature to track income and expenses for specific farm enterprises. You might have Classes set up for each of the crops or types of produce you raise (Corn, Soybeans, Wheat, Sweet Corn, Tomatoes, etc.), for livestock production stages (Farrowing, Nursery, Finishing; Cow/Calf, Backgrounding, Feedlot; etc.), or for any farm business "department" you want to identify.

If you raise grain or forage that is fed to livestock, you may want to credit crop Classes with income for the raised feed, and charge livestock Classes with an expense for the grain or forage they consume. The goal is to measure profitability separately for each part of the farm business, to help you decide which parts are more profitable, or where changes are needed. For instance, you might find that your Corn enterprise is barely profitable and that you would be better off financially to stop raising corn and purchase the feed you need.

Accounting for the internal (within the farm business) income and expenses is referred to as *managerial accounting* or *cost accounting*, and is an advanced topic which is beyond the scope of this book. It can be done in QuickBooks but requires a lot of accounting effort and a solid understanding of the accounting concepts involved.

# Closing Out a Raised Inventory

**Problem**  We delivered the last of the soybeans a week ago—the bins are empty now. But after entering all of the soybean sales QuickBooks says we still have 189 bushels on hand. How do I fix that?

**Solution**  Enter a quantity adjustment for the Soybeans Item, to reduce its inventory quantity to zero.

**Discussion**  When you close out an inventory (when sell or use all of it) the inventory quantity in QuickBooks *very often will not be zero* after you have entered all sales or other transactions for the Item.

In this example QuickBooks shows an inventory of 189 bushels of soybeans, though the bins are empty and all of the soybean transactions have been entered. QuickBooks could just as easily have shown a *negative* 189 bushel inventory. Discrepancies like this happen often and for many reasons: inaccurate bin measurements, inventory shrinkage, livestock death losses that didn't get recorded, grain test weight differences, and so on. The simple fact is that an accounting system's inventories are *always just an estimate* of what you actually have on hand.

Handling this situation is easy: simply adjust the Item's inventory quantity to zero. This is no different from other inventory adjustments—you are simply correcting the inventory quantity to match the actual physical quantity on hand.

1. **Open the Adjust Quantity/Value On Hand window** (Vendors > Inventory Activities > Adjust Quantity/Value on Hand).

2. **Fill in the header fields,** as appropriate.

Chapter 6 - Production, Sales, and Common Transactions

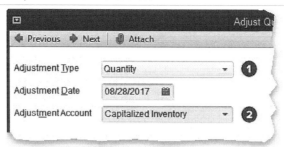

① **Adjustment Type.** You only need to correct the quantity, so select *Quantity* as the adjustment type.

② **Adjustment Account.** Use Capitalized Inventory 65 or another equity account you have reserved for raised inventory adjustments.

3. **Select the Item you want to adjust**—Soybeans in this example.

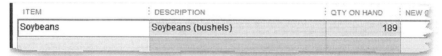

4. **Update the Item's quantity** by entering a New Quantity of 0 (zero), then pressing the tab key.

## Closing Out a Raised Inventory

After you do, the Item Info box in the lower left corner of the window should show that the Item's quantity and value are now zero:

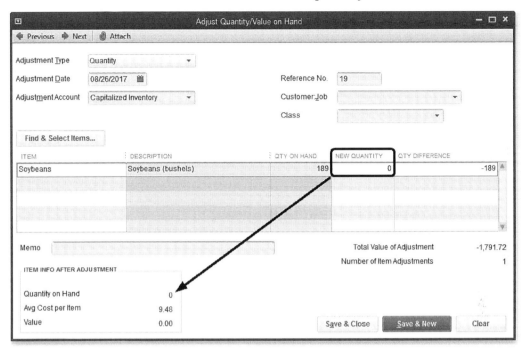

5. **Click the Save & Close button** to save the inventory adjustment and close the window.

This page is intentionally blank.

CHAPTER 7

# Other Inventory Adjustments and Transactions

| **About this chapter** | This chapter shows how to enter miscellaneous inventory adjustments and less-common transactions. |

## How to Value Raised Inventories

Often when you make an inventory adjustment [97] you will need to assign a value to the inventory. For instance, if you have just finished wheat harvest and now have 9,000 bushels of wheat in storage, you need to make an adjustment for the Wheat Item to update its quantity and value. But what value should you assign? ...market price? ...per-bushel cost of production? ...something else? This section will help you decide how to value raised inventories.

 **The ideas in this section apply to *raised* inventories but not to *resale* inventories.** Resale inventories should be valued at their purchase cost, for income tax recordkeeping purposes.

### Why place a value on inventories?

As you make inventory adjustments throughout the year, sometimes you might only adjust an Item's quantity or only its value. Sometimes both.

Quantity adjustments are necessary to keep QuickBooks' inventories in synch with the actual physical inventories you have on hand. But why adjust an Item's value? The entire reason is because Item values show up as assets on the farm balance sheet. Raised inventories are usually considered current assets of the farm business.

## Valuing Raised Inventories

Farmers and ranchers traditionally value raised inventories—growing crops, grain in storage, growing market livestock, etc.—based on their market value. This may or may not be correct from an accounting standpoint, depending on who is the main "consumer" of your financial reports; that is, depending on who is using them as a source of information about the farm business.

## The Lower of Cost or Market Rule

Accountants often apply what is known as the Lower of Cost or Market (LCM) rule when valuing inventories, which says that inventories should be valued at *the lower of* either their cost (purchase, replacement, or production cost) or their *net market value* (market value less any selling costs).

>  **See the Accounting 101** [151] discussion of the Lower of Cost or Market rule for more information.

In agriculture though, applying the LCM rule is usually hindered by a lack of cost information. Few farming operations have a detailed record of production costs for a crop or a group of market livestock. One reason is that cash basis accounting makes tracking production costs difficult to do in a general-purpose accounting system like QuickBooks. It is *possible* to do with full accrual accounting, but the job is never simple.

>  **Some ag-specific accounting packages** have features for tracking production costs for raised farm inventories. Even with these however, production cost accounting requires more time and accounting effort than most people are willing to spend.

Because cost information is lacking, valuing farm inventories based on market prices has essentially become the standard approach in most of agriculture. Lenders—who are typically the main consumers of balance sheet information outside of the farm business—are accustomed to, and expect, their customers to value farm inventories based on market prices.

**Agricultural lending practices are well adapted** to analyzing market value-based balance sheets. Market-valued inventories are well suited for making short-term lending decisions because they predict the farm business' near-term cash situation reasonably well. For longer-term lending, rules of thumb lenders apply in analyzing loans (required equity percentages, equity growth over time, and others) automatically make some allowances for the way farm assets are typically valued.

### Accounting 101: The Lower of Cost or Market rule

Generally accepted accounting principles(GAAP) are the commonly agreed to standards adopted by accountants in the U.S. They specify that inventories should be valued according to the Lower of Cost or Market (LCM) rule, which states that inventories should be valued at *the lower of* either their cost (purchase, replacement, or production cost) or their net market value (market value less any selling costs).

Applying the LCM rule is meant to avoid:

- **Overstating the *net realizable value* of assets.** If you value soybean inventories at $15.00 per bushel when their market price is only $12.00 you are overstating the income you could realize by selling them, and thus overstating their asset value.

   Further, if trucking the soybeans to market would cost $0.25 per bushel, the *net realizable value* of the soybeans would actually be $12.00 - $0.25 = $11.75 per bushel. Transportation and other selling costs reduce the net amount of income that could be realized from selling the soybeans.

- **Overstating your *investment* in assets.** Suppose the current market price of soybeans is $12.00 per bushel and your production costs are about $8.00 per bushel. If you value soybean inventories at $12.00 you are overstating your investment in them by $4.00 per bushel. When inventories are valued at no more than you have invested in producing them, the balance sheet portrays farm business assets at their *earned value,* rather than market value—which may be inflated due to current market prices.

This explanation oversimplifies how accountants apply the LCM rule. To learn more, do an Internet search for "lower of cost or market" and "net realizable value".

## OK, so <u>how should I</u> value raised inventories?

To best answer this question, first consider who are the "consumers" of the information on your balance sheet reports, and how they would prefer assets to be valued. Whether that consumer is your lender, yourself, or someone else, most people expect agricultural inventories to be valued at *net market value:* market price less transportation or other selling costs. If the current wheat price at an elevator where you typically sell wheat is $4.75 per bushel, but the hauling costs to get it there are $0.25 per bushel, the wheat's *net market value* is $4.50 per bushel.

Valuing inventories based on market prices is usually the easiest approach, but not always. For some inventories a market price is not readily available, but an estimate of production costs may be fairly easy to put together. For example, what if you need to place a value on a growing crop of wheat? Coming up with a market price is difficult because not much wheat is sold that way—you cannot simply phone your local elevator and find out today's price for an acre of growing wheat, five months ahead of harvest.

However, a quick look through past bills for fertilizer, seed, and chemicals used on the wheat crop would let you estimate per-acre input costs. And your knowledge of local custom rates, or a custom rate guide published by a university, would let you estimate your investment in tillage, planting, and other field operations. Spending a few minutes with a calculator or spreadsheet would let you arrive at a reasonable estimate of production costs for the growing crop of wheat.

When a market price is difficult to obtain, estimating production costs may be the best way to come up with an inventory value.

 **Work in Process (WIP) inventory** is the accounting term for inventories which are still in production and not yet complete, like a growing crop of wheat or 100-pound market hogs. A companion term is Finished Goods inventory, which refers to inventories that are complete and ready for sale, such as harvested grain in storage.

## Updating Inventory Values for Preparing a Balance Sheet

If you want the balance sheet to be as current as possible, here are steps you should consider taking:

1. **Take an inventory count** [91] or estimate, to have up-to-date information about your actual, physical inventories.

   This is important to do if you have not updated inventories in QuickBooks for quite a while. However, if you are confident that your inventories are current, you can bypass this step.

2. **Compare the physical inventory count to the inventory quantities in QuickBooks.** The Inventory Valuation Summary report (Reports > Inventory > Inventory Valuation Summary) gives you an easy way to do that:

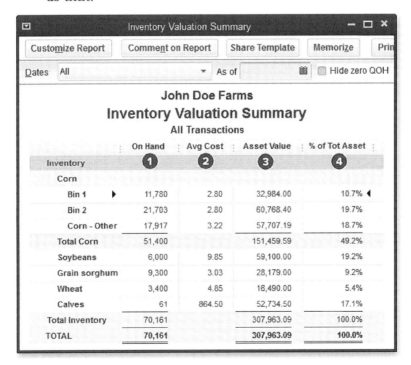

❶ **On Hand** is the inventory quantity for each Item.

## Chapter 7 - Other Inventory Adjustments and Transactions

② **Avg Cost.** For raised inventory Items this column does not actually show average costs; but rather, *average values*—calculated by dividing the Asset Value by the On Hand quantity for each Item. This is helpful information for considering whether the value currently assigned to an Item is acceptable.

③ **Asset Value** is the total value of an Item's inventory quantity. Amounts in this column will appear on balance sheet reports, included in the balance of the asset account associated with each Item, such as Inventory:Grain or Inventory:Market Livestock.

④ **% of Tot Asset** (percentage of total assets) is one of many additional columns you may include in the report, by customizing it.

3. **Make inventory adjustments as needed,** to update the quantity and/or value of your inventory Items.

   See: *How to Make an Inventory Adjustment* 97 in Chapter 5.

4. **Prepare the balance sheet** (Reports > Company & Financial > Balance Sheet Standard).

> **Do not adjust the value of *resale* inventory Items!**
>
> Unlike raised inventories, resale inventories should not have their values changed in QuickBooks except to fix accounting errors. A resale Item's value represents its purchase cost, which must be kept intact for income tax accounting purposes.
>
> **To prepare a market value balance sheet when resale inventories are involved,** special techniques are necessary. One approach is to create a balance sheet report in QuickBooks, export it to a spreadsheet, then replace the values of resale inventories with market values before printing the report.

# Purchasing "Raised" Inventory

The title of this section may have you asking "How can I *purchase* something that I *raise* (produce)?" The answer has to do with the fact that farm production is not always sold: sometimes it may be consumed in the farm business; used for producing something else.

Feed grains are a typical example. Some producers sell part of the corn or grain sorghum they raise but also feed part of it to livestock. Due to drought, flooding, lack of sufficient storage space, or any number of reasons, they may run short of grain to use for feed and may need to purchase more.

## The Inventory Part Item Type and Inventory Purchases

Here's the problem: the Inventory Part Item type works fine for *sales* of things your farm produces, but it does not work as you might expect for *purchases* because QuickBooks—and the Inventory Part Item type—were designed with accrual accounting in mind. (See the Accounting 101 explanation below.) For this reason, when an Inventory Part Item which represents inventories of farm production is used in a purchase transaction, the transaction must be handled in a special way. Otherwise, the Item's inventory quantity and value won't be updated as they should be.

 **Inventory Part Items *do* work as expected for *resale inventories*** —things which are purchased and then resold, such as feeder livestock —but that discussion will be part of a future edition in the QuickBooks Cookbook™ series.

### Accounting 101: The problem with the Inventory Part Item type

The problem really is not with the Inventory Part type itself but with the fact that we set it up in a nonstandard way for cash basis accounting.

In accrual accounting, the inventory value of an Item is based on its cost—purchase cost if it was purchased, or its manufacturing/production cost if the Item was created/raised/grown/produced. While an Item is in production, the production costs associated with it are accumulated in a Work In Process (WIP) inventory account. Then when the item is completed those costs get transferred to a

155

Finished Goods account as the item's inventory (asset) value. Flatly stated, in accrual accounting an item's inventory value consists of the actual costs involved in producing it or purchasing it. Those are real financial costs, not some notion of what the item might currently be worth or some estimate of its market value.

Things are different with cash basis accounting because production costs are expensed at the time of purchase, not accumulated in an asset account. When the time comes to add a harvested crop or raised livestock to inventory, there is no accumulated cost-of-production balance available somewhere to assign to it as inventory value. In an accounting sense, raised inventories "magically appear" in cash basis accounting: no trail of accounting entries exist to describe the production costs invested in them.

Things are different with cash basis accounting because production costs are expensed at the time of purchase, not accumulated in an asset account. So when the time comes to add a harvested crop to inventory there is no accumulated cost-of-production balance available to assign to the crop as its inventory value. In other words, raised inventories "magically appear" in the accounting system: no trail of transaction entries exists to describe the production costs invested in them.

This is why we use inventory adjustments  to get farm production into inventory in QuickBooks, and why inventory values are typically based on market prices or other estimates of value. From an accounting standpoint, raised inventories just "happen" as of the day you make an inventory adjustment to get them into inventory.

## Cash Purchases of "Raised" Inventory

**Problem** We usually sell about two-thirds of the corn we raise and use the rest to feed cattle. But with last year's drought a lot of what we raised had to be delivered on cash sale contracts. Now, here in late summer I'm running out of corn for feed. I will need to buy a couple truckloads to get by until harvest when we will have our own corn to feed again. I know how to enter a purchase of corn, but how do I get the corn into inventory?

**Solution** If you write a check for the corn, enter it as you normally would but add two additional lines to get the corn into inventory.

## Purchasing "Raised" Inventory

***Discussion*** In cash basis accounting, grain you purchase for feed is a expense. So when you enter the check in QuickBooks the corn purchase needs to be posted to an expense account; maybe an account named Purchased Feed for example. Or you could have an Item named Feed Corn Expense which posts to the Purchased Feed account. (You can enter expenses using accounts, or Items, or both.)

But recording an expense does not update inventories for the Corn Item. To get that done, you need additional lines on the check, as described below.

> ★ **This example assumes you want to track inventories for the purchased corn...which may not be so.** Having current inventories may be important when making corn sales, but you might not care whether inventories are current or not during a time when you are purchasing corn for feed. In that case you could just enter the purchased corn as an expense and not bother with getting it into inventory. Later—maybe after the next corn harvest—you can again adjust inventories in QuickBooks to match the quantity of corn you have on hand.

## Creating the necessary Items

The Write Checks form gives you the option of entering expenses by selecting accounts on the Expenses tab, or Items on the Items tab:

For the inventory activities which need to happen we need to use the Corn Item, and it can only be used on the Items tab. So to keep the example simple (to keep all parts of it on the Items tab) we will use only Items in this transaction, not accounts. Here are the Items we will need:

- **Corn**  is an Inventory Part Item representing inventories of raised corn (the same Item used in prior examples).
- **Capitalized Inv Item** [84] is an Other Charge Item which represents Capitalized Inventory [65], the equity account used as an off-

setting account for raised inventory transactions throughout this book.

❖ **Feed Corn** is a Non-inventory Part Item for recording purchases of corn for feed. It posts expense to an account named Feed:Grain Purchased, and is set up this way:

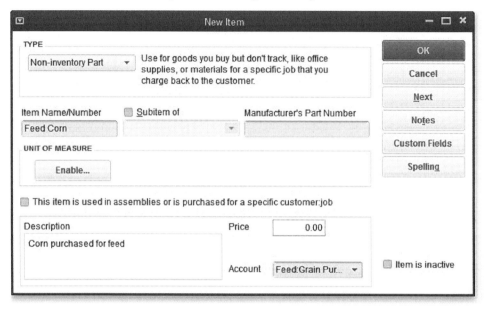

## How to enter a purchase of "raised" inventory

1. **Open the Write Checks window** (Banking > Write Checks).

2. **Fill in the form's header fields** by selecting a checking account, payee, date, and amount.

3. **Click on the Items tab** in the lower part of the form.

4. **Select Items, and enter quantities and costs (prices)** as shown below.

## Purchasing "Raised" Inventory

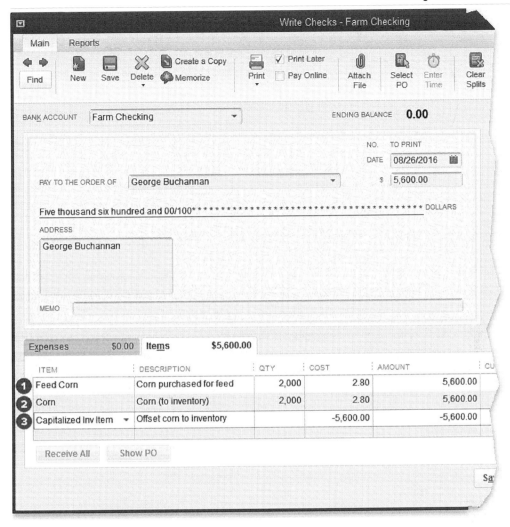

① **Feed Corn** posts expense to Feed:Grain Purchased, an expense account.

② **Corn.** This line increases the Corn Item's inventory by 2,000 bushels and its value by $5,600. It also increases the balance of the Grain Inventories account (the asset account associated with the Corn Item) by $5,600.

③ **Capitalized Inv Item.** Because the amount on this line is negative it offsets the $5,600 amount on line ②. Combined, lines ② and ③ leave the net amount of the check unaffected. This line *increases* the balance of the Capitalized Inventory [65] account by $5,600. (For equity accounts, a negative amount on a Check or Bill increases the account's balance.)

5. **Click the Save & Close button** to save the check and close the Write Checks form.

# Transferring Raised Items to Fixed Assets

***Problem*** We are keeping 20 of the heifers we raised, for breeding. How do I transfer them from market livestock inventory to the cow herd (fixed asset inventory)?

***Solution*** Use an inventory adjustment to decrease raised market livestock inventory and increase the breeding herd inventory.

***Discussion*** While the heifers were growing you may have valued them at net market value for balance sheet purposes. But what value should you assign when you move them to the breeding herd—to fixed assets?

The answer to that question depends how you have chosen to maintain fixed asset records in QuickBooks. Several approaches are possible, with their most important difference being whether fixed assets are valued at market value or book value. A full discussion of valuing fixed assets is beyond the scope of this book, so rather than getting bogged down in the details let's just identify the essential things which need to happen when you transfer raised inventories to fixed assets:

1. **Move the raised inventory to a fixed asset Item.** The 20 heifers need to be moved from the raised livestock inventory Item to a different Item, which will then represent them as a fixed asset. This topic's example uses Inventory Part Items to represent fixed assets.

     **Using the Inventory Part Item type for fixed assets** makes it possible to update asset values any time you want, simply by making an inventory adjustment [97]. So the Inventory Part type is a good choice when

## Transferring Raised Items to Fixed Assets

fixed assets are being valued based on their market values. Other Item types work better when fixed assets are being maintained at book value.

2. **Assign a value to the fixed asset Item** based on the approach you have chosen to use for valuing fixed assets. This topic's example assumes fixed assets are being valued based on market values, which is the simplest approach and makes preparing market value balance sheets easier.

 **For a discussion of different ways to value fixed assets** see the gray note later in this section, titled *Three ways to value fixed assets* 167.

### Wait a minute...why not use the Fixed Asset Item type?

In the the Pro and Premier editions of QuickBooks the Fixed Asset Item type seems like an incomplete or unfinished feature. The reason is that Intuit's Fixed Asset Manager software is not included in those QuickBooks editions. Fixed Asset Manager can access the data fields in Fixed Asset Items and is capable of calculating depreciation, updating asset information, and more. But as this is written, only the Accountant and Enterprise editions of QuickBooks include Fixed Asset Manager.

Plainly stated, the Fixed Asset item type is not very useful for Pro and Premier users. Other Item types are often a better choice. Here are some pros and cons related to the Fixed Asset Item type:

- The setup window for Fixed Asset Items has several additional fields not used for any other Item type. Surprisingly, most of those fields *are not connected to anything within QuickBooks!*

  If you set up a new Fixed Asset Item and then use it in a purchase transaction, the amount paid will not update the Item's Cost field. The same is true if you sell the asset: neither the Sales Price nor the Sales Date fields of the Item will be updated with the selling price or date of the sale. The only way to get information into these fields (and several others) is to type it in manually.

  Without the Fixed Asset Manager software, only the Asset Account field is connected to anything useful: it identifies the asset account which will include the Item's value on balance sheets.

- Fixed Asset Items do not support quantities. If you purchased 20 cows *you would need to set up a separate Fixed Asset Item for each of them!* Why?

161

> Because selling part of a Fixed Asset Item is not possible. This is a major drawback of the Fixed Asset Item type for many farm businesses.
>
> ❖ Fixed Asset Items cannot have subitems. Without subitems, you cannot control how fixed assets are grouped on reports, as you can with most other Item types, so Fixed Asset Items cannot be grouped into categories such as livestock, machinery, buildings, and land.
>
> ❖ Does your tax preparer directly access your QuickBooks company file when preparing taxes? If you send the file on a flash drive, or upload it to the tax preparer's Web portal, or allow access to it via a file sharing service, the preparer likely accesses your QuickBooks file directly. If so, and your preparer uses Fixed Asset Manager for depreciation calculations, he or she may prefer that you use the Fixed Asset Item type. (Be sure to ask before setting up any Items for fixed assets, so you can set them up as your tax preparer prefers.)

## Setting Up a New Item for the Fixed Asset

Each fixed asset or fixed asset group should be represented by its own QuickBooks Item. If you own three tractors for instance, a separate Item should be used for each tractor. But if you buy a group of cows, does, ewes, or other breeding animals, use a single Item to represent the entire group. This also applies to animals transferred from raised inventory to fixed assets, such as the group of raised heifers in this example.

Here are steps for setting up an Inventory Part Item to represent the heifers as fixed assets.

1. **Open the Item List window** (Lists > Item List).

2. **Select** Item > New from the button menu at the bottom of the window.

# Transferring Raised Items to Fixed Assets

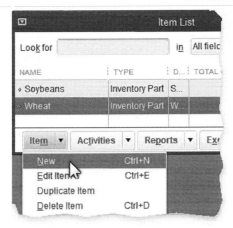

The New Item window will open.

3. **Fill in details for the new Item:**

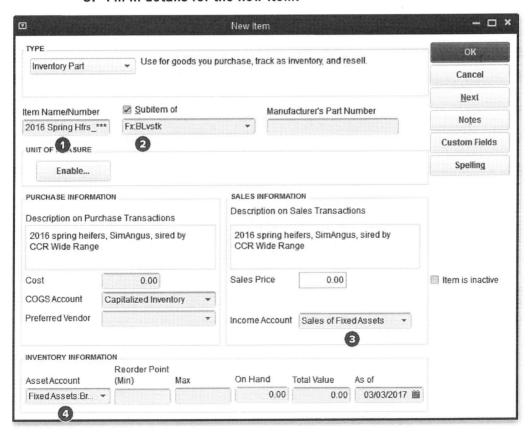

## Chapter 7 - Other Inventory Adjustments and Transactions

① **Item Name/Number.** The Item name should usually be a shortened description of the Item. In this case, *2016 Spring Hfrs_\*\*\** identifies the group as heifers born in the spring of 2016.

> 🔧 **The _\*\*\* on the end of the Item name is a reminder** that it should be edited later, after income taxes have been prepared, to add the tax preparer's asset number in place of the "\*\*\*". Including the asset number in fixed asset Item names can avoid confusion later, when a fixed asset you have sold needs to be matched up with the tax preparer's asset list.

② **Subitem of.** *Optional.* You can structure the Item list to make fixed asset reports easier to get and more useful. In this example, the Item is being set up as a subitem of *Fx:BLvstk*.

- **Fx** is a top-level parent Item for all fixed assets. In other words, all fixed assets are grouped under the *Fx* Item. Having a single "master" parent Item makes it easy to filter Item reports to include only fixed assets.

- **BLvstk** (short for "breeding livestock") is one of several subitems of *Fx* representing groups of related fixed assets. Others might be *Mach* (for "machinery") or *Land*. This causes fixed assets to be grouped on reports into categories like Breeding Livestock, Machinery, and Land.

③ **Income Account.** Sales of Fixed Assets is an account of the Other Income type. Its purpose is to accumulate fixed asset sales during the year, for easy reporting at tax time.

④ **Asset Account.** The asset account selected for this Item is Fixed Assets:Breeding Livestock. On balance sheets, the asset value of the heifers will be included as part of this account's balance.

4. **Click the OK button** to save the new Item and close the window.

# Moving the Heifers from Raised Livestock Inventory to Fixed Assets, and Assigning an Asset Value

These are raised heifers, so no *financial* transaction (purchase or sale) is involved in moving them to fixed assets. All you need is an inventory adjustment to (1) decrease the inventory for the raised livestock Item representing the heifers, and (2) increase the inventory for their fixed asset Item.

1. **Open the Item List window** (Lists > Item List).

2. **Select** Activities > Adjust Quantity/Value on Hand from the button menu at the bottom of the window.

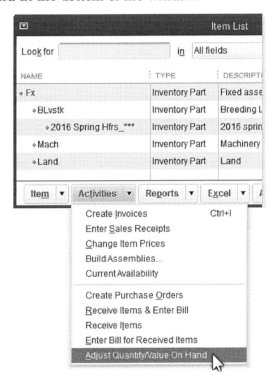

The Adjust Quantity/Value on Hand window will open.

3. **Fill in the inventory adjustment details** as shown below.

## Chapter 7 - Other Inventory Adjustments and Transactions

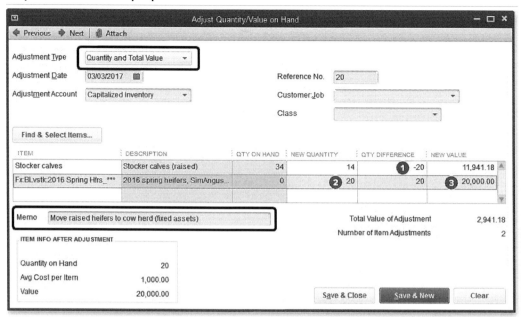

① **Qty Difference.** The heifers have been part of the Stocker calves inventory. A Quantity Difference of -20 will decrease the inventory for that Item.

② **New Quantity.** The New Quantity for the fixed asset Item is 20, the number of heifers being transferred to fixed assets.

③ **New Value.** As fixed assets, the heifers are being assigned a value of $20,000 ($1,000 per head). That value will be included in the amount shown for Fixed Assets:Breeding Livestock on the farm's balance sheet.

⭐ **If fixed assets were being valued for income tax purposes** the heifers' book value would be $0, assuming costs of raising the heifers had been expensed up to this point. However, the assumption in this example is that asset values for income tax purposes are maintained outside of QuickBooks (typically, by a tax preparer).

4. **Click the Save & Close button** to save the inventory adjustment and close the window.

**Three ways to value fixed assets**

Fixed assets can be valued based on market values or book values, and at least two book value approaches are possible depending on your purpose for maintaining fixed asset information.

**Market value basis.** Maintaining fixed assets at *net market value* (estimated market value, less any selling costs) makes it easy to prepare a market value balance sheet directly from QuickBooks. This is the simplest approach, partly because it does not place any requirements on you to do accounting for tax-related asset details: you don't have to keep track of accumulated depreciation, remaining undepreciated asset value, etc.—those are maintained entirely outside of QuickBooks (typically by the farm business' tax preparer).

The Inventory Part Item type is a good choice for representing fixed assets valued at net market value because it allows updating asset values at any time, simply by making an inventory adjustment 97. (Inventory adjustments are not available for other Item types.)

**Income tax basis** is a book value approach in which fixed assets are valued at their income tax basis, or book value. A tractor, for instance, would be valued at its original purchase price minus accumulated deprecation (and things like Section 179 expense deductions, if any). For raised items such as the heifers in the example above, tax basis is normally $0—assuming the costs of raising them (feed, vaccines, veterinary care, etc.) were expensed along the way, before they were moved to fixed assets.

When this approach is used, things like depreciation are usually calculated outside of QuickBooks (typically by a tax preparer) then entered in QuickBooks to update fixed asset values. The result is fixed asset book values in QuickBooks which match the remaining undepreciated values of fixed assets maintained by your tax preparer. With this approach you can, for example, quickly look up the tax basis of a particular piece of machinery in QuickBooks. However, the same information is easy to get from your tax preparer's fixed assets list, so maintaining income tax book values in QuickBooks seldom provides enough benefit to overcome the accounting effort it requires.

**Economic basis** is another book value approach. With this approach, the goal is to write off the cost of a fixed asset over a period of time (depreciate it) at a rate which mimics the asset's actual decline in value or usefulness. The keys to getting this done are (1) choosing an appropriate depreciation method, and (2) using realistic estimate of the asset's useful life as the time period for depreciating the asset. If you have ever taken a basic accounting class you probably learned about this—how different depreciation methods relate to annual depreciation expense, asset replacement, and declines in asset value over time.

Economic book values are calculated the same as all other book value approaches: an asset's accumulated depreciation (total depreciation so far) is subtracted from the original investment in the asset (dollars paid for it, plus the book value of any trade-ins). However, though the calculation is done in a similar way, it is important to understand that economic book values are often very different from book values for income tax purposes. The main reason is that income tax-based depreciation is determined by the tax laws and sometimes has little relationship to the economic value of a fixed asset, or to the costs of owning it over a period of time.

 **A good example of this is the Section 179 deduction** currently allowed by the U.S. Federal income tax law. With it, you may buy a tractor for $100,000 and deduct the entire amount in the year of purchase, leaving the tractor with a tax-based book value of $0—which obviously has no relationship to the tractor's remaining economic value.

This reveals why some farm businesses prepare balance sheets and (accrual) profit and loss reports based on an economic basis for asset values rather than an income tax basis. Economic depreciation is an attempt to realistically estimate fixed asset ownership costs, and the resulting economic book values support more accurate measurements of business progress, such as return on equity.

# Moving Inventories from One Stage of Production to Another

**Problem** We moved 284 pigs from farrowing unit B to the south nursery unit today. How should I adjust the inventory for my Farrowing Pigs and Nursery Pigs Items?

**Solution** Make an inventory adjustment which reduces the quantity for Farrowing Pigs by 284 and increases the quantity for Nursery Pigs by the same number.

**Discussion** Many farm enterprises involve multiple stages of production. Livestock enterprises in particular often have two or more stages—like farrowing, nursery, and finishing in a swine operation; or cow/calf, stocker calves, and feeder cattle in a beef operation.

## Moving Inventories from One Stage of Production to Another

When production involves multiple stages, consider using a different QuickBooks Item for the inventory at each stage: Farrowing Pigs, Nursery Pigs, and Finishing Pigs; Calves, Stockers, Feeders; and so on. This approach (1) makes your QuickBooks inventories more useful for management information (they can show how many pigs are in each production stage at any point in time, for instance) and (2) makes it easier to accurately value inventories for preparing a balance sheet, compared to having all production lumped together and represented by a single Item.

Many crop enterprises have multiple stages too. A harvested crop (the first stage) undergoes some kind of processing (a second stage) to result in a different product or something that is marketed differently. For example, you might raise wheat and sell most of it as grain but run part of it through a seed cleaner to sell as seed. In that case, you should probably have separate QuickBooks Items for commodity wheat and for seed wheat. Or maybe you raise high-quality oats and sell part of them as a bulk commodity but also process some with other ingredients to make a sweet feed for horses, which you bag and sell wholesale to feed stores. Obviously, bulk (commodity) Oats and Sweet Feed inventories should be represented as separate Items.

Here are the steps for moving inventories between stages of production:

1. **Open the Adjust Quantity/Value On Hand window** (Vendors > Inventory Activities > Adjust Quantity/Value on Hand).

2. **Fill in the header fields,** as appropriate.

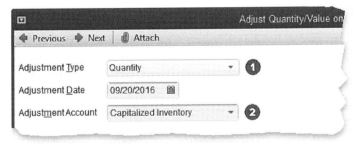

① **Adjustment Type.** Normally, you will make a *Quantity* adjustment.

## Chapter 7 - Other Inventory Adjustments and Transactions

❷ **Adjustment Account.** Use Capitalized Inventory 🔖 or another equity account you have reserved for raised inventory adjustments.

3. **Enter or select the Items to adjust;** Farrowing Pigs and Nursery Pigs in this example.

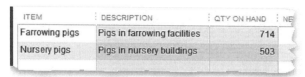

4. **Update the quantity for both Items.**

   The easy way is to enter the Qty Difference for each Item:

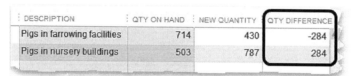

**When you adjust the quantity for an Item...**

QuickBooks automatically adjusts its total value, too. Compare the two Item Info boxes shown above. Before the quantity adjustment the Value for Farrowing Pigs is $12,852. After the adjustment, the Value will be $7,740.

5. **Add a comment in the Memo field** as a reminder of the purpose of the adjustment.

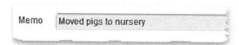

6. **Click the Save & Close button** to save the inventory adjustment and close the window.

# Questions, Answers, and Special Situations

## Questions & Answers

### Should I use Inventory Part Items for things we produce but don't plan to keep on hand as an "inventory"?

Generally, no. Set up Items of the Non-inventory Part type [72] for things you produce and sell but don't expect to inventory. Non-inventory Part Items record income or expense without affecting balance sheet accounts (assets, liabilities, or equity) the way Inventory Part Items do.

If you someday change your mind and want to start keeping inventories for a Non-inventory Part Item, you can change it [73] to the Inventory Part type.

See: *Can I change an Item's type?* [73] in Chapter 5

### How can I know when to set up separate Items for two things which are similar?

When two things are similar, set up separate Items for them only if you want to separately keep track of *sales* or *inventories* for them.

For example, suppose you have been using an Inventory Part Item named Corn for corn inventories and sales. But this year you will also be growing some food-grade white corn. You should set up a separate Item for the white corn—maybe named White Corn, or as a subitem of Corn, named Corn:White—to have inventory and sales information which is separate for the specialty corn.

### Is it possible to calculate total production of a crop, from my QuickBooks inventory records?

Yes. For an example see *Estimating production from inventory records* [41] in Chapter 4.

## Gifting: Giving Away Raised Inventory

***Problem*** One of my hay customers was dissatisfied with a few bales of hay in the load they picked up recently. So I gave them 10 extra bales (small square bales of bromegrass hay) for free as a good will gesture. How should I enter this in QuickBooks?

***Solution*** You can make an inventory adjustment [97] to decrease your inventory of bromegrass hay by 10 bales. Because the quantity is small though, it may make more sense to wait until the next time you take a physical inventory count or estimate to make the adjustment.

***Discussion*** Gifting something doesn't result in income but does decrease the inventory you have on hand, so entering an inventory adjustment would be appropriate. But does it always make sense to bother with making small inventory adjustments? Well, it depends...

If you are making an effort to have very accurate inventory information in QuickBooks, then you certainly should make an inventory adjustment. But most hay producers who sell small square bales begin with thousands of bales on hand, which makes it unlikely that their *original* physical inventory count [97] (i.e., when the hay was put in storage) was completely accurate. If the original count was only a rough estimate, making small inventory adjustments probably is not warranted.

### Larger Gifts, and Gifts to Charity

Many producers routinely gift grain or livestock to a church or other charitable organization, or to family members or others. The inventory effect is the same as described above. If the gift is of a material (significant) quantity or if you are trying to maintain accurate inventories in QuickBooks, you should make an inventory adjustment [97] to record the inventory decrease caused by the gifting.

More important from a tax standpoint, is that you properly document the gift and meet IRS requirements for transferring ownership of the gifted item(s) to the recipient. *Be sure to consult a competent tax advisor* if you are unfamiliar with IRS requirements for gifting farm production.

## Harvesting Raised Livestock for Food

***Problem*** We took a market lamb we had raised to the local slaughterhouse to have it butchered. How should I record this in QuickBooks?

***Solution*** Make an inventory adjustment  to decrease your market lamb inventory by 1. Because the quantity is small though, it may make more sense to wait until the next time you take a physical inventory count or estimate to make the adjustment.

***Discussion*** You should make an inventory adjustment whenever a change or loss of inventory has materially affected the inventory you have on hand, or if you are making an effort to have very accurate inventory records in QuickBooks.

However, making small inventory adjustments is not always necessary or worthwhile. If you are fattening 1,000 market lambs, making an adjustment for 1 lamb may not be important to do—the adjustment could wait until the next time you take an inventory count or adjust inventories for other reasons.

★ **Don't forget the income tax implications of livestock harvested for personal consumption.** The costs of raised livestock you harvest for food are reportable as income for tax purposes. *Consult your tax preparer for details and reporting requirements.*

This page is intentionally blank.

# CHAPTER 8
# Depositing Payments You Have Received

| About this chapter | This chapter is not about farm inventories! Its purpose is to "complete the circle" for you: to show how payments you receive for sales of inventory (and other Items) make their way into a bank deposit in QuickBooks. |
|---|---|

## Making Deposits, and the Undeposited Funds Account

**Problem** I have entered several sales in QuickBooks, and all of them were sent to the Undeposited Funds account. How do I get them into a bank deposit?

**Solution** Use the Make Deposits window to prepare a deposit. When the Make Deposits window opens, the Payments to Deposit window will also open if there are any amounts in Undeposited Funds. Select payments to include in the deposit by checkmarking them.

**Discussion** One of the most important aspects of entering deposits in QuickBooks is making sure the dollar amount of each deposit entry matches the deposit amounts on your bank statements. When those amounts differ, reconciling the bank account can become a tedious, hair-pulling job.

What would be the problem? Suppose you made only one bank deposit for the month, totaling $4651.03 and consisting of three payments; checks received for these amounts: $398.48, $4001.52, and $251.03. If each of these checks were entered as a separate deposit in QuickBooks, would you know at a glance whether the total of the three deposit entries equaled the $4651.03 amount on the bank statement? (Most of us would not—we would need to use a calculator to find out.)

OK, so adding up three checks isn't too difficult. But what if you had made six different bank deposits during the month, each comprised of two to five payments? And what if you had entered each of those payments in QuickBooks—maybe 25 checks or so—as *individual* deposit entries? Suddenly the job of reconciling the six deposits on the bank statement with the 25 deposit entries in QuickBooks would be a big problem. There is no quick way to figure out how the 25 deposit entries should be grouped together to match up with the six bank deposits.

The easy way to prevent problems like this is to *always* have sales income (from Sales Receipts, and from the Receive Payments window) posted to the Undeposited Funds account. That way, later you can select payments from Undeposited Funds to include in a bank deposit, which lets you group received payments in your QuickBooks deposit entries *in exactly the same way* as they are grouped in the physical deposits you send to the bank. This makes reconciling the bank account a whole lot easier.

 **Think of Undeposited Funds as a temporary "holding tank" for payments you have received;** a place to keep them until you are ready to include them in a deposit.

## Assuring received payments go to Undeposited Funds

The payments you receive for sales are normally entered on either the Sales Receipts form or the Receive Payments form. Sales Receipts are for recording cash sales, as when the buyer pays you at the time of the sale. Receive Payments is for recording payments you receive for invoiced sales, as when you enter an invoice at the time of the sale, then the buyer pays you later.

Both forms have an optional *Deposit To* field, which is hidden by default. When it is hidden, the payments you enter on either form are *automatically* posted to Undeposited Funds. When the *Deposit To* field is visible, you can select the account to which a payment will be posted.

**You can control whether *Deposit To* is visible or hidden** with the Preferences setting at: Edit > Preferences > Payments > Company Preferences [tab] > Use Undeposited Funds as a default deposit to account.

Why would anyone want to make the *Deposit To* field visible? Experienced accountants may like the flexibility of posting received payments directly to a specific bank (or other) account—maybe a different checking account, a savings or money-market account, etc.

 ***Most* QuickBooks users should post received payments to Undeposited Funds.** From there they can be included in a deposit entry for any account, grouped the same way as they will appear on bank statements.

## Selecting amounts from Undeposited Funds, to include in a deposit

Here are the steps for selecting payments stored in the Undeposited Funds account, to include them in a deposit.

1. **Open the Make Deposits window** (Banking > Make Deposits).

   When the Make Deposits window opens, the Payments to Deposit window will also open if there are any undeposited payments in Undeposited Funds.

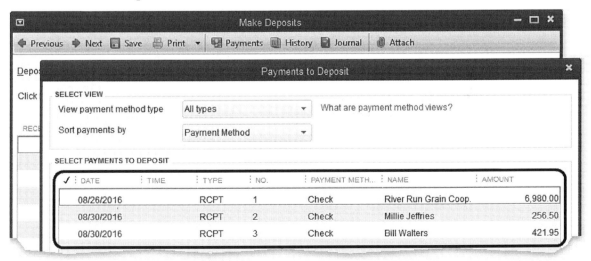

## Chapter 8 - Depositing Payments You Have Received

2. **Select the payments you want to include in the deposit,** by check-marking them:

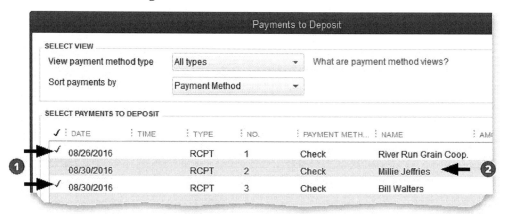

① **The first and third payments** are checkmarked, to include in the deposit.

② **The second payment** is not checkmarked. Millie Jeffries asked that her check be held for a week before cashing or depositing it.

3. **Click the OK button** in the Payments to Deposit window, to close the window and move the checkmarked payments into the Make Deposits window:

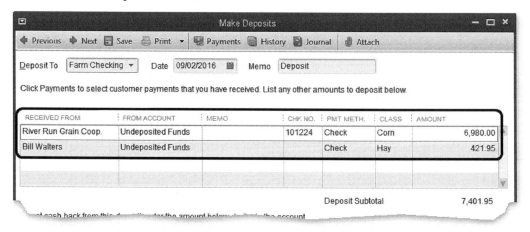

**If you decide to include additional Undeposited Funds amounts in the deposit,** you can reopen the Payments to Deposit window by clicking the Payments icon in the ribbon bar:

4. **Click the Save & Close button** to save the deposit entry and close the Make Deposits window.

## Including other payments in a deposit

Besides payments entered through the Sales Receipts or Receive Payment forms, you can also enter payments directly in the Make Deposits window. (However that is not the preferred way to enter sales transactions, for reasons listed in the gray note below.)

For example, suppose a neighbor gave you a check for $200 for hauling cattle to the local sale barn. If you rarely do custom hauling you may prefer not to set up an Item to record the income. Without an Item, the payment cannot be entered on a Sales Receipt, which also means it won't be posted to Undeposited Funds. You can simply include the payment in a deposit by adding another line to the deposit and selecting an appropriate account for the income.

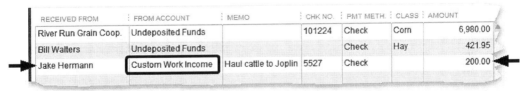

 **Why not just enter _all_ sales directly in Make Deposits?**

Though it is _possible_ to always enter sales directly on the Make Deposits form (Banking > Make Deposits), you should generally enter them on either a Sales Receipt or an Invoice. Why? Because the Make Deposits form:

1. Does not give you a place to enter sales quantities (bushels, head, pounds, etc.).

> **2.** Does not support using Items in sales transactions. Using Items is essential if you want to track inventories!
>
> **3.** Does not support many of the sales and inventory reports available in QuickBooks, because many of them are only available for transactions in which Items were used.

## About online banking and bank deposits in QuickBooks

Deposits should nearly always be entered in QuickBooks (1) before you send a physical deposit to the bank, and (2) before you download bank transactions from the bank's Web site, into QuickBooks. You generally should not allow deposit entries to be created automatically by capturing them from downloaded bank transactions.

Why? Because a downloaded deposit transaction contains sparse details about the individual checks or cash amounts in the deposit. That makes it difficult to know which account(s) should be credited with income or which invoices were paid by which customers. Also, if you don't have a detailed record of deposits you cannot know whether some are still outstanding (have not yet cleared the bank) or may have been lost in the mail—rare, but it does happen.

Without having your own record of bank deposits (in QuickBooks), you cannot know your current bank balance with any accuracy, and reconciling the bank account may not be possible.

**CHAPTER 9**

# Inventory Information and Reports

| About this chapter | This chapter shows where to find various sources of Item and inventory information in QuickBooks, plus reports you may use often when working with inventories. |

## Where to Find the Information You Want

When you want information about an Item—or current inventories or inventory values—you can usually find it in several places in QuickBooks. The same information may be available in a couple different reports, and sometimes in the Item List or the Inventory Center too.

Here are several kinds of information you might want, along with the places where you can find each one:

### Current inventory quantity

The current quantity on hand for an inventory Item.

- ❖ Item List 183
- ❖ Inventory Center 187
- ❖ QuickReport 185
- ❖ Inventory Stock Status by Item report 189

### Current inventory value

The asset value of an Item's current inventory.

181

- ❖ Inventory Valuation report 190

## Sales by Item

The quantity and/or dollars of sales for an Item.

- ❖ Sales by Item report 192

## Sales by customer

The quantity and/or dollar amount of an Item sold to each customer, or to a specific customer.

- ❖ Sales by Customer report 193

## Contracted quantities

Inventory quantities contracted for sale, and quantities on hand but not contracted (available to sell).

- ❖ Inventory Center 187—shows contracted ("On Sales Orders") quantities only

- ❖ Inventory Stock Status by Item report 189—shows contracted quantities (entered on Sales Orders), and remaining quantities (uncontracted; available to sell).

    ★ **See Chapter 11 - Tracking Cash Sales Contracts** 215 for details on keeping track of sales contracts for inventory Items.

# The Item List

The Item List window displays all Items except Fixed Asset Items, and can serve as a quick source of Item information.

❖ **To open the Item List window,** select Lists > Item List.

The Item List can show (among other things) the quantity on hand for Inventory Part Items, as highlighted in the screenshot above. If the window does not show the information you want, you can customize it to choose which columns are displayed.

❖ **To customize columns displayed in the Item List window,** right click anywhere in the window, then select Customize Columns... from the pop-up menu:

## Chapter 9 - Inventory Information and Reports

The Customize Columns window will open, where you can select columns to display, and their display order. (The order of column names in the Chosen Columns box controls their left-to-right order in the Items List.)

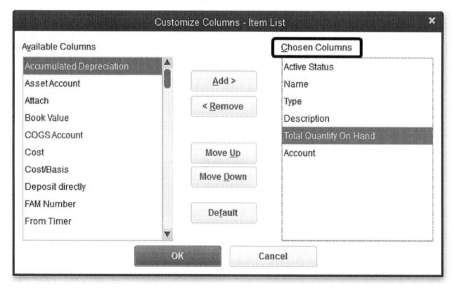

## Getting QuickReports, from the Item List

A QuickReport gives you inventory information for a single Item and its subitems, if any. To open a QuickReport window for an Item:

1. **Click on the desired Item** in the Item List window, to select it.

2. **Select** Reports > QuickReport **from the button menu** at the bottom of the window. Or, you may simply type *Ctrl-Q*.

A QuickReport window will open for the selected Item. The example below is for the Corn Item, including its subitems Bin 1 and Bin 2. The Corn - Other section lists transactions in which just the Corn Item was used, without a subitem.

## Chapter 9 - Inventory Information and Reports

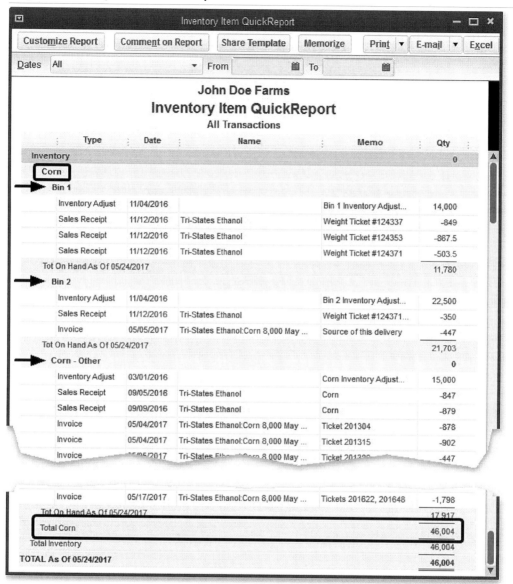

# The Inventory Center

*The Inventory Center is available in QuickBooks Premier and higher editions.* It displays quantity and value information for Inventory Part Items and provides quick access to transactions which refer to those Items.

> **QuickBooks Pro users:** the Inventory Center is handy but is not a sufficient reason for upgrading to QuickBooks Premier, because all of the information in the Inventory Center is available in reports common to all QuickBooks editions. Other Premier features such as Sales Orders, however, *may* be a sufficient reason to upgrade—if you want to do the things they allow, such as keeping track of cash sale contracts 215.

❖ **To open the Inventory Center window,** select Vendors > Inventory Activities > Inventory Center.

Here are general descriptions of Inventory Center features:

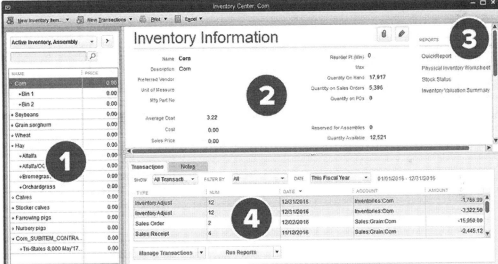

① **The left pane** of the Inventory Center window lists Inventory Part Items. Information displayed in other panes is specific to the Item you select here.

② **The upper right pane** shows details about the currently selected Item, such as average value, quantity on hand, contracted quantities ("Quantity on Sales Orders"), and more.

**③ Report links** give you quick access to reports for the currently selected Item.

**④ The lower right pane** lists transactions involving the selected Item.

## Getting QuickReports, from the Inventory Center

QuickReports are available for any Item in the Inventory Center, just as they are in the Item List window. To open a QuickReport for an Item:

1. **Click on the desired Item** in the left pane of the Inventory Center, to select it.

2. **Type** *Ctrl-Q* **to open a QuickReport** for the Item.
   or...
   **Click on the QuickReport link** in the upper right pane of the Inventory Center window:

Either way, a QuickReport window will open for the selected Item. For an example, see the Corn QuickReport shown earlier 185 in this chapter.

# Common Reports

Here are examples of common inventory and sales reports. This is not an exhaustive list, because many other reports also include Item, inventory, or quantity information or can be customized to include it.

## Inventory Reports

### QuickReports

Though discussed elsewhere QuickReports deserve a mention here, because they are one of the quickest ways to get transaction details for an inventory Item. They are usually generated from either the Item List 183 or the Inventory Center 187. (See those topics for details on how to get a QuickReport for an Item.)

### Inventory Stock Status by Item report

This report shows the on-hand quantities, contracted quantities (on Sales Orders), available quantities (not contracted; available for sale), and more, for Inventory Part Items.

❖ **To open the report,** select Reports > Inventory > Inventory Stock Status by Item.

Chapter 9 - Inventory Information and Reports

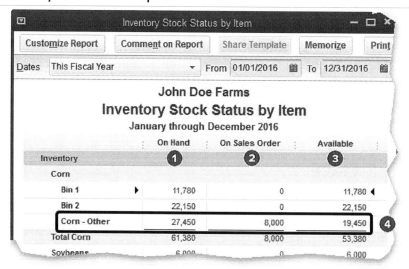

① **On Hand** is the current inventory quantity on hand for each Item.

② **On Sales Order** represents the quantity which has been contracted for sale.

③ **Available** is the difference between On Hand and On Sales Order. It represents the inventory which is not contracted for sale, and therefore is available to sell.

④ **The Corn - Other line** shows quantities for the Corn Item. There are 27,450 bushels of Corn in inventory (On Hand), 8,000 bushels contracted for sale (On Sales Order), and 19,450 bushels available to sell (Available).

## Inventory Valuation report

The Inventory Valuation report has several uses but is especially helpful when updating inventory values, because it displays information which will let you quickly decide which Items may be overvalued or undervalued.

Summary and Detail versions are available, with the Detail version listing individual transactions.

# Common Reports

❖ **To open the Summary version of the report,** select Reports > Inventory > Inventory Valuation Summary.

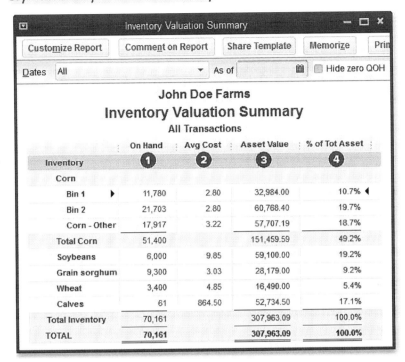

① **On Hand** shows the current inventory quantity for each Item.

② **Avg Cost.** For raised inventories, the Avg Cost column does not really show a cost; but rather, the average value per unit for each Item. This information is helpful for considering whether the value assigned to an Item is appropriate.

③ **Asset Value.** The Asset Value of each Item will be included on balance sheet reports as part of the balance of the asset account assigned to the Item, such as Inventory:Grain.

④ **% of Tot Asset** (percentage of total assets) is one of many columns you may include, by customizing the report.

**Memorizing reports**

If you find yourself making the same customizations each time you open a particular report—filtering it for specific Items, adding or removing columns, etc.—memorizing the report would be a good idea. That saves all of your customizations un-

191

## Chapter 9 - Inventory Information and Reports

der a memorized report name of your choosing, so that you can recall the report at any time from the Memorized Reports list (Reports > Memorized Reports). Memorized reports let you avoid re-applying the same report customizations over and over again.

To memorize a report, click the Memorize button in the report's menu bar:

[ Memorize ]

Then follow the prompts to assign a name to the memorized report, and save it.

# Sales Reports

## Sales by Item report

As the name implies, this report is handy for seeing sales information for Items. Summary and Detail versions are available, with the Detail version listing individual transactions.

❖ **To open the Detail version of the report,** select Reports > Inventory > Sales by Item Detail.

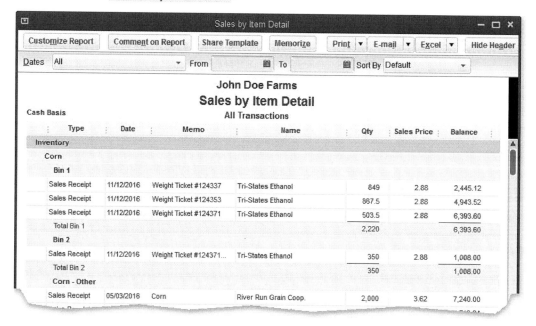

# Common Reports

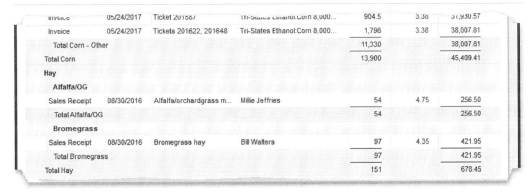

## Sales by Customer report

As the name suggests, the Sales by Customer report lists the dollar amount of sales to each customer, over the period of time covered by the report. Summary and Detail versions are available, with the Detail version listing individual transactions.

Because it groups sale transactions by customer, this report is handy for answering questions like "How many bushels did we deliver to the ethanol plant last month?".

❖ **To open the Detail version of the report,** select Reports > Inventory > Sales by Customer Detail.

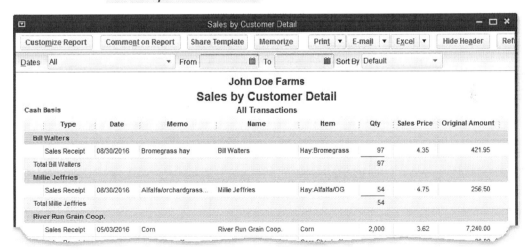

## Chapter 9 - Inventory Information and Reports

| | | | | | | | |
|---|---|---|---|---|---|---|---|
| **Tri-States Ethanol** | | | | | | | |
| *Corn 8,000 May 2017 $3.38* | | | | | | | |
| ① Invoice | 05/24/2017 | Ticket 201304 | Tri-States Ethanol:Corn... | Corn | 878 | 3.38 | 2,967.64 |
| Invoice | 05/24/2017 | Ticket 201315 | Tri-States Ethanol:Corn... | Corn | 902 | 3.38 | 3,048.76 |
| Invoice | 05/24/2017 | Ticket 201389 | Tri-States Ethanol:Corn... | Corn | 447 | 3.38 | 1,510.86 |
| Invoice | 05/24/2017 | Tickets 201498, 201... | Tri-States Ethanol:Corn... | Corn | 2,674.5 | 3.38 | 9,039.81 |
| Invoice | 05/24/2017 | Ticket 201587 | Tri-States Ethanol:Corn... | Corn | 904.5 | 3.38 | 3,057.21 |
| Invoice | 05/24/2017 | Tickets 201622, 201... | Tri-States Ethanol:Corn... | Corn | 1,798 | 3.38 | 6,077.24 |
| Total Corn 8,000 May 2017 $3.38 | | | | | 7,604 | | |
| *Tri-States Ethanol - Other* | | | | | | | |
| ② Sales Receipt | 09/05/2016 | Corn | Tri-States Ethanol | Corn | 847 | 2.92 | 2,473.24 |
| Sales Receipt | 09/09/2016 | Corn | Tri-States Ethanol | Corn | 879 | 2.95 | 2,593.05 |
| Sales Receipt | 11/12/2016 | Weight Ticket #124337 | Tri-States Ethanol | Corn:Bin 1 | 849 | 2.88 | 2,445.12 |
| Sales Receipt | 11/12/2016 | Weight Ticket #124353 | Tri-States Ethanol | Corn:Bin 1 | 867.5 | 2.88 | 2,498.40 |
| Sales Receipt | 11/12/2016 | Weight Ticket #124371 | Tri-States Ethanol | Corn:Bin 1 | 503.5 | 2.88 | 1,450.08 |
| Sales Receipt | 11/12/2016 | Weight Ticket #1243... | Tri-States Ethanol | Corn:Bin 2 | 350 | 2.88 | 1,008.00 |
| Sales Receipt | 11/12/2016 | Corn Checkoff | Tri-States Ethanol | Corn Checkoff | -2,570 | 0.01 | -25.70 |
| Sales Receipt | 03/07/2017 | Corn | Tri-States Ethanol | Corn_SUBITEM... | 888 | 2.94 | 2,610.72 |
| Total Tri-States Ethanol - Other | | | | | 2,614 | | |
| Total Tri-States Ethanol | | | | | 10,218 | | |
| **TOTAL** | | | | | **8,369** | | |

**① Invoices.** These invoices were entered for deliveries [226] on a cash sale contract [215]. The contract is represented as a Job for the Tri-States Ethanol customer, and the Job's name is *Corn 8,000 May 2017 $3.38*.

**② Sales Receipts.** Normal (not contracted) sales are entered as sales receipts.

# Preparing Income Tax Reports

QuickBooks was designed with a number of accrual features which cash basis record keepers can use. The Bills feature, for example, can help you keep track of amounts you owe to others, and Invoices can help you keep track of amounts others owe to you.

The good news is that using the accrual features *does not* prevent you from producing cash basis income and expense reports, which are essential if you file income taxes on a cash basis. All you need to do to prepare a cash basis report is select the *Cash* report option. When you do, QuickBooks removes the effect of accrual transactions (unpaid Bills and Invoices) from the report, as if they had never been entered.

# Preparing Income Tax Reports

**Cash basis reports are truly cash based *in most cases* but not all...**

Here is what you need to know:

- **Cash basis profit and loss reports (and income tax reports)** should be cash based in all cases, so long as Bills and Invoices are the only sources of accrual transactions. QuickBooks knows how to reverse the accrual effects of Bills and Invoices to produce cash basis reports; however it cannot do so when, for instance, a General Journal entry was used to record accrual income or expense.

- **Cash basis balance sheet reports** *are not always* truly cash based. The reason is that QuickBooks must keep the balance sheet in balance in all cases, guaranteeing that assets = liabilities + equity. That is why a "cash basis" balance sheet report may sometimes include an accounts payable or accounts receivable amount—neither of which should be present in a truly cash based report.

    *Example:* Suppose you purchase a hay rake for $11,000 in December and enter the purchase in QuickBooks as a Bill, which you won't be paying until January. On December 31st you prepare a cash basis balance sheet. Because the hay rake is a fixed asset, its $11,000 value will be included in the Assets section of the balance sheet. To keep the balance sheet in balance, QuickBooks must include an $11,000 accounts payable amount (for the unpaid Bill) in the Liabilities section of the balance sheet.

**A sensible reporting approach:**

1. **Prepare balance sheets on an accrual basis**—yes, even the balance sheets you provide to others outside the farm business, such as your lender. If you are using any of QuickBooks' accrual features, an accrual balance sheet will provide a more accurate picture of the business's assets, liabilities, and equity.

2. **Prepare profit and loss reports on either a cash or accrual basis,** depending on how you want income and expense information presented. However, always prepare cash basis profit and loss reports (or income tax reports) for income tax preparation if you are a cash basis tax filer.

**The *Accrual* report option does not "magically" do accrual accounting**

Selecting the *Accrual* report option causes QuickBooks to include transactions entered on accrual forms, such as Bills and Invoices, but *it does not convert a set of records created with cash basis accounting methods into a set of accrual re-*

**195**

> *cords*. True accrual accounting reports are only possible if you use accrual accounting methods, which involve more than simply using the Bills and Invoices forms.

## How to Prepare a Cash Basis Income Tax Report

QuickBooks has several reports which organize income and expenses for income tax preparation:

- **Income Tax Summary** (Reports > Accountant & Taxes > Income Tax Summary) provides income and expense totals by account and by tax line—if you have assigned tax lines to income and expense accounts.

- **Income Tax Detail** (Reports > Accountant & Taxes > Income Tax Detail) is essentially the same as the Summary version except that it also lists the transactions which contributed to each income or expense total.

- **Income Tax Preparation** (Reports > Accountant & Taxes > Income Tax Preparation) provides income and expense totals by account, rather than by tax line.

The steps below show how to prepare a cash basis Income Tax Summary report. The same steps would apply to preparing other income tax reports or a profit and loss report on a cash basis. (Some people prefer to use a profit and loss report for tax preparation rather than one of the income tax reports.)

1. **Open an Income Tax Summary report** (Reports > Accountant & Taxes > Income Tax Summary).

   The Income Tax Summary report window will open.

2. **Click the Customize Report button** at the top of the report window.

   The Modify Report window will open.

3. **Select the** *Cash* **option on** the Display tab of the Modify Report window.

# Preparing Income Tax Reports

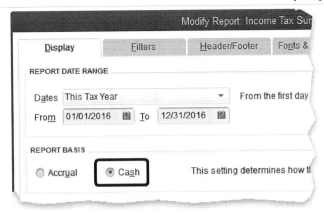

4. **Click the OK button** to close the Modify Report window and update the report.

    The report will be redisplayed on a cash basis:

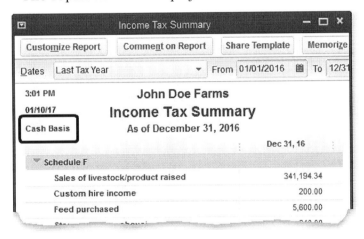

**How does QuickBooks reverse the effects of accrual transactions to prepare a cash basis report?**

In accrual accounting, expenses are reported as of the date they were incurred (the Bill date), and income is reported as of the date it was earned (the Invoice date). When you select the *Cash* option for a report, expenses are reported as of the date they were *paid* (not the Bill date), and income is reported as of the date it was *received* (not the Invoice date; but instead, when payment was actually received on the Invoice).

This change in the timing of income and expense reporting is only in effect for the current report—no changes are made to any transactions.

CHAPTER 10

# Tracking Inventory by Location

| About this chapter | This chapter shows how to keep separate inventories for the same Item stored in different locations. It is simple to do and involves *very little* additional effort beyond what is required for keeping a single, combined inventory for an Item. |
|---|---|

## Why track inventory by location in QuickBooks?

How do you keep track of things in different storage locations—bushels of grain in various bins and at commercial storage sites, for instance? Do you use a paper ledger sheet, a spreadsheet, or a smartphone app? Or do you just keep track of it all in your head? You may wonder why anyone would want to do the job in QuickBooks. Here are some reasons:

❖ If you use QuickBooks to keep track of inventories but also keep separate inventory records outside of QuickBooks, you are having to enter bushels, pounds, or whatever, in two places. If you use QuickBooks for storage location records, you only need to enter the information once, in one place.

❖ QuickBooks automatically keeps track of remaining quantities at each location—no math required. You can get a report of quantities on hand by location at any time. All you have to do is identify a source location when entering sales.

❖ You can see the quantity on hand for any storage location at a glance, in the Inventory Center (Vendors > Inventory Activities > Inventory Center; *available in QuickBooks Premier and higher editions*).

199

❖ When the time comes to prepare a balance sheet, having inventories in QuickBooks makes the job quicker and easier. You won't need to take a physical count or make an estimate for each storage location—no bin measurements or "eyeball guesses" will be needed to know what you have on hand. You may only need to make an inventory adjustment 97 to update the value of those inventories.

# Setting Up Subitems for Inventory Locations

All QuickBooks editions let you set up subitems in the Item List, in the same way that you can set up subaccounts in the Chart of Accounts. For instance:

> **Parent Item**
>   First subitem
>   Second subitem
>   Third subitem

 **QuickBooks supports up to five Item levels.** In other words, any Item can have subitems nested up to four levels deep. Having too many subitem levels, however, can make the Item List more complicated and confusing to use. Generally it's best to have no more than one or two subitem levels.

You can use subitems to represent different storage locations for a parent Item:

> **Corn**
>   **Bin 1**
>   **Bin 2**
>   **Tri-State Elevator**

This arrangement allows Item reports to automatically show the inventory quantity at each location (i.e., for each subitem) as well as a grand total quantity at the parent Item level:

## Setting Up Subitems for Inventory Locations

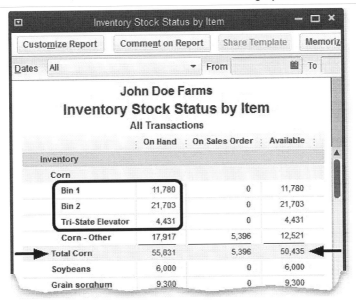

As you can see in this report example, subitem quantities and values contribute to totals for their parent Item, Corn. But this is only the case *on reports!* QuickBooks maintains a separate inventory quantity and value for each subitem, independent of the parent Item. Said differently, when a subitem is used in a transaction, the inventory quantity and value of parent Item levels *is not affected.*

## Organizing the Item List for Storage Locations

How you arrange Items and subitems determines the kinds of information you can keep track of, and the detail you will get on reports. There is no single "right way" to organize the Item List; only different ways, to support different information goals.

You need a parent Item for each major product or commodity you produce. If you raise corn and soybeans for example, you probably need a Corn Item and a Soybeans Item:

>**Corn**
>**Soybeans**

Here are the same two Items, with subitems added for storage locations:

**Corn**
    Bin 1
    Bin 2
    Tri-State Elevator
**Soybeans**
    Bin 1
    Bin 2
    Tri-State Elevator

Identical subitem names have been added to both the Corn and Soybean Items, because the same storage locations may be used for storing either corn or soybeans. However, duplicate subitems is not always necessary. If Bin 1 is only used for corn, for instance, then the Soybeans Item would not need to have a Bin 1 subitem.

Other Item arrangements may be useful depending on the kinds of things you produce and the inventory information you want to track. For instance, if you grow regular yellow corn, popcorn, and food-grade white corn you might set up Items like these:

**Corn**
    No. 2 yellow
        Bin 1
        Bin 2
        Tri-State Elevator
    Popcorn
        Bin 1
        Bin 2
        Tri-State Elevator
    White
        Bin 1
        Bin 2
        Tri-State Elevator

This arrangement would let you get reports of the quantity on hand at each storage location, with separate subtotals for each type of corn plus a grand total for all corn (all types combined).

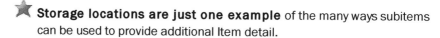 **Storage locations are just one example** of the many ways subitems can be used to provide additional Item detail.

# Setting Up Subitems for Inventory Locations

## How to Set Up Subitems

You can set up subitems for storage locations as shown for this subitem of Corn, named Bin 1:

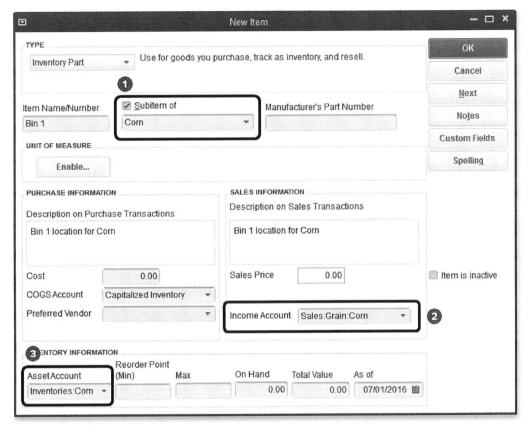

① **Subitem of.** The only real requirement for setting up a subitem is to checkmark the *Subitem of* box and select a parent Item in the box below it.

② **Income Account.** The Bin 1 subitem will post income to the same account as its parent Item, Corn. Tracking inventories by location is unrelated to how income is recorded: all of Corn's subitems could post income to the same account, or to different accounts if you want.

203

③ **Asset Account.** The value of the inventory for this Item—the value of the corn in Bin 1—will be included in the same asset account as for its parent Item, Corn ⌐81⌐. Location subitems usually refer to the same asset account as their parent Item, though you may choose a different asset account for them if you want.

See also: *Setting Up Raised Inventory Items* ⌐80⌐.

# Adding Production to Inventory, by Location

*Problem* — We finished filling Bin 1 and Bin 2 with corn today. They have about 14,000 and 22,500 bushels in them, respectively. How should I record that in QuickBooks?

*Solution* — Make an inventory adjustment, and assign the appropriate quantity and value to each location subitem.

*Discussion* — Adjusting quantities for individual inventory locations (subitems) works the same as adjusting quantities for a single Item ⌐123⌐. However, the timing of when you make inventory adjustments may be different when several locations are involved. For instance, you may want to adjust the inventory for each location separately as they become "completed" in some way—as each grain bin is filled, for example.

Here is an example inventory adjustment to record the quantity of corn stored in Bin 1 and Bin 2:

## Adding Production to Inventory, by Location

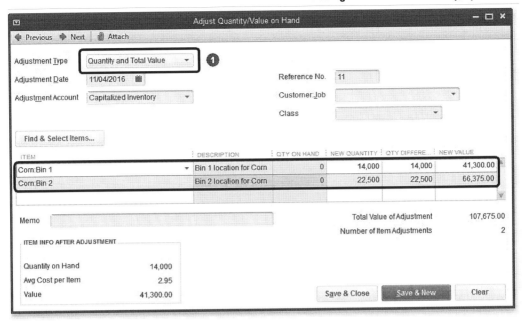

**① Adjustment Type.** The first time you adjust inventories for any location subitem, use a Quantity and Total Value adjustment to establish both a quantity and a value for the inventory.

## Entering Sales, by Location

**Problem** I received a check today for three truckloads of corn we sold last week. Two loads and part of the third load came from Bin 1; the rest of the third load was from Bin 2. (Problems with the unloading auger on Bin 1 forced us to finish out about 350 bushels of the third load from Bin 2.) How should I enter the sale for the three loads of corn?

**Solution** Enter the sale on a Sales Receipt, with the quantity from each location (each subitem) on a separate line.

**Discussion** Use the Sales Receipts form because you have received payment for the sale. (If you had delivered the corn with payment to be received later, you could use an Invoice instead. Or, you might just wait until you received the check and enter it then, on a Sales Receipt.)

## Chapter 10 - Tracking Inventory by Location

To keep inventories current for each location you must enter *at least* one line for each location involved in the sale. In the example below a separate line is entered for each load except for the third load, which is split onto two lines because it came from two different bins.

## How to Enter a Cash Sale of Inventory from Two Locations

1. **Open the Sales Receipts form** (Customers > Enter Sales Receipts).
2. **Fill in the form** as shown below.

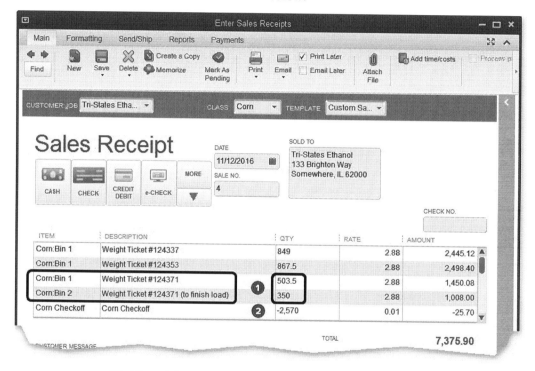

- ❶ The third load is split onto two lines, because it was filled partly from Bin 1 and partly from Bin 2.

- ❷ The Qty on the Corn Checkoff line is entered as the *negative* of the number of bushels sold so the Amount on that line (-$25.70) will subtract from the sales receipt's total.

You are not required to enter corn checkoff (or other) deductions as shown here. Assuming the buyer's settlement sheet

### Entering Sales, by Location

shows the corn checkoff amount, it could have simply been entered in the Amount column.

The only requirement for tracking inventories by location is that transactions show the quantity removed from each location. So the first three lines of the Sales Receipt above could have been combined and entered as a single line, like this:

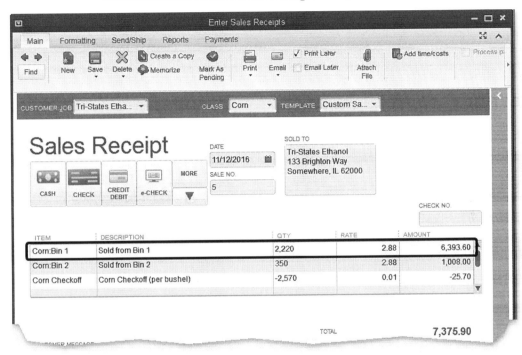

3. **Click the Save & Close button** to save the transaction and close the form.

## Depositing the payment (check)

Besides posting income, a sales receipt also posts the payment amount (the check received for corn, in this example) to an account called Undeposited Funds—a sort of "holding tank" for payments you have received but not yet deposited in the bank. When you are ready to prepare a bank deposit, QuickBooks lets you select the payments you want to include in it from the Undeposited Funds account.

See: *Depositing Payments You Have Received* 175.

**207**

**Have a good paper trail**

To be successful at keeping inventories for different locations you need to have a good paper trail—a reliable system for identifying the source location for every sale or delivery.

For example either you, another family member, or an employee may haul loads of grain or other items from storage. To keep track of where each load came from, the driver could note the source location on the weight ticket received at the time of delivery. Or, all weight tickets for grain hauled from a particular storage location could be stapled or paper clipped together. Or...there are many options for coming up with a system that works well for you.

# Reports by Inventory Location

*Problem* How can I get a report that shows inventory quantities for each location (subitem) of an Item?

*Solution* The information is available in several different QuickBooks reports, two of which are described below.

*Discussion* Both the Inventory Stock Status by Item Report, and QuickReports, are good sources of quantity information for inventory locations. (If you have QuickBooks Premier or higher, you can also find the quantity information in the Inventory Center, Vendors > Inventory Activities > Inventory Center).

## How to Get an Inventory Stock Status by Item Report

The Inventory Stock Status by Item report shows quantities on hand for all Items and subitems, making it a good source of inventory information for different locations.

❖ **To open the report,** select Reports > Inventory > Inventory Stock Status by Item.

# Reports by Inventory Location

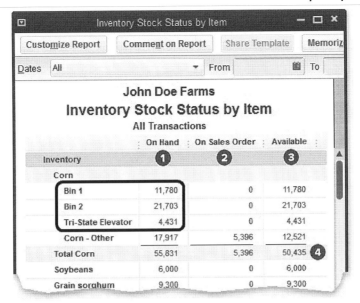

① **On Hand** is the current inventory quantity on hand. As this screenshot shows, the report provides on-hand quantities for each location subitem as well as a total for the parent Item, Corn.

② **On Sales Order** represents contracted quantities yet to be delivered. (Numbers only appear in this column if you are using Sales Orders to track contracted quantities 215.)

In this example, 5,396 contracted bushels remain to be delivered on contracts, as shown on the Corn - Other line. Corn - Other represents transactions where the Corn Item was used without a subitem. (That is typical, because quantities are usually contracted for the parent Item, not for a specific location—a contract may be filled by delivering corn from any of the storage locations.)

③ **Available** is the difference between On Hand and On Sales Order. In this example it represents the bushels of corn in inventory which are not contracted for sale; i.e., the number of bushels available to sell.

④ **Total Corn.** This line shows that there are 55,831 bushels in inventory but only 50,435 available to sell, because of the

209

## Chapter 10 - Tracking Inventory by Location

5,396 bushels contracted for sale.

## How to Get a QuickReport of Inventories by Location

1. **Open the Item List window** (Lists > Item List).

2. **Click on the Item you want to report on,** to select it; Corn in this example.

3. **Select** Reports > QuickReport **from the button menu** at the bottom of the window.

A QuickReport window will open for Corn, showing detail for individual transactions, inventories for each subitem (Bin 1 and Bin 2), and the total inventory for all corn:

# Reports by Inventory Location

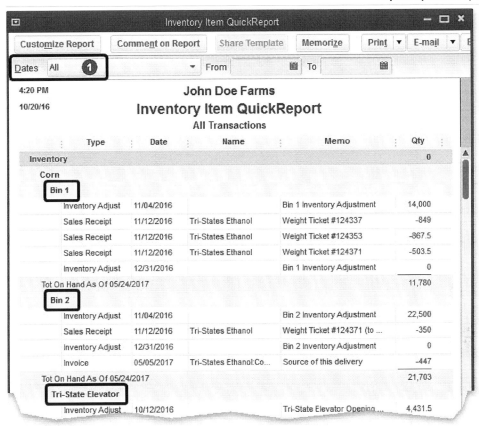

**① Dates.** By default, the report only shows transactions for the current fiscal year to date. If you don't see all of the transactions you want to see, expand the report's date range. This example shows "All" transactions.

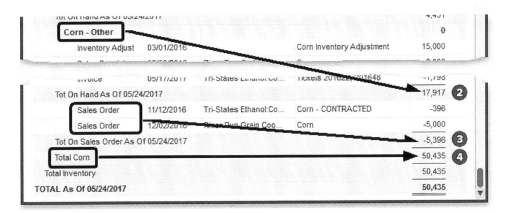

**②  Corn - Other.** This section lists transactions in which the Corn parent Item was used without a subitem. (In QuickBooks reports "- Other" added to an Item name identifies amounts for the parent Item, separate from amounts for subitems.)

You may wonder, "Where is the Corn - Other inventory stored?" Because these transactions don't specify a subitem, they do not identify the storage location.

**③  Sales Order transactions.** If you use Sales Orders to track contracted quantities 215 they will be listed in a separate report section, as shown here. The total for that section will subtract from available inventory, because contracted quantities are considered committed for sale and thus not available to sell by other means.

**④  Total Corn.** This is the total inventory of Corn available for sale—for all storage locations combined, minus contracted quantities.

# Other Activities for Location Subitems

## Making Inventory Adjustments

Adjusting quantities and values for location subitems is the same as making inventory adjustments 97 for any Inventory Part Item. Just remember that the quantity and value of each subitem is separate from the parent Item's quantity and value. That means you must use separate adjustment lines for each subitem—and also for the parent Item (if it is being used to represent other inventories, not connected with a specific location).

Here is an inventory adjustment to update only the inventory *value* of Corn and its subitems, as you might do for preparing a balance sheet:

## Other Activities for Location Subitems

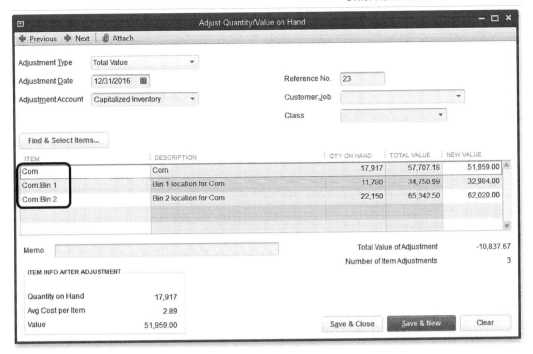

## "Closing Out" Location Inventories

When a storage location is empty, zeroing out the quantity for the Item which represents that location is important to do. It will prevent stray/incorrect inventory information from affecting future inventory reports.

See *"Closing Out" a Raised Inventory* 145, in Chapter 7.

This page is intentionally blank.

# CHAPTER 11
# Tracking Cash Sales Contracts

| About this chapter | This chapter shows how to use Jobs and Sales Orders to keep track of cash sales contracts for farm inventory items, including contract quantities and prices, deliveries, and a lot more. |
|---|---|

A *sales contract* is a contract you enter into to sell something to someone, which specifies the item being sold, the quantity, the price (or a formula for determining the price), delivery dates, and often the payment terms. In the commodities markets, sales contracts for physical commodities are often referred to as *cash sale contracts* (as opposed to futures or options contracts).

This chapter gives you procedures for tracking cash sale contracts for raised inventories⌐16⌐ and managing information about them, with examples for grain sale contracts. These procedures *can be used for all kinds of sales contracts;* they are not limited to working with grains.

They are also suitable for working with cash sales contracts for resale inventories⌐23⌐.

## QuickBooks Premier and Enterprise

The Premier and Enterprise editions have a Sales Orders feature which you can use along with Jobs (also called *Job codes* or *Customer:Jobs*), to track sales contracts.

❖ Setting up a Job for a sales contract makes reporting easy and links the contract with a particular Customer (buyer—the other party in the contract).

215

❖ Entering a Sales Order for the contract establishes contract details (items to be sold, quantity, price, etc.) and makes it possible for QuickBooks to automatically keep track of delivered and yet-to-be-delivered quantities for the contract.

## QuickBooks Pro

QuickBooks Pro has the Jobs (also called *Job codes* or *Customer:Jobs*) feature but does not have Sales Orders. However, if you have QuickBooks Pro you can use subitems for tracking sales contracts—if you are not already using them for some other purpose, like tracking inventory by location 199. Sales orders are superior for tracking sales contracts, but using subitems yields nearly as much information and requires about the same amount of effort. The last section 274 of this chapter shows how to use subitems for sales contracts.

 **QuickBooks Pro users:** you can skip ahead to the subitems section 274, then visit other parts of the chapter for additional information, as needed.

## Basic sales contract steps

Here are the main steps involved in using Jobs and Sales Orders to work with contracts:

❖ **Add a new Job** 218 to represent each contract.

Set up a new Job each time you enter into a sales contract. Using the Job on sales orders, invoices, and other transactions will link them to the contract, making all of the contract's transactions easy to find.

❖ **Create a sales order** 220 to record details of the contract.

Include the contracted Items, quantities, prices, delivery dates, and other relevant details on the sales order.

Sales orders are non-posting transactions, which means they don't affect income or expenses—they are just a record of what you have agreed to sell to someone. However, QuickBooks inventory reports *do* show sales order quantities as inventories committed for sale, which makes it easy to find out how much of your inventory is contracted and how much is still available to sell.

- **Create invoices** [226] **to record deliveries on the contract.**

    When you make a delivery, open the contract's sales order and create an invoice from it for the quantity delivered. This (1) records the fact that the buyer owes you for what you have delivered (an accounts receivable amount), and (2) allows Quick-Books to *automatically keep track of the quantities delivered and remaining to deliver* on the contract.

- **At contract settlement, enter a final invoice** [249] **if needed.**

    When you receive payment from the buyer, enter a final invoice to record any deliveries you have not yet entered in QuickBooks, minus any fees or charges the buyer has deducted from the payment. (Fees are often listed on a settlement sheet [250] received from the buyer, with the buyer's payment. This is standard practice for most grain contracts, for instance.)

- **Reconcile your invoices with the settlement sheet** [249] or other payment documentation. Compare the combined total of your invoices against the payment amount, and make corrections if they do not match.

- **Receive payment** [263] **on the invoice(s),** to close out the contract in QuickBooks.

    After all invoices have been entered for the contract, use the Receive Payments window to record the payment you have received from the buyer. This step will close or "pay off" the invoices, so their amounts are no longer included in Accounts Receivable. (Accounts Receivable represents amounts owed to the farm business by others).

Chapter 11 - Tracking Cash Sales Contracts

# Using Jobs to Represent Contracts

In QuickBooks, *Jobs* (also called *Job codes,* or *Customer:Jobs*) are a way to identify and keep track of projects related to individual customers. They are often used in the construction and building trades but are also a good fit for tracking sales contracts: a sales contract is essentially a "project" you have undertaken with a specific customer —the buyer of the contracted items.

You create Jobs by adding them in the Customer list (sometimes called the Customer:Jobs list). Each Job is specific to a customer, and all of the Jobs defined for a Customer will be listed below the customer's name. Here are examples of different ways you might set up Job names for corn and soybean cash sale contracts with River Run Grain Cooperative, a customer in the Customers list:

> **River Run Grain Coop.**
>    Corn May 2017 $3.38
>    Soybeans Dec 2016 $9.34

Or:

> **River Run Grain Coop.**
>    Corn 8,000 May 2017 $3.38
>    Soybeans 5,000 Dec 2016 $9.34

Or:

> **River Run Grain Coop.**
>    May'17 8,000 Corn $3.38
>    Dec'16 5,000 Soybeans $9.34

Including contract details in Job names helps identify each Job with a specific contract, at a glance. You can include things like the commodity name, contract quantity, contract price, delivery month, the contract number assigned by the buyer, etc.

Here are steps for setting up a Job in the Customer Center:

1. **Open the Customer Center** (Customers > Customer Center).

2. **Click on the customer name** for which you want to add the Job, to select it.

### Using Jobs to Represent Contracts

3. **Select** New Customer & Job > Add Job from the button bar at the top of the Customer Center window:

The New Job window will open.

4. **Enter a Job Name and other details** on the Job Info tab:

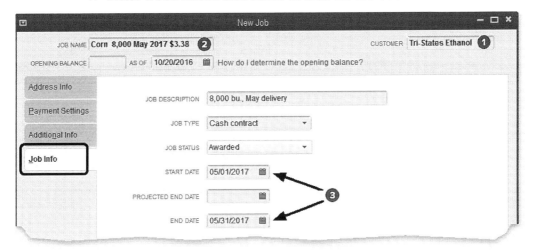

① **Customer.** The Customer name should be preselected for you, but if not, select the customer offering the contract (the buyer).

219

**② Job Name.** As mentioned above, include details in the job name which help identify the contract.

**③ Start Date** and **End Date.** If the contract specifies a delivery period, enter the beginning and ending delivery dates. In this example the contract delivery period is May 1 - May 31, 2017.

★ **Only a Job Name is required** for setting up a new Job. However, if you add contract details on the Job Info tab, such as a Start Date and an End Date, some of those details will be displayed in the Customer Center when you select the Job.

5. **Click the OK button** to add the new Job.

Another way to add a new Job is by entering it directly in the Sales Orders form when you add a new contract, as shown in the next section [220] of this chapter.

# Entering a Sales Contract

**Problem** Today I contracted 8,000 bushels of corn for delivery to Tri-States Ethanol in May 2017, at $3.68 per bushel. How do I enter the contract in QuickBooks?

**Solution** Add a new Job for the customer (buyer) Tri-States Ethanol, to identify the contract, and enter a sales order for the contract quantity and price.

**Discussion** Creating a Job for each sales contract links all contract-related transactions to the Job (and thus to the Job's parent customer). It lets you easily get reports on the status of all contracts (Jobs) for a particular customer, for instance. You can create a Job in the Customer Center as described earlier [218] or set one up "on the fly" as you create a sales order for the contract, as shown in the steps below.

Sales orders are non-posting transactions (they don't affect income or expense) but QuickBooks gives them special handling for inventory purposes. Once you've entered a sales order for a contract, QuickBooks can provide information such as the quantity delivered to date, the quantity remaining to be delivered on the contract, the portion of your total inventory which is contracted, and so on.

## Entering a Sales Contract

Here are steps for entering a sales order for the contract described above, and creating a new Job at the same time:

1. **Open the Sales Orders form** (Customers > Create Sales Orders).

2. **Select the customer name** in the Customer:Job field, **then add a colon ":"** after the customer name, **followed by the new Job name** you want to use.

   In this case "Tri-States Ethanol" was selected, then ":Corn 8,000 May 2017 $3.38" was added. The Customer:Job field may be too short to show both names completely, as shown in this example:

### What if a Customer is also a Vendor?

If Tri-States Ethanol could be selected in step 2 above, that means it must be in the Customer list: QuickBooks only allows Customers (and not Vendors) to be selected on sales forms (Sales Orders, Sales Receipts, and Invoices). But what if you also buy distiller's grains from Tri-States Ethanol for livestock feed, and you enter those purchases as Bills? If that is so, Tri-States Ethanol must also be added to the Vendors list: QuickBooks only allows Vendors (and not Customers) to be selected on the Bills form.

This creates a problem: QuickBooks requires Customer names and Vendor names to be *unique across both lists*. If "Tri-States Ethanol" is a name in the Customer list, QuickBooks *will not* let you add "Tri-States Ethanol" to the Vendor list too.

The solution is to vary the names a bit in the two lists. You might add Tri-States Ethanol to the Vendor list as "Tri-States Ethanol-V". Adding a "V" or a "C" to the end of a name is a common approach for entering the same name in both the Vendors list and the Customers list.

3. **Press the Tab key** or **click elsewhere** on the Sales Orders form.

   QuickBooks will display a Not Found message to let you know that the name does not exist and to ask what to do:

**221**

## Chapter 11 - Tracking Cash Sales Contracts

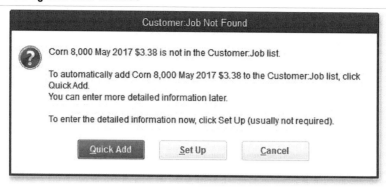

4. **Click the Quick Add button.**

   QuickBooks will add the new Job name to the Customer:Jobs list, and allow you to continue working with the Sales Order.

5. **Fill in the rest of the Sales Order** as shown below.

   Mainly you need to select the contracted Item(s), and enter the contracted quantity and price for each of them.

# Entering a Sales Contract

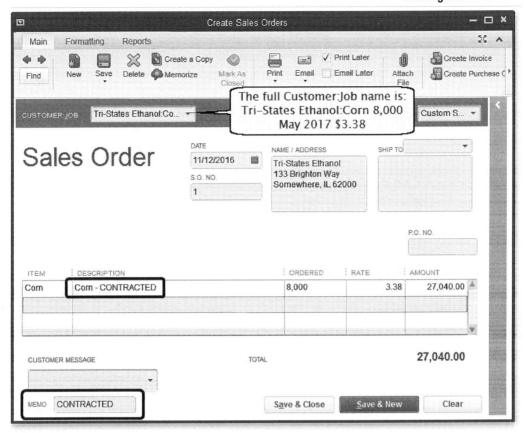

Though the Job name in the Customer:Job field identifies this sales order as a corn contract, adding a comment in the Description column or the Memo field makes it clear that the sales order represents a cash sale contract.

6. **Click the Save & Close button** to save the sales order and close the form.

## Seeing the Sales Order's Effect on Inventory

A good place to see the sales order's effect on inventories is in the Inventory Stock Status by Item report. Before preparing the report though, you *must* have the *Quantity on Sales Orders* Preference setting turned on. Otherwise, contract (sales order) quantities will be omitted from the report.

**How to enable the** *Quantity on Sales Orders* **setting:**

1. **Select** Edit >Preferences > Items & Inventory > Company Preferences [tab].

2. **Checkmark** *Quantity on Sales Orders* on the Company Preferences tab:

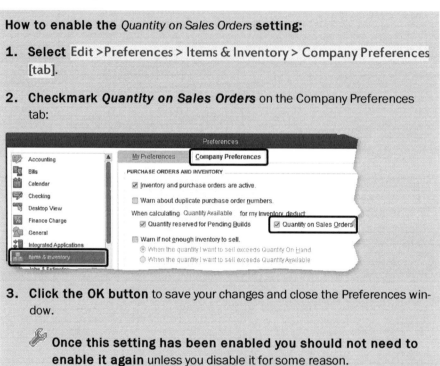

3. **Click the OK button** to save your changes and close the Preferences window.

   *Once this setting has been enabled you should not need to enable it again* unless you disable it for some reason.

With the *Quantity on Sales Orders* setting enabled, the Inventory Stock Status by Item report (Reports > Inventory > Inventory Stock Status by Item) will have an On Sales Orders column which shows contracted quantities. More correctly, it shows the quantity *remaining to be delivered* on each contract, which in this case is the entire contracted quantity, 8,000 bushels:

### Entering a Sales Contract

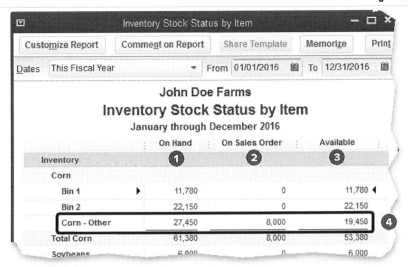

① **On Hand** is the current inventory quantity on hand.

② **On Sales Order** represents the quantity of corn that has been contracted—8,000 bushels in this example.

③ **Available** is the difference between On Hand and On Sales Order. Here, it represents the bushels of corn in inventory which are not contracted for sale—the number of bushels available to sell.

④ **The Corn - Other line** shows a 27,450 bushel inventory for the Corn Item (excluding subitems). With 8,000 bushels contracted for sale, 19,450 bushels are available to sell.

## Modifying or Canceling a Contract

***Problem*** There was some confusion at Tri-States Ethanol and their office staff failed to get the contract recorded. The market price moved higher after that, so we mutually agreed to cancel the contract. Can I just delete the sales order I entered for it, or will that cause problems?

***Solution*** You may delete or modify a sales order any time you want.

225

## Chapter 11 - Tracking Cash Sales Contracts

***Discussion*** Editing or deleting a sales order is safe to do at any time; for instance, you might need to make a correction after noticing that the quantity or price was entered incorrectly.

As for the Job you added to represent the contract, you may *rename* a Job at any time, but you cannot *delete* a Job if any transactions have been entered which refer to it. Even if you cannot delete a Job though, you can prevent it from showing in the Customer:Jobs list by editing the Job and marking it Inactive:

1. **Open the Customer Center** (Customers > Customer Center).
2. **Right click on the Job you want to make inactive,** to open a pop-up menu for it.
3. **Select *Make Customer:Job Inactive*** from the pop-up menu.

   The Job (contract) will then be hidden.

To show the Job again, select *All Customers* from the drop-down list at the top of the Customers & Jobs tab in the Customer Center:

## Recording Deliveries on a Contract

***Problem*** **I delivered two loads of corn on the contract with Tri-States Ethanol this week—878 bushels, and 902 bushels. Should I enter these deliveries in QuickBooks? If so, how?**

***Solution*** As you make deliveries, enter them in Quick-Books by creating invoices from the sales order which represents the contract 220.

### Recording Deliveries on a Contract

**Discussion**  From an accounting standpoint the correct approach is to enter an invoice for each delivery, but that is not always necessary, and whether you do it or not is your choice. You also have other options, discussed in this section.

To correctly maintain contract quantities in QuickBooks delivery inventories *must be created from the sales order representing the contract* 📖. A sales order records the *possibility* of a sale, but an invoice records the *fact* that a sale has been made—or at least that Items have been transferred to the purchaser, as when grain has been delivered to a buyer.

If you have never created an invoice from a sales order it may seem strange and unfamiliar at first, but it is easy to do. It only takes a few mouse clicks, and accomplishes several important things: it (1) decreases the inventory of the delivered Item, (2) decreases the quantity remaining to be delivered on the contract (the sales order), (3) records the fact that the buyer owes for what you have delivered (it adds to accounts receivable), and (4) records income.

Here are the steps for creating an invoice to record a delivery, on a contract:

1. **Open the Sales Orders form** (Customers > Create Sales Orders).
2. **Find the sales order for the delivered-on contract, and open it.**

   To find the desired sales order you can:

   ❖ Use the Previous and Next buttons at the top of the form.

   ❖ Use the Find button (immediately below the Previous and Next buttons) to search by customer name, date, etc.

   ❖ Locate the sales order in a report such as Open Sales Orders by Customer (Reports > Sales > Open Sales Orders by Customer),

227

then double-click it in the report window to open it in the Sales Orders form.

3. **Click the** Create Invoice **icon** on the Main tab of the ribbon bar.

A window will open, giving you the option to create an invoice for the entire sales order or just for selected Items.

4. **Select the** Create invoice for selected items **option, then click the OK button.**

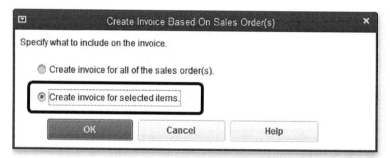

 **Selecting this option is important** because it will allow you to specify quantities for the invoice. Selecting the other option would create the invoice for the entire remaining quantity on the sales order.

The Specify Items and Quantities for Invoice window will open.

5. **Select the delivered Item(s)** by checkmarking them, then **enter the quantities that were delivered.** Finally, **click the OK button.**

In this example two loads of corn were delivered. *You can either create a separate invoice for each load or a single invoice for both.* Separate invoices are easier to compare against scale tickets and/or the settlement sheet you will receive from the buyer. However, creating one invoice for several loads can reduce the number of invoices you have to enter. (See: *I'd like to combine deliveries...* 235 later in this section.)

For this example we will enter a separate invoice for each load delivered. The first one had 878 bushels on it:

After clicking OK, QuickBooks will close the Sales Orders form and open the Create Invoices form, pre-filled with the Item or Items you selected (just the Corn Item here).

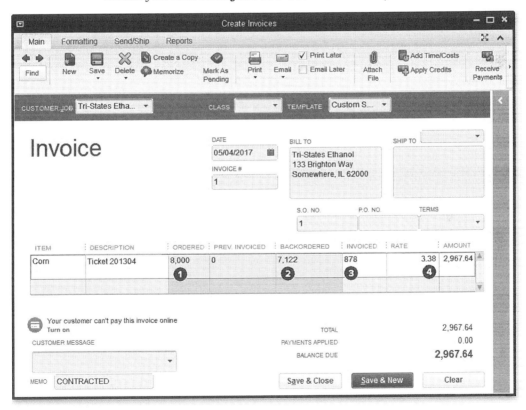

① **Ordered** shows the originally contracted quantity. (Invoices created from sales orders remain "connected" to the sales order, allowing them to display information about the sales order.)

② **Backordered** shows what the remaining quantity to deliver will be after the invoice is saved. ("Backordered" may seem like a strange term here, but remember, QuickBooks was designed for retail inventories.)

③ **Invoiced** is the quantity that was entered in the Specify Items and Quantities for Invoice window (the screenshot prior to the one above).

④ **Rate (price)** is the contracted price, filled in directly from the sales order when the invoice was created.

6. **Click the Save & Close button** to save the invoice and close the window.

7. **Open the Sales Orders form again** (Customers > Create Sales Orders). (The form must be reopened because QuickBooks automatically closed it when the invoice was created.)

   ★ **A quick way to return to a particular sales order** is to create an Open Sales Orders by Customer report (Reports > Sales > Open Sales Orders by Customer) and keep the report open. You can double-click any sales order in it to open the sales order for viewing or editing.

8. **Repeat steps 2 through 6**, but this time create an invoice for 902 bushels—the second load of corn.

# Recording Deliveries on a Contract

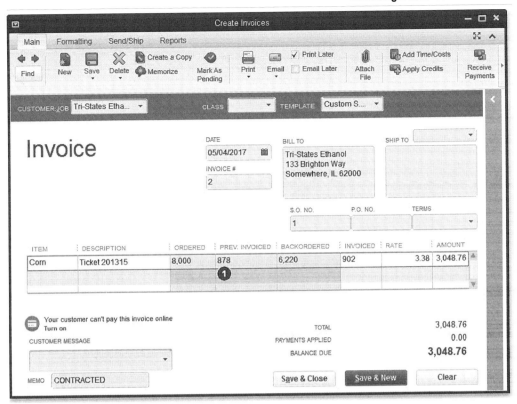

① **Prev. Invoiced.** This invoice has a piece of information which was not present on the prior one. Prev. Invoiced is the total quantity which has been invoiced from the sales order so far. Here, it is the quantity from the invoice created earlier—the number of bushels invoiced so far, as deliveries on the contract.

*"Won't using invoices sometimes put income in the wrong tax year?"*

As an astute cash basis recordkeeper you may be concerned about this, and rightfully so. An invoice records income *as of the invoice date*. But in cash basis accounting, income should only be recorded *when payment is received*. If you enter an invoice for a sale made "this year" but don't receive payment until "next year", income will be recorded in the wrong year; or it would be, if QuickBooks didn't have a solution for the problem...

Enabling the *Cash* option when you prepare a report will cause QuickBooks to prepare it on a cash basis. Income will only include sales for which payment was *received* during the time period covered by the report. So if you entered invoices in December but then didn't receive payment on them until January, the income from those invoices would be included as income in January, not December. This only happens when a report is prepared with the *Cash* option.

 **Using the *Cash* option on a report** causes QuickBooks to move income into the accounting period when it was received, and expenses into the accounting period when they were paid. However, this mostly applies to income or expense transactions entered on the Bills, Invoices, or Credit Memos forms. And there are limitations: QuickBooks cannot move amounts posted to balance sheet accounts, for instance. If a report contains amounts you believe should or should not be present and you cannot figure out why, consult a QuickBooks professional for help.

 **Accounting 101: Why use multiple invoices?**

Whether you enter one invoice or several for contract deliveries is your choice. But if you want to keep inventories updated in QuickBooks *and* make an accountant happy somewhere, you will create multiple invoices along the way as you make deliveries.

The accountant will be happy because he or she understands **the main reason for using invoices:** to maintain accounting control over the business' assets—an accurate record of what the business owns (such as inventories) versus what is owed to the business (accounts receivable). Purely from an accounting standpoint, you should create an invoice whenever goods are transferred to a customer or services are provided to a customer. (Does your supplier for chemicals, feed, or seed ever fail to create an invoice when they deliver products to you? Probably not often.)

In most farm businesses though, creating invoices as soon as goods change hands may not always be practical. More often, you may just wait until you receive payment for something before making any kind of accounting entry at all, and that works OK most of the time. In fact, the systems we commonly use to "maintain control over business assets" are things like a pile of scale tickets fluttering on the dashboard of a semi, or trying to remember that Gary Jones still owes for 40 big round bales of hay.

From a practicality standpoint, you need to strike a balance between minimizing accounting effort (the number of invoices you enter) versus having current inventory information. If you want up-to-date inventory quantities in QuickBooks—

## Recording Deliveries on a Contract

or especially if you will be preparing a balance sheet soon—you need to get invoices entered to record the quantities and dollar value of inventories which have left the farm business.

At times when you *are not* concerned with keeping inventories current, you can "drag your feet" a bit about getting invoices entered. You might enter one invoice for all deliveries made on a contract during the week instead of entering an invoice every day, or for each load delivered.

### Seeing how the deliveries affected inventories

A good place to see how deliveries have affected the contract's status is in the contract's sales order. If you open the Sales Orders form (Customers > Create Sales Orders), then navigate to the sales order for the desired contract, here is what you will see in the sales order's detail area:

| ITEM | DESCRIPTION | ORDERED | RATE | AMOUNT | BACKORDERED | INVOICED |
|------|-------------|---------|------|--------|-------------|----------|
| Corn | Corn - CONTRACTED | 8,000 | 3.38 | 27,040.00 | 6,220 | 1,780 |

❶ **Ordered** shows the originally contracted quantity, 8,000 bushels in this example.

 **The Ordered column is editable but *should not* be changed** unless the wrong quantity was entered when the sales order was originally created.

❷ **Backordered** shows the quantity remaining to be delivered on the contract, 6,220 bushels.

❸ **Invoiced** shows the quantity delivered on the contract so far: 878 + 902 = 1,780 bushels. (Only deliveries *which have been entered on invoices* are included here—QuickBooks cannot know about deliveries you have not entered!)

To see how deliveries affected inventories for the Corn Item, go to the Inventory Center (Vendors > Inventory Activities > Inventory Center; *available in QuickBooks Premier and higher editions*), click on the Corn Item, then click on the QuickReport link in the right pane of the window.

## Chapter 11 - Tracking Cash Sales Contracts

A QuickReport window will open for Corn:

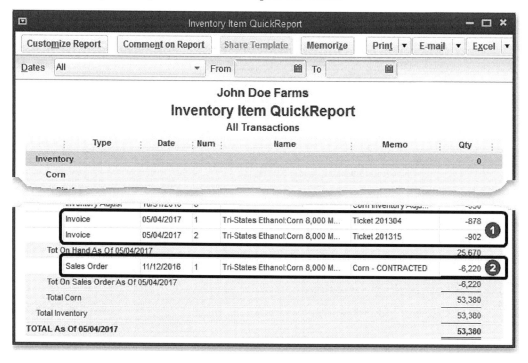

① **Invoices** for the two deliveries reduced corn inventories by 878 and 902 bushels.

② **Sales Order.** The undelivered portion of the sales order is a negative number because sales orders (contracts) reduce the number of bushels available to sell, so they are deducted from inventory on this report.

**Another way to get the same QuickReport** is to go to the Item List (**Lists > Item List**), click on the Corn Item, then select **Reports > Quick-Report** from the button menu at the bottom of the window:

## Questions & Answers

### Couldn't I just enter one invoice, for everything delivered on the contract?

You could, but then there wouldn't have been much value in bothering to enter a sales order for the contract 220 at all. The sales order would mostly just be a record of the contracted quantity and price, providing about as much information as a sticky note on your computer screen!

Entering a single invoice at contract settlement is the simplest option *but also yields the least information.* Without entering invoices as you make deliveries, QuickBooks cannot show how much has been delivered on a contract or how much remains to be delivered. Note however, that this *is* a viable option if all of the deliveries on a contract will happen over a short period of time and you are not concerned with keeping QuickBooks' inventories updated during that time.

The steps for creating a single invoice are the same as for multiple invoices, except that you create the invoice for the entire sales order—the entire contract quantity—at once. For details, see: *Contract Settlement / Payment / Closeout* 249.

### I'd like to combine deliveries on fewer invoices. How should I do that?

Enter an invoice for the combined quantity of all the deliveries you want to enter—maybe everything delivered over a few days' time, for instance. The steps are the same as for entering a separate invoice for each delivery, but with the following differences:

In step 5 (see page 228), you would enter the total quantity delivered. If you want, you can calculate the total using the QuickBooks calculator, like this:

## Chapter 11 - Tracking Cash Sales Contracts

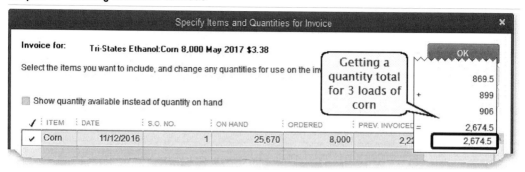

The invoice then, will be for the total quantity:

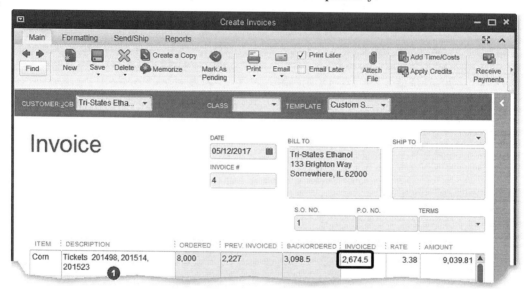

① **Description.** When an invoice represents several deliveries it is a good idea to include scale ticket numbers or other documentation. The information may be helpful later, if you are trying to figure out an error or problem.

## How should I enter discounts or premiums for quality factors?

Deductions for quality factors like low test weight, excess moisture, or heat damage, or premiums for things like oil content can be entered as separate Item lines:

## Recording Deliveries on a Contract

① **Item.** DamageDiscnt 87 is an Item used for entering grain damage discounts.

② **Amount.** Enter discounts as negative numbers in the Amount column, so they will subtract from the invoice total.

### However...

Waiting until contract settlement 249 to enter discounts or premiums is usually best. That lets you enter the net total amount of all discounts or premiums shown on the settlement sheet 250, as a single line on the final invoice. That approach is simpler than entering a discount or premium on each delivery invoice. Also, you may not know the exact amount of discounts or premiums until contract settlement—another good reason for waiting until then to enter them.

### What about weight-for-weight or shrinkage deductions?

Some quality factors are discounted by reducing the gross quantity to a smaller net quantity, then basic contract fulfillment (and payment) on the net quantity. Foreign matter in grain, for example, is sometimes discounted weight-for-weight. If 1,000 bushels of grain were delivered and found to contain 2% foreign matter, the gross quantity

(1,000 bushels) would be reduced by 2% (1,000 * .02 = 20 bushels), resulting in a net quantity of 980 bushels (1,000 - 20 = 980).

Excess moisture is sometimes discounted in a similar way, using a shrink factor. Corn, for example, might be shrunk by 1.4% for each percentage point of moisture over 15%. If 1,000 bushels of corn are delivered at 16% moisture, the shrinkage would be 1000 * 0.014 = 14 bushels, resulting in a net quantity of 1000 - 14 = 986 bushels.

As discussed above, you may not have the necessary information available for including discounts like these on each delivery invoice, and unless they are likely to be significant it is usually not important to do so. If you do include them however, do that by creating the invoice for the *net quantity* instead of the gross quantity, because contract fulfillment is usually based on the net quantity delivered.

## "How should I enter contract deliveries if I'm using subitems for storage locations?"

⭐ **This discussion assumes you are using subitems for storage locations,** not for representing contracts 274. You may use subitems for either purpose but they should not be used for both, because that will greatly complicate the recordkeeping involved.

You can represent storage locations as subitems  of a parent Item. For instance:

    **Corn**
        **Bin 1**
        **Bin 2**
        **Bin 3**

Arranged this way, each subitem can be assigned the inventory quantity for a location. To keep inventories current for each location, invoices for contract deliveries must identify the location (subitem) that was the source of the delivery. For instance, if a load of corn delivered on a contract came from bin 2, then the Corn:Bin 2 Item needs to be used on the invoice for that load of corn.

The problem is that when you create an invoice from a sales order it *must* contain the same Item(s) as are on the sales order. If you use different Items the linkage QuickBooks maintains between the

## Recording Deliveries on a Contract

sales order and the invoice will be broken, and the sales order will no longer recognize the invoice as a delivery made on that sales order (contract).

If you enter a sales order for a corn contract and use the Corn Item on it, the delivery invoices you create from that sales order must have the Corn Item on them as well. So how can an invoice be for both Corn and for Corn:Bin 2, for instance? The solution is to use two more Item lines to the invoice, to reverse the inventory decrease for the original Item (Corn), and apply it to the location subitem (Corn:Bin 2).

Here is an example:

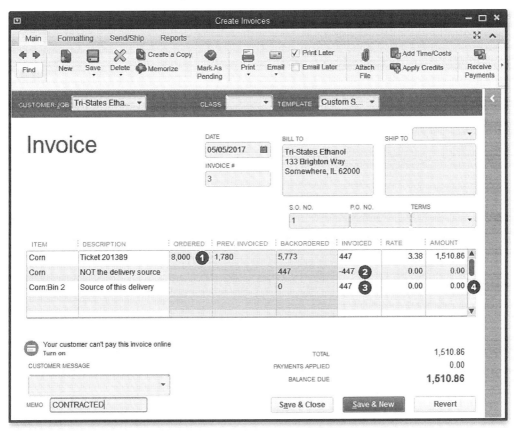

1. **The first line** is the one connected to the sales order. You can tell that by the fact that the Ordered column has a number in it on that line—the number of bushels contracted.

**② The second line** is for a negative quantity, so it reverses the first line's effect on inventories for the Corn Item. Together, the first and second lines cancel each other out (in terms of inventory quantity) so that this invoice will not change Corn's inventory quantity.

**③ The third line** assigns the invoiced quantity to Corn:Bin 2, decreasing its inventory by 447 bushels.

**④ Amount.** The Amount column represents income from the corn sale. So why is the Amount for Corn:Bin 2 zero? Assuming both Corn and Corn:Bin 2 post income to the same account, only one line needs to record income for this corn sale, and the first line does that.

If Corn and Corn:Bin 2 had been set up to post income to *different* accounts, then the Amount would need to be moved from the first line to the third line.

# Entering Progress Payments & Advances

***Problem*** The corn contract with Tri-States Ethanol lets me request an advance payment on delivered bushels. I have a loan payment coming due soon, so I asked for an advance and they sent me a check for $7,000. How do I enter the payment so that it will be linked to the contract?

***Solution*** Enter the payment in the Receive Payments window, and apply it to the invoices you have entered for deliveries on the contract.

***Discussion*** A *progress payment* or *advance* is a partial payment received before contract completion. Not many commodity contracts provide for progress payments, but some do, and other special situations can arise which may require applying a payment to a contract before it is completed/settled.

Below are the steps for entering a progress payment.

### Entering Progress Payments & Advances

⚠️ **This progress payment is just an example.** It *is not* included in reports shown later in this chapter, for the Corn 8,000 May 2017 $3.38 contract.

1. **Open the Receive Payments window** (Customers > Receive Payments).

2. **Select the contract's Customer:Job name** in the Received From field.

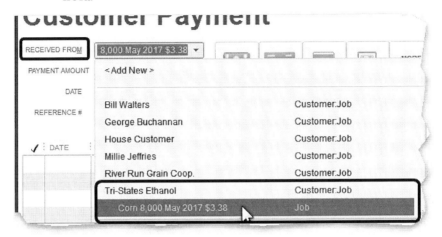

This will limit the invoices displayed in the lower part of the window to ones for the Corn contract with Tri-States Ethanol.

3. **Fill in the rest of the form** as shown below.

## Chapter 11 - Tracking Cash Sales Contracts

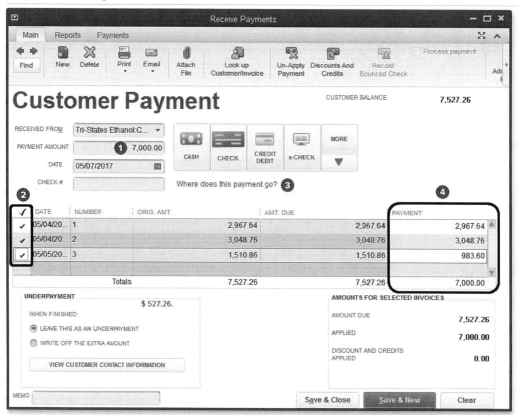

① **Payment Amount.** When you enter the payment amount, QuickBooks will immediately checkmark (②) as many invoices as it can, from oldest to newest, until the payment has been fully applied to invoices. If the payment is larger than the dollar amount of the available invoices you can leave the remainder of the payment as a credit on the customer's (buyer's) account—something which is not likely to happen with a progress payment, because they are usually for less than the value of what has been delivered so far.

If you want the payment applied to invoices other than the ones QuickBooks has checkmarked, you can change which invoices are checkmarked.

② **√ (check marks)** Checkmark the invoice(s) to which you want the payment applied. If you want it applied to invoices other than the ones QuickBooks has selected, you can change which invoices are checkmarked.

**❸ Where does this payment go?** If Receive Payments window displays this message, the payment will be posted to the Undeposited Funds [176] account. If not, the window will have a *Deposit To* field in it, where you can select a destination account for the payment.

**❹ Payment.** The Payment column shows the payment amount that will be applied to each invoice.

4. **Click the Save & Close button** to record the payment, apply it to the checkmarked invoice(s), and close the window.

# Getting Information about Contracts and Deliveries

*Problem* — How can I get information about the contract—things like the number of bushels contracted, how many bushels are delivered vs. remaining to deliver, and so on?

*Solution* — Most of the information about the status of contracts is available in the Customer Center, the Inventory Center, and in sales reports and inventory reports.

*Discussion* — The examples below show how to get answers to specific questions about the status of a contract or inventories.

*How many bushels were contracted in a particular contract?*
*How many total bushels are contracted (across all contracts)?*
*How many bushels have been delivered on contracts?*
*How many bushels remain to be delivered?*

A place to find some of this information is in the contract's sales [220] order [220] (**Customers: Create Sales Orders**):

## Chapter 11 - Tracking Cash Sales Contracts

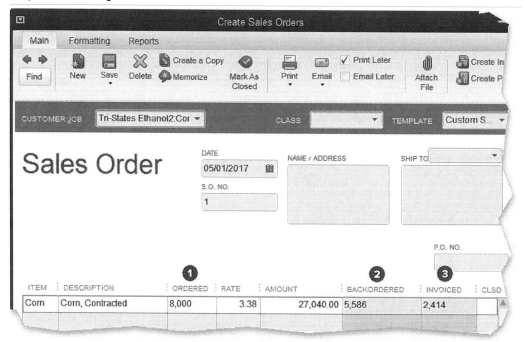

① **Ordered** is the contracted quantity.

② **Backordered** is the quantity remaining to be delivered on the contract.

③ **Invoiced** is the quantity delivered so far. More correctly, it is the delivered quantity *which has been entered in QuickBooks* by creating invoices from the sales order.

Another place to find the same information is in the Open Sales Orders by Item report (Reports > Sales > Open Sales Orders by Item), which shows contract quantities for all open (net-yet-filled) contracts. Here is an example of the report, with two open contracts:

### Getting Information about Contracts and Deliveries

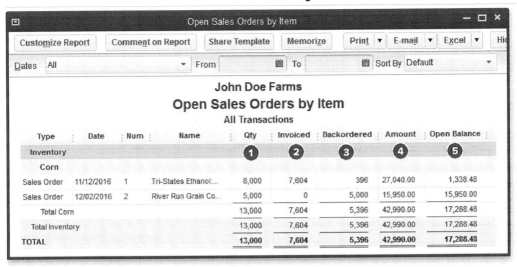

1. **Qty** is the contracted quantity.

2. **Invoiced** shows the total quantity delivered on each contract. More correctly, it shows the delivered quantity *which has been entered in QuickBooks* by creating invoices from the contracts' sales orders.

3. **Backordered** shows the quantity remaining to be delivered on each contract—again, assuming all deliveries made so far have been entered as invoices.

4. **Amount** is the dollar value of the contract: the contracted quantity multiplied by the contract price.

5. **Open Balance** is the contract value remaining to be delivered: the Backordered quantity multiplied by the contract price.

🟊 **You can get similar information from a QuickReport:** click on an Item in either the Item List (**Lists > Items**) or the Inventory Center (**Vendors > Inventory Activities > Inventory Center**), then type *Ctrl-Q* to open a QuickReport window for the Item.

## How many bushels are contracted with each buyer?

If you have described contract quantities in the Job names which represent contracts, you can see contracted quantities for any buyer

## Chapter 11 - Tracking Cash Sales Contracts

(customer) with a quick glance at the Job names in the Customer Center window (**Customers > Customer Center**):

You can also get contract information for a buyer (customer) in the Open Sales Orders by Item report (**Reports > Sales > Open Sales Orders by Item**), shown in the topic above 244. If you want to filter the report to limit it to a single customer, here's how:

1. **Click the Customize Report button** at the top of the report.

   The Modify Report window will open.

2. On the Filters tab, **select Name in the Filter box, then select the buyer's (customer's) name** from the dropdown list in the center of the window.

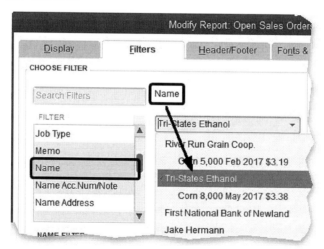

   🔧 Selecting a customer name but *not* a particular Job will include all Jobs (all contracts) for the customer.

3. **Click the OK button** to close the window and apply the filter to the report.

### Getting Information about Contracts and Deliveries

Here is the same report as shown earlier, but filtered to include only contracts for Tri-States Ethanol:

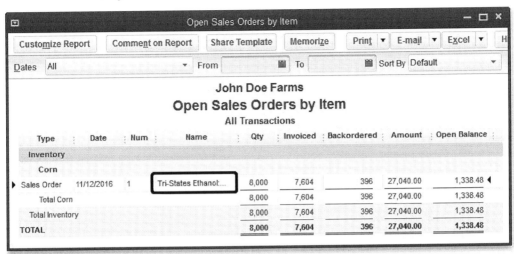

## How many *un*-contracted bushels do I have?

If your QuickBooks edition has the Inventory Center (Vendors > Inventory Activities > Inventory Center), clicking on an Item name in the left pane, such as Corn, will reveal inventory information for that Item in the right pane. Here is a partial view of the right pane for the Corn Item:

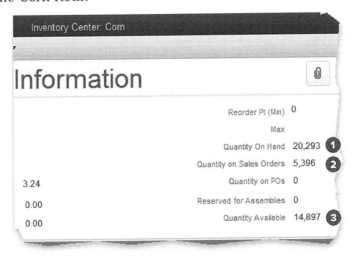

① **Quantity on Hand** is the total corn inventory on hand.

② **Quantity on Sales Orders** is the remaining (undelivered) quantity on contracts for this Item

③ **Quantity Available** is the difference between ① and ②. It is the portion of the quantity on hand which is available to sell, because it is not contracted.

If your edition of QuickBooks does not have the Inventory Center, you can get the same information from an Inventory Stock Status by Item report. Before preparing the report though, you *must* have the *Quantity on Sales Orders* Preference setting turned on (see below). If you don't, the report will not include contracted (sales order) quantities.

**How to enable the** *Quantity on Sales Orders* **setting:**

1. **Select** Edit > Preferences > Items & Inventory > Company Preferences [tab].

2. **Checkmark** *Quantity on Sales Orders* on the Company Preferences tab:

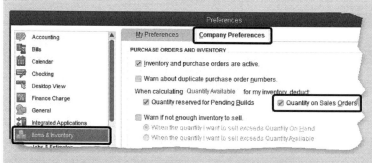

3. **Click the OK button** to save your changes and close the Preferences window.

 **Once this setting has been enabled you should not need to enable it again** unless you disable it for some reason.

With the *Quantity on Sales Orders* setting enabled, the Inventory Stock Status by Item report (Reports > Inventory > Inventory Stock Status by Item) will have columns with the same information as described above for the Inventory Center:

### Getting Information about Contracts and Deliveries

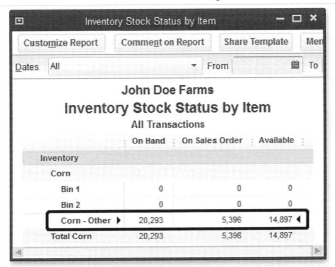

## Contract Settlement/Payment/Closeout

***Problem*** I finished delivering the contracted corn last week and received a settlement sheet and check in the mail today. What should I do to enter the payment and close out the contract in QuickBooks?

***Solution*** Enter a final invoice for the contract. It should include any deliveries you have not yet recorded, any discounts or deductions, and charges for storage, drying, commodity checkoff programs, or other fees. Then compare the total for all of the contract's invoices against the amount of the payment. If they do not match, correct the final invoice until they do. Finally, receive payment against all of the invoices to close ("pay off") the invoices.

***Discussion*** The main things you need to get done are: (1) if the contract's sales order has an undelivered (not yet invoiced) quantity, create an invoice from the sales order to zero it out, and (2) make sure that the total dollar amount of invoices for the contract matches the amount of the payment you received.

249

# Contract Settlement Entries

*Settlement* is the process of reconciling the buyer's settlement sheet and payment with your copies of weight tickets or other delivery documentation and with the invoices you have entered for deliveries. Often, settlement also involves entering discounts and fees charged by the buyer as deductions from the payment. The main goals of contract settlement are to (1) discover errors, if any, and (2) assure that the total amount of invoices you have entered for the contract matches the payment you have received.

*Closeout* involves making sure the quantity associated with the contract is zero in QuickBooks, so the contract will be closed out (no longer active; no longer "on the books"), and is usually just a part of the settlement process.

## The Settlement Sheet

Here is the settlement sheet provided by Tri-States Ethanol:

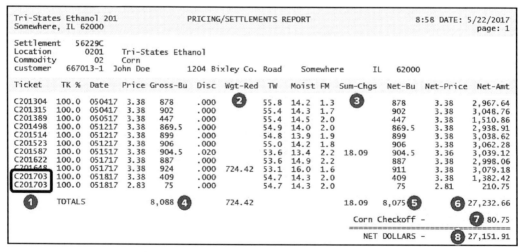

**① Split load.** The last two detail lines represent a single load of corn (both have the same ticket number). The first of the two lines fills out the remaining bushels of the contract, at the contract price of $3.38 per bushel. The last line is for an ex-

## Contract Settlement/Payment/Closeout

cess 75 bushels over the contracted quantity of 8,000 bushels, sold at that day's cash corn price of $2.81 per bushel.

**②** **Wgt-Red** stands for Weight Reduction. One load had a weight reduction of 724.42 pounds due to moisture content (16%) above the standard accepted by the buyer (15%). The gross quantity on that line is 924 bushels, but the net quantity is only 911 bushels because of the weight reduction.

**③** **Sum-Chgs** is the total of per-bushel charges for things like damaged grain, low test weight, excess foreign matter, etc. This column's total is deducted from

**④** **Gross bushels** delivered.

**⑤** **Net bushels** delivered, after weight reductions (see **②**.)

**⑥** **Gross dollars** to be paid, after deducting discounts (Sum-Chgs **⑥**) but before subtracting fees for things like storage or commodity assessments (see Corn Checkoff **⑦**).

**⑦** **Corn checkoff** is a "below the line" deduction, meaning a fee deducted from the gross amount of the sale.

**⑧** **Net dollars** to be paid.

If you have been entering invoices to keep track of deliveries 227, the most important part of closing out the contract is entering a final invoice for the contract and (if necessary) correcting prior invoices until the invoice total matches the amount of the payment you have received.

## Here is the likely situation at this point:

- **You may not yet have created invoices for some deliveries.** One or more may still need to be entered in QuickBooks.

- **Your invoices most likely have been entered for the *gross quantity* delivered, and at the *gross price* (contract price),** which may be different from the *net quantity* and *net price*.

  In grains for example, the net quantity may be less because of weight-based deductions from the gross quantity for things like foreign matter or excess moisture. Likewise, the net price may be lower or higher than the contract price after discounts or premiums for quality factors like test weight, heat damage, or oil content have been applied. (Delivery invoices are usually entered at the gross quantity and gross price because the exact amount of discounts or premiums may not be known until contract settlement.)

❖ **You have not yet entered other charges** which the buyer has subtracted from the final payment amount for things like storage, commodity checkoff assessments, and so on.

## Here is what needs to happen:

❖ **You need to enter a final invoice** for the quantity remaining on the sales order.

 **You must invoice the _entire_ remaining sales order quantity** to close out the sales order (and thus the contract) in QuickBooks.

❖ **The final invoice needs to include charges** which the buyer has subtracted from the gross payment amount.

❖ **The combined total for all of the contract's invoices (including the final one) must match the payment amount.** If they don't match, then either (A) one of the invoices won't be closed when you receive payment on them (the invoice will be left with a partly unpaid balance), or (B) the buyer's accounts receivable account (in QuickBooks) will be left with a credit balance. Either would be incorrect. You may need to adjust quantities and/or prices on one or more invoices to make the amounts match.

## Here are your options for making these things happen:

Assuming you have entered more than one invoice for deliveries made on the contract, and that each may not be for the exact settlement quantity and price (they were entered for the gross quantity and price, not the net quantity and net price), you could either:

A. Edit each invoice, correcting them to the net quantity and net price shown on the settlement sheet, or

## Contract Settlement/Payment/Closeout

B. Make adjustments for any quantity and price differences on the final invoice only, leaving the others unchanged.

Option B is usually the more workable choice and is the one described by the steps below. It is a bit "messy"—it will seem complicated the first time you do it—but requires the least time and effort to accomplish.

## Finding out what has been invoiced so far

You need to find out the total quantity and dollar amount entered on delivery invoices so far, so you can enter a final invoice for the *remaining* quantity and dollar amount. A good place to find this information is in a Sales by Customer Detail report. Here is how to prepare the report, filtered for the contract you want to close out—limiting the report to transactions for that contract, to prevent confusion with other contracts:

1. **Open the Sales by Customer Detail report** (Reports > Sales > Sales by Customer Detail).

2. In the Dates box, **select a date range** which will include all of the contract's delivery invoices.

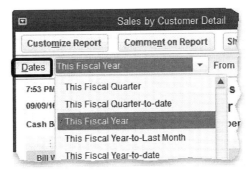

3. **Click the Customize Report button.**

    The Modify Report window will open.

4. On the Filters tab, **click on Name in the Current Filter Choices box, then select the contract's Customer:Job name** from the drop-down list in the center part of the window:

# Chapter 11 - Tracking Cash Sales Contracts

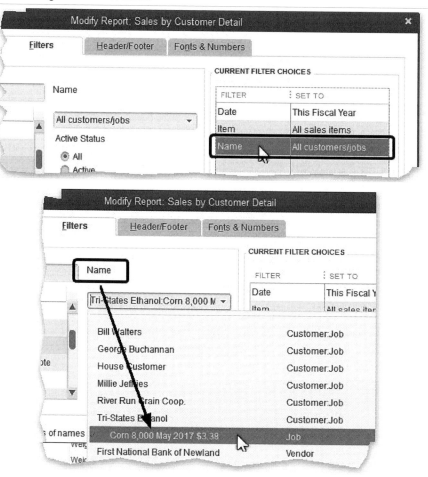

5. On the Display tab, **select the Accrual report basis** if it is not selected already. (Unpaid invoices are involved, and the report won't include them if it is prepared on a Cash basis.)

## Contract Settlement/Payment/Closeout

6. **Click the OK button** to close the Modify Report window.

   The report will be redisplayed, showing only transactions for the Customer:Job (contract) you selected.

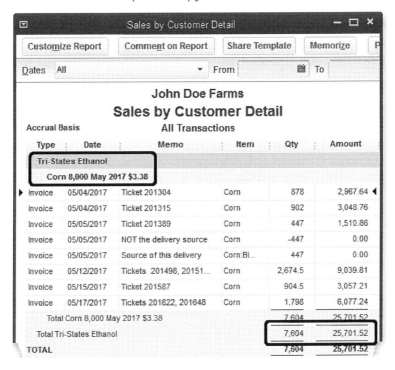

In the report example above, the quantity and dollar value of corn invoiced so far are 7,604 bushels and $25,701.52, respectively. This information will be necessary for figuring out how many bushels and dollars must be on the final invoice.

## Entering the final invoice

The purpose of the final invoice is to complete entry of the contracted bushels, adjust for any overage or shortage (quantities delivered above or below the contracted quantity), adjust for quality discounts or premiums, and deduct fees for things like storage charges or commodity checkoff assessments.

1. **Open the Sales Orders form** (Customers > Create Sales Orders).

2. **Find the contract's sales order, and open it.**

   To find the desired sales order you can:

   ❖ Use the Previous and Next buttons at the top of the form.

   ❖ Use the Find button (immediately below the Previous and Next buttons) to search by customer name, date, etc.

   ❖ Locate the sales order in a report such as Open Sales Orders by Customer (Reports > Sales > Open Sales Orders by Customer), then double-click it in the report window to open it in the Sales Orders form.

3. **Click the Create Invoice icon** on the Main tab of the ribbon bar at the top of the form.

   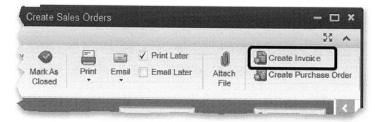

   A window will open, giving you the option to create an invoice for the entire sales order or just for selected Items.

4. **Select the** *Create invoice for all of the sales order(s)* **option, then click the OK button.**

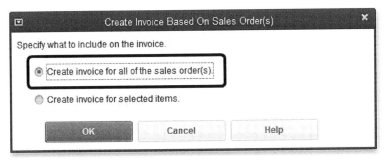

QuickBooks will close the Sales Orders form and open the Create Invoices form, filled in with an Item line for the remaining (not yet invoiced) quantity from the sales order:

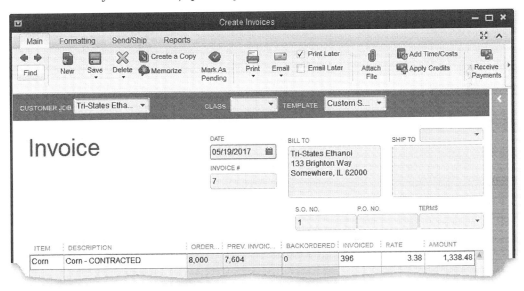

5. **Add any contract overage or shortage on a separate line.**

The first Item line completed invoicing of the contract's 8,000 bushels, but the settlement sheet is for 8,075 net bushels (see item ❺ on the settlement sheet 250), which means 75 bushels more were delivered than were contracted. The overage *must be entered on a separate Item line* to update corn inventories for the additional quantity sold and to record income from its sale. **Do not simply include the overage in the first line's quantity!**

## Chapter 11 - Tracking Cash Sales Contracts

> **Why not?** Because QuickBooks filled in the first Item line from the contract's sales order, it maintains a linkage between that line and the sales order. Changing the quantity on that line would change the sales order's record of how much had been invoiced from it, leaving the sales order with a non-zero quantity and preventing it from being closed out.

| ITEM | DESCRIPTION | ORDER... | PREV. INVOIC... | BACKORDERED | INVOICED | RATE | AMOUNT |
|---|---|---|---|---|---|---|---|
| Corn | Corn - CONTRACTED | 8,000 | 7,604 | 0 | 396 | 3.38 | 1,338.48 |
| Corn | Over contract | | | | 75 | 2.81 | 210.75 |

|  |  |
|---|---|
| TOTAL | 1,549.23  |
| PAYMENTS APPLIED | 0.00 |
| BALANCE DUE | 1,549.23 |

A contract shortage would be entered the same way, but as a negative quantity and Amount.

6. **Add a line to adjust for quality discounts or premiums,** if any.

   When quality discounts or premiums are involved, usually the *net price* received will be different from the *contract price*. Assuming you have been entering delivery invoices at the contract price, you need to add a line to adjust for discounts or premiums. The goal is to make the combined total of the contract's invoices up to this point equal to the gross payment amount (⑥ on the settlement sheet 250, before deductions for "below the line" fees like storage charges or commodity assessments). Here is how to calculate the adjustment for quality discounts or premiums:

   ❖ The total on the current invoice is $1,549.23 so far (① in the screenshot above).

   ❖ The total of all prior invoices is $25,701.52 (from the Sales by Customer Detail report on page 255).

   So up to this point, the total of all invoices is:

   $$1{,}549.23 + 25{,}701.52 = \$27{,}214.57$$

   ❖ The gross payment amount from the settlement sheet is $27,232.66 (⑥ on the settlement sheet 250).

So the difference between the total of all invoices and the gross payment amount is:

27,232.66 - 27,214.57 = -$18.09

So the invoice needs a line with an Amount of -$18.09 (negative, to deduct from the invoice's total).

> ⭐ **This matches the Sum-Chgs amount shown on the settlement sheet** ⟦250⟧ **at** ❸. That should be the case if all delivery invoices for the contract have been entered at the contract price (without including quality discounts or premiums).

| ITEM | DESCRIPTION | ORDERED | PREV. INVOICED | BACKORDERED | INVOICED | RATE | AMOUNT |
|---|---|---|---|---|---|---|---|
| Corn | Corn - CONTRACTED | 8,000 | 7,604 | 0 | 396 | 3.38 | 1,338.48 |
| Corn | Over contract quantity | | | | 75 | 2.81 | 210.75 |
| Discounts | Grain quality discounts | | | | | -18.09 | -18.09 |

TOTAL 1,531.14
PAYMENTS APPLIED 0.00
BALANCE DUE 1,531.14

Now the total for this invoice ($1,531.14) plus prior invoices should equal the gross payment amount of $27,232.66 (❻ on the settlement sheet ⟦250⟧). But this is not the *net* payment amount—a few more steps are necessary to get there.

7. **Add Item lines for "below the line" fees,** if any.

    > *"Below the line" fees* means fees deducted from the gross amount of the sale, such as for storage charges or commodity check-off assessments.

Enter each fee as a negative amount on a separate Item line. Here is a Corn Checkoff deduction (from ❼ on the settlement sheet ⟦250⟧):

## Chapter 11 - Tracking Cash Sales Contracts

| ITEM | DESCRIPTION | ORDERED | PREV. INVOICED | BACKORDERED | INVOICED | RATE | AMOUNT |
|---|---|---|---|---|---|---|---|
| Corn | Corn - CONTRACTED | 8,000 | 7,604 | 0 | 396 | 3.38 | 1,338.48 |
| Corn | Over contract quantity | | | | 75 | 2.81 | 210.75 |
| Discounts | Grain quality discounts | | | | | -18.09 | -18.09 |
| Corn Checkoff | Corn Checkoff (per bushel) | | | | -8,075  | 0.01 | -80.75 |

Your customer can't pay this invoice online
Turn on

CUSTOMER MESSAGE

TOTAL 1,450.39
PAYMENTS APPLIED 0.00
BALANCE DUE **1,450.39**

> **❶ Invoiced.** The Invoiced quantity is entered as the negative of the net bushels sold. QuickBooks automatically multiplied it by the Rate for the Corn Checkoff Item ($0.01 per bushel) to calculate the checkoff amount—a negative number, so it subtracts from the invoice total.
>
> A simpler approach would be to just enter the corn checkoff amount shown on the settlement sheet, as a negative number:

| Discounts | Grain quality discounts | | | | | -18.09 | -18.09 |
|---|---|---|---|---|---|---|---|
| Corn Checkoff | Corn Checkoff | | | | | | -80.75 |

### Why put fees on a separate line?

Why not simply include things like a corn checkoff deduction in the Amount on the first line? You *can* do that, but there may be tax reasons for keeping assessments and fees separate from sales.

If the buyer is a cooperative, the cooperative may pass along an income tax deduction to you, called the Domestic Production Activities Deduction (DPAD). It is based on the gross value of commodities you sold to them during the year *excluding* commodity checkoff deductions and other such indirect fees. Keeping gross sales dollars separate from "below the line" fees makes it easier to compare your QuickBooks records against the form 1099-PATR form you will receive from the cooperative at year's end.

Also, some fees should be recorded separately so they can be deducted as expense. A storage fee, for instance, should be entered on a separate line because storage and warehousing is a separate expense deduction on Federal income tax forms.

# Contract Settlement/Payment/Closeout

**What if charges and fees are more than the invoice amount?**

QuickBooks won't let you enter an invoice for a negative dollar amount. If charges and fees would make the final invoice amount negative, enter them on the Credit Memos form (Customers > Create Credit Memos/Refunds) instead, but as *positive* amounts. (A negative amount on an invoice has the same effect as a positive amount on a credit memo.)

8. **Click the Save & Close button** to save the invoice and close the window.

## Verifying Invoice Totals

After entering a final invoice for the contract, the total amount for all of the contract's invoices combined should match the payment amount (❽ on the settlement sheet 250). You can verify that by opening a Sales by Customer Detail report (Reports > Sales > Sales by Customer Detail) and filtering it 253 to show only transactions for the contract:

261

## Chapter 11 - Tracking Cash Sales Contracts

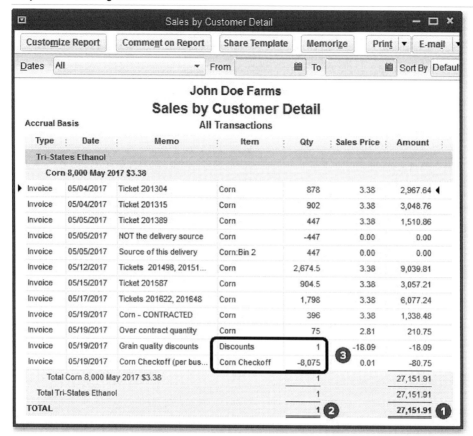

① **Amount.** The report's total should match the payment amount from the settlement sheet, $27,151.91. If they don't match, make corrections by editing the final invoice (or other invoices) as necessary.

② **Qty.** *The report's quantity total is irrelevant and meaningless,* because it includes quantities for other Items besides Corn—in this example, for Discounts and Corn Checkoff as shown at ③.

## Verifying Contract Closeout

From a QuickBooks standpoint, a contract is closed when the entire quantity on the sales order has been invoiced. This happens automatically if you apply the entire remaining sales order quantity to the contract's final invoice.

If you want to verify that a contract is closed, find its sales order in the Sales Orders window (Customers > Create Sales Orders). If closed, the sales order will be marked *Invoiced in Full* and each Item line will have a checkmark:

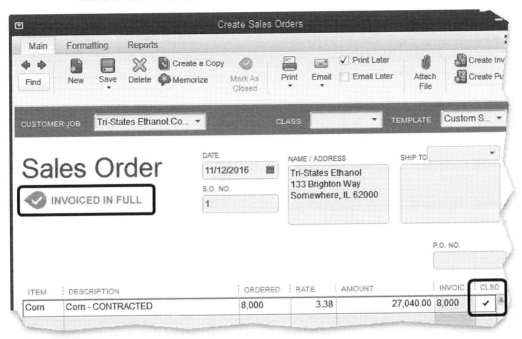

## Receiving Payment on the Invoice(s)

Whether you have entered one invoice or several, you need to receive payment on all of them to close them, and to make the income they represent available for cash basis reporting.

> ⭐ **Cash basis income and expense reports** only include income from an invoice if payment has been received on it.

1. **Open the Receive Payment window** (Customers > Receive Payments).

2. **Select the Customer:Job name for the contract** in the Received From field.

## Chapter 11 - Tracking Cash Sales Contracts

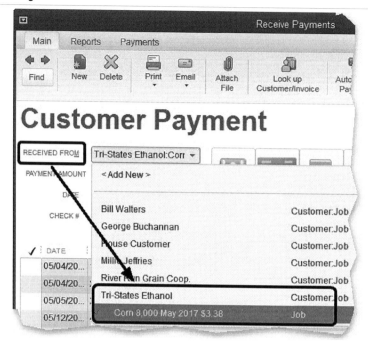

QuickBooks will list all invoices for the Customer:Job (Tri-States Ethanol:Corn 8,000 May 2017 $3.68), in the lower part of the window.

3. **Enter the payment amount** in the Payment Amount field, **then press the Tab key.**

   When you do, QuickBooks will checkmark as many invoices as the payment will fully or partially pay off. (If the total of the contract's invoices matches the payment amount, all invoices will be paid off.)

4. **Enter the Date** of the payment, and **click on the appropriate payment type icon** (Cash, Check, Credit/Debit, etc.).

   The window should then appear as follows:

### Contract Settlement/Payment/Closeout

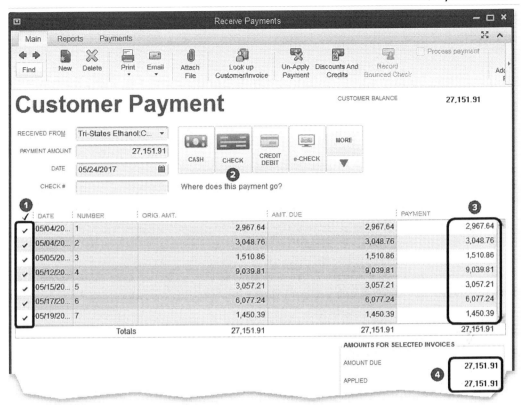

1. **√ (checkmarks).** All invoices are selected for payment (checkmarked).

2. **Payment type.** The Check icon is selected, to show that the payment was received as a check.

3. **Payment.** The Payment column shows the amount applied to each invoice.

4. **Amount Due** and **Applied.** When these amounts are equal it means the payment exactly paid off all of the invoices.

5. Click the **Save & Close button** to save the payment and close the window.

   ⭐ **Receiving payment on an invoice stores the payment in the Undeposited Funds account,** by default. To deposit the payment in the bank, see *Depositing Payments You Have Received* 175.

## Hiding Inactive Contracts (Jobs)

If you enter very many sales contracts the Customer Center (Customer:Jobs list) will eventually become cluttered with Job names representing old, closed contracts. However, QuickBooks will not let you delete Job names which have been used in transactions. The solution is to mark old Jobs inactive. That hides them from normal viewing in the Customer Center without deleting them.

To mark a Job inactive, open the Customer Center (Customers > Customer Center), right-click the Job name, then select *Make Customer:Job inactive* from the pop-up menu:

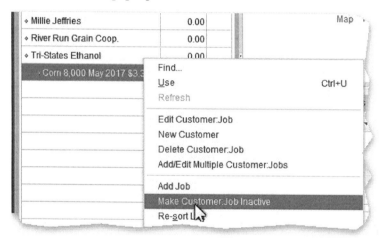

After you do this, the Job will be hidden. To show hidden Jobs, select *All Customers* from the drop-down list at the top of the Customers & Jobs tab:

Contract Settlement/Payment/Closeout

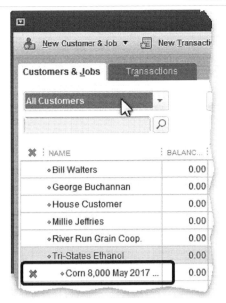

# More about Contract Shortages

A contract *shortage* occurs when a contract is settled for less than the full contract quantity. Shortages are sometimes handled the same way as contract overage 257, but not always. And sometimes the buyer may charge a penalty, depending the contract's provisions for shortages and on the good will of the buyer.

When a contract shortage occurs, either of two things may happen. You may rarely have to deal with contract shortages in QuickBooks, but this section shows how to handle both situations.

## Writing Off the Shortage

The buyer may simply "write off" (ignore) the shortage by settling the contract for the quantity you delivered. For example, if the contract was for 8,000 bushels but you delivered 7,967 bushels—a 33 bushel shortage—the payment will be for 7,967 bushels if the buyer is willing to write off the shortage.

This is more likely to happen if:

❖ The delivery shortage is small, and/or

## Chapter 11 - Tracking Cash Sales Contracts

- ❖ The shortage benefits the buyer, and/or
- ❖ The buyer simply wants to maintain a good business relationship with you.

To update inventories and income correctly you need to show the shortage on the sales contract's final invoice 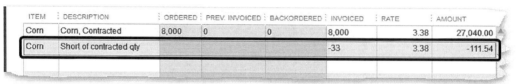 on a separate Item line, using the same Item name but with the quantity entered as a *negative* number. That will cause QuickBooks to calculate a negative Amount on that line, thus subtracting the shortage from the invoice (and from income).

| ITEM | DESCRIPTION | ORDERED | PREV. INVOICED | BACKORDERED | INVOICED | RATE | AMOUNT |
|---|---|---|---|---|---|---|---|
| Corn | Corn, Contracted | 8,000 | 0 | 0 | 8,000 | 3.38 | 27,040.00 |
| Corn | Short of contracted qty | | | | -33 | 3.38 | -111.54 |

 **Enter shortages on a *separate* invoice line.** *Do not* simply adjust the quantity on the line which came from the sales order (the first line in the screenshot above). If you do, the sales order will be left with an un-invoiced quantity, preventing it from being closed out in QuickBooks.

 **Alternatively, you can enter the shortage on a credit memo** as a *positive* number, if you prefer.

## Entering a Penalty

Some contracts specify a penalty to be charged when the contract is settled for less than the contracted quantity. The penalty should be listed as a separate amount on the contract's settlement sheet, and needs to be entered on the final invoice for the contract—or in a credit memo if you prefer.

### What Item should you use for a penalty fee?

You could set up an Item specifically for contract fees and penalties, but unless you pay a penalty often—rare in most farm businesses—it makes sense to use a general-purpose Item you have set up for commissions, selling fees, and miscellaneous marketing expenses. Typ-

## More about Contract Shortages

ically this would be a Service or Other Charge Item which posts to an expense account. For example:

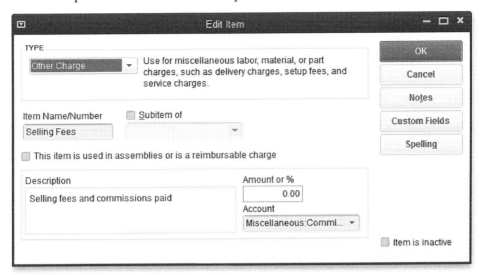

The penalty needs to be added on a separate invoice line, as a negative amount:

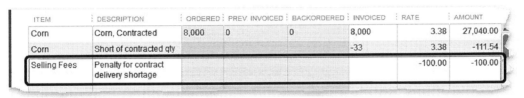

Chapter 11 - Tracking Cash Sales Contracts

# Handling Other Contract Types

***Problem*** Most of this chapter deals with basic cash sale contracts. What about other cash contract variations, like basis contracts or price-later contracts? How should those be handled?

***Solution*** The steps for handling other contract types are essentially the same as for plain cash sale contracts, with slight differences in some cases.

***Discussion*** Most of the contract types described in this section are just slightly different from "plain-vanilla" cash sale contracts in terms of how they should be handled in QuickBooks. Here are the general steps for handling all cash sale contracts. Details about specific contract types are discussed in this section's topics.

❖ **Add a new a Job** [218] when you enter into a contract.

❖ **Create a sales order** [220] to represent the contract and record details like quantity and price.

❖ **Create invoices** [226] **from the sales order,** to record deliveries you make on the contract.

❖ **Enter a final invoice** [249] **at contract settlement,** if needed, and enter charges and deductions as negative amounts on the invoice.

❖ **Reconcile your invoices with the settlement sheet** [249] or other documentation received from the buyer, and make corrections if needed.

❖ **Receive payment** [263] on the invoice you have entered for the contract, to close them in QuickBooks.

## Basis contracts

A *basis contract* is a contract for sale of a commodity, in which delivery dates and local basis are specified when the contract is agreed to but the net contract price is determined later (by a specified date) when the seller selects a futures price to use for calculating the price.

When you enter the sales order 220 for a basis contract you will have to use an estimated price, because the contract price won't be determined until later when you select a futures price. Once the contract price has been determined, edit the invoices you have entered for the contract and change their price to the contract price.

## How to enter a cash advance

Some buyers will issue a partial cash advance on grain delivered on a basis contract; for example, bushels delivered x 75% of the current cash price. If you receive a cash advance, enter it by receiving payment 263 on the invoices you have entered for deliveries on the contract.

What if you have not yet entered any invoices for deliveries on the contract? Then you *must* enter at least one, so the cash advance can be applied to it. Why? Because the cash advance is taxable income in the year received. It must be applied to an invoice so the income will be included on cash basis tax reports.

>  **Don't use a sales receipt to record a cash advance.** Though sales receipts are commonly used for recording cash income, unlike invoices they cannot have a connection with a sales order. Using a sales receipt to record a cash advance would not update the contract's status (bushels delivered, bushels remaining to be delivered, etc.).

## How to roll a basis contract forward to a later month

Usually, the only information you might keep in QuickBooks about contract dates may be notes in the Memo or Description field of the contract's sales order, or in the date fields of the contract's Job. If any contract terms—such as delivery dates—are changed, you just need to update the sales order and/or Job information. No accounting transactions are needed.

## Price-later contracts

A *price-later contract* is a contract for sale in which the commodity (e.g., grain) is delivered to the buyer but the price will not be established until later. Whenever the seller chooses (within a date range specified by the contract) he or she can set the contract price at the buyer's posted cash price for that date.

Until the contract price is known, use an estimated price when you enter a sales order[220] or invoices[226] for the contract. Once the contract price has been set, edit the invoices you have entered for deliveries on the contract and change them to the contract price.

Use the same procedures as for a cash contract, except that if all of the grain has already been delivered when the contract is entered into, there is no need to use a sales order. In that case you can enter a single invoice for the delivered grain, at an estimated price. When the contract price is determined, edit the invoice and change the price to the contract price.

## Service fees

If the buyer charges a service fee and it is deducted from the payment you receive, include it as a negative amount on the final invoice for the contract. If you pay the service fee separately, you may enter a check or a bill for it.

## Delayed payment contracts

In a *delayed payment contract,* the commodity is delivered, title is transferred to the buyer, and the price is established when the contract is entered into. However, payment does not occur until the payment date specified in the contract. Delayed payment contracts are often used to defer tax liability: grain is delivered in one tax year, and payment occurs in the next tax year.

Handle delayed payment contracts in the same way as other cash contracts in QuickBooks. When you finish making deliveries you should have one or more open (unpaid) delivery invoices[226] on the books, and the amount owed to you will be included in accounts receivable on balance sheet reports. When the payment arrives, receive payment[263] on the invoices the same as you would for any cash contract.

## Hedge-to-arrive (or "basis later") contracts

In a *hedge-to-arrive contract* the seller locks in the futures market portion of the contract price at the time the contract is entered into, then sets the basis portion later (within a time period specified by the contract) by selecting a date on which to use the buyer's basis.

Because the contract price is unknown when the contract is entered into, just use an estimated price when you enter a sales order[220] or invoices[226] for the contract. Once the contract price has been set, edit the invoice(s) you have entered for the contract and change the estimated price to the contract price.

## Minimum price contract

A *minimum price contract* establishes a guaranteed minimum price but lets you lock in a higher price if market prices move higher. The delivery period, quantity, and minimum price are established in the contract. You can lock in a price above the contract's minimum if the market goes higher *and* you exercise your option to lock in the price before a deadline date specified in the contract.

Handle minimum price contracts the same as other cash contract types, entering sales orders[220] and invoices[226] at an estimated price. Later when the contract price has been determined, edit the invoices and replace the estimated price with the actual contract price.

## Premium cost and service fees

Any costs you pay separately or up front, such as premium cost paid at contract signing, will normally be entered as a check or a bill. *Only fees deducted from the contract payment should be entered as deductions on an invoice.*

# QuickBooks Pro: Using Subitems to Account for Cash Sale Contracts

Compared to sales orders, using subitems to represent cash sale contracts is a bit less desirable, but that does not mean they are inadequate for the job! No, the problem is that subitems have *many other* potential uses, such as tracking inventory by location 199. Consequently, using subitems to track contracts may conflict with one of those other uses. But if you are not using subitems for some other purpose, they will work fine for tracking sales contracts.

Sales orders *do* have an advantage when it comes to reporting: you can get more contract-related reports and information if you use sales orders. But QuickBooks Pro does not have the Sales Orders feature, and subitems are a workable alternative.

This section briefly tells how to use subitems for tracking cash sale contracts. In a few cases, you will need to refer to other parts of the chapter if you want detailed explanations.

## Using Subitems to Represent Contracts

For each sales contract you enter into, define a new *subitem* of the Item which represents the commodity you are contracting for sale. For example, here are Corn and Soybeans parent items, each with a subitem for one contract:

**Corn**
    Tri-States 8,000 May'17 $3.68
**Soybeans**
    JCB 5,000 Dec'16 $9.34

To set up a contract subitem, open the Item List window (Lists > Item List), then select Item > New from the button bar menu at the bottom of the window, and fill in the detail as shown in this corn contract subitem:

## QuickBooks Pro: Using Subitems to Account for Cash Sale Contracts

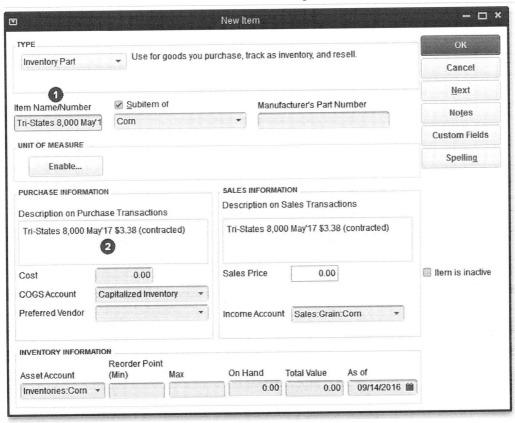

① **Item Name/Number.** The full subitem name here is "Tri-States 8,000 May'17 $3.38". Always make the subitem name as descriptive as possible. It should identify the buyer (customer) in some way, and should also include the contract quantity, price, delivery month, or other details, as you choose.

⚠️ **Subitem names for contracts _really really really_ should identify the buyer.**

When using sales orders 220 and Jobs 218 the act of selecting a Job on a sales order "connects" it to the contract, because the Job identifies the contract. Then when invoices are created from the sales order they automatically have a connection to the same Job. So, every contract-related transaction is automatically connected to a specific Job—and to the Customer by way of the Job.

275

But subitems are only automatically connected *to their parent Item*—Corn in the example above. If you had several Corn subitems representing contracts with different buyers but none of the subitem names identified the buyer, selecting the wrong subitem when entering a transaction would be easy to do. That is why subitem names should identify the buyer in some way. You don't have to use the buyer's full name; just use anything that will let you identify the subitem with a particular buyer (customer).

**❷ Description.** The subitem's description, likewise, should contain information to identify the buyer, and any other contract details you find useful.

For details on setting up Items, see: *Setting Up Raised Inventory Items* [80].

## What about using Jobs too?

Subitems are fully adequate to identify contracts within QuickBooks, so using Jobs is optional (and a bit redundant). However, if you set up a Job for each contract and are careful to select the correct job when entering invoices, you can have the same information described earlier in this chapter for Jobs—such as direct access to contract information in the Customer Center window.

For details on setting up Jobs see *Using Jobs to Represent Contracts* [218].

# Entering a Sales Contract

To enter the contract in QuickBooks, use an Inventory Adjustment [97] to move the contracted quantity from the parent Item to the contract subitem, like this:

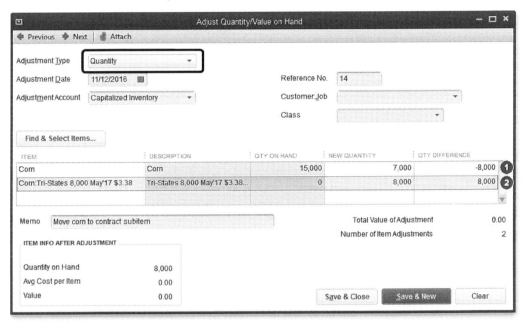

① **The first line** decreases the Corn inventory by 8,000 bushels.

② **The second line** increases inventory for the contract subitem by the same amount—8,000 bushels, the contracted quantity.

★ **What if the parent Item does not have enough inventory available to move to the contract subitem?** Sometimes you may be entering a contract before you actually have the inventory on hand—as when entering a contract ahead of crop harvest, for example. In that case, only adjust the subitem's quantity, to make it equal to the contracted quantity. Later when you actually have inventory on hand, adjust the parent Item's inventory to match the on-hand quantity *minus the quantity which is contracted.*

## Recording Deliveries on a Contract

The same as when using sales orders you should create invoices as you make deliveries on the contract. This keeps your QuickBooks inventories updated while you are making deliveries, rather than just after the contract is filled. Typically you might enter an invoice every few days—recording several deliveries in each invoice—to strike a balance between having current inventory information versus the accounting effort required.

Entering an invoice (1) decreases the inventory quantity for the contract subitem, (2) records the dollar amount the buyer owes for what you have delivered (accounts receivable), and (3) records income.

> **"Won't using invoices sometimes put income in the wrong tax year?"**
>
> As an astute cash basis recordkeeper you may be concerned about this, and rightfully so. An invoice records income *as of the invoice date*. But in cash basis accounting, income should only be recorded *when payment is received*. If you enter an invoice for a sale made "this year" but don't receive payment until "next year", income will be recorded in the wrong year; or it would be, if QuickBooks didn't have a solution for the problem...
>
> Enabling the *Cash* option when you prepare a report will cause QuickBooks to prepare it on a cash basis. Income will only include sales for which payment was *received* during the time period covered by the report. So if you entered invoices in December but then didn't receive payment on them until January, the income from those invoices would be included as income in January, not December. This only happens when a report is prepared with the *Cash* option.
>
>  **Using the *Cash* option on a report** causes QuickBooks to move income into the accounting period when it was received, and expenses into the accounting period when they were paid. However, this mostly applies to income or expense transactions entered on the Bills, Invoices, or Credit Memos forms. And there are limitations: QuickBooks cannot move amounts posted to balance sheet accounts, for instance. If a report contains amounts you believe should or should not be present and you cannot figure out why, consult a QuickBooks professional for help.

Below is an invoice with two detail lines, to record two deliveries on a contract. They could have been entered as a combined quantity on a single line but this approach shows the bushels for each load, which may be useful for knowing which loads have been entered.

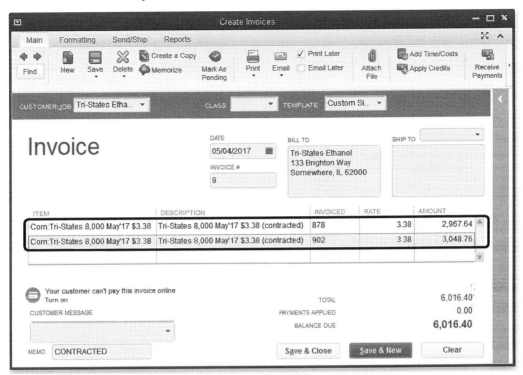

# Getting Information about Contracts and Deliveries

## Bushels delivered

The Sales by Item Summary report (Reports > Sales > Sales by Item Summary) shows the total quantity and dollar amount of sales for each Item. The quantity on the contract subitem's line represents the total quantity delivered on the contract, to date:

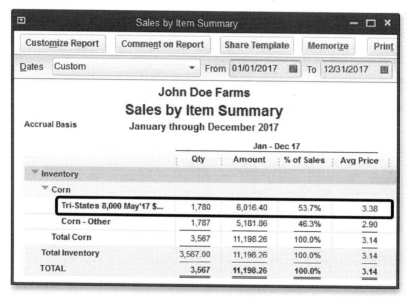

If you want to verify delivery quantities, use the Sales by Item Detail report (Reports > Sales > Sales by Item Detail). The Detail version of the report lists individual sales for an Item, subtotaled separately for each subitem:

# QuickBooks Pro: Using Subitems to Account for Cash Sale Contracts

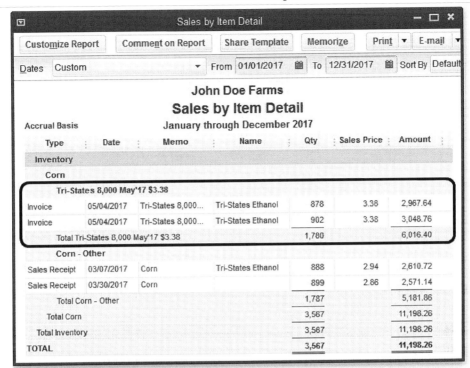

## Contract Settlement / Payment / Closeout

Contract settlement and closeout are activities you need to do after receiving the buyer's payment on the contract along with (usually) a settlement sheet listing the individual deliveries, price, and any fees or deductions from the payment.

Here is the detail portion of a final invoice, for the remaining un-invoiced contract quantity, including contract overage, and various discounts and fees as described earlier in *Contract Settlement/Payment/Closeout* 249.

## Chapter 11 - Tracking Cash Sales Contracts

| ITEM | DESCRIPTION | INVOICED | RATE | AMOUNT |
|---|---|---|---|---|
| Corn:Tri-States 8,000 May'17 $3.38 | Tri-States 8,000 May'17 $3.38 (contracted) | 396 | 3.38 | 1,338.48 |
| Corn | Over contract quantity | 75 | 2.81 | 210.75 |
| Discounts | Grain quality discounts | | -18.09 | -18.09 |
| Corn Checkoff | Corn Checkoff (per bushel) | -8,075 | 0.01 | -80.75 |

Your customer can't pay this invoice online
Turn on

CUSTOMER MESSAGE

TOTAL 1,450.39
PAYMENTS APPLIED 0.00
BALANCE DUE **1,450.39**

## Contract closeout

Invoicing the remaining quantity on the contract should leave the subitem with an inventory quantity of zero, but mistakes and contract differences can occur. So if a subitem has a non-zero quantity after all contract transactions have been entered, make an inventory adjustment to move the remaining subitem inventory back to the parent Item—or if the difference is small, simply zero out the subitem's inventory.

## Receiving Payment on the Invoice(s)

After entering the last invoice for the contract, don't forget that you must receive payment (Customers > Receive Payment) on the invoices. If you entered them correctly, the total of the invoices should equal the payment amount received, and receiving payment on the invoices should completely close ("pay off") all of them.

For details, see *Receiving Payment on the Invoice(s)* 263.

## Hiding Inactive Contracts (Subitems)

After a contract has been settled and is not longer active you can mark its subitem inactive. That will leave the subitem in place in the Item List but hides it from normal viewing, reducing clutter in the Item List and reducing the likelihood of selecting the wrong subitem when entering a transaction.

# QuickBooks Pro: Using Subitems to Account for Cash Sale Contracts

To mark a subitem inactive:

1. **Open the Item List window** (Lists > Item List).

2. **Right-click on the Item** (or subitem) to display its pop-up menu.

3. **Select Make Item Inactive** from the pop-up menu.

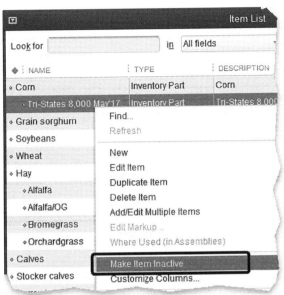

283

This page is intentionally blank.

CHAPTER 12

# Tracking Inventories for Others (Landlords, etc.)

| About this chapter | This chapter extends ideas introduced earlier in this book to the problem of tracking inventories for others outside of the farm business, such as landlords. It is a "mostly visual" chapter: the examples are based mostly on screenshots, with expanded details where more explanation is needed. |
|---|---|

This chapter shows how you can keep track of inventories for people who are outside of the farm business, but related to it, such as landlords. It shows how to manage inventories for outside parties in the same QuickBooks company file—alongside the farm business' records—without co-mingling funds or financial information.

The entire chapter is based on a common example: keeping inventories for a crop of corn, for multiple landlords. The same techniques could be applied to any kind of inventory or any number of inventory items—you might track corn *and* soybean inventories, for instance, and for any number of landlords, off-farm relatives, or others.

Transactions shown in the examples have been kept simple to demonstrate the fundamentals of third-party inventories, without getting bogged down in details for things like commodity checkoff deductions or grain storage fees. Once you've grasped the basics, you can easily add the necessary details when entering your own transactions.

# Chapter 12 - Tracking Inventories for Others (Landlords, etc.)

## John Doe Farms' Business Situation

John Doe Farms owns part of the cropland it farms, cash rents some cropland, and also has several crop-share landlords, with land rented for 50/50, 55/45, and 60/40 shares of the crop.

The local market for corn is not good—a river terminal elevator 40 miles away usually offers much better prices. So during harvest, John Doe Farms typically stores most or all of the production from the corn acreage it farms, including landlords' shares of the crop, then hauls the corn to the river terminal later. John does not charge landlords for storage, and feels it is well worth the efficiency he gains by being able to store the entire crop in his own bins: he avoids harvest-time moisture dockage discounts, long-distance hauling bottlenecks, and the wide basis (low prices) of local markets at harvest.

All corn harvested is weighed on the farm's scales before making its way into the farm's bins. Weights, plus moisture information from the combine's yield monitor, allows John to co-mingle his own corn and landlord corn in the farm's storage system. Mary Doe uses the weight and moisture information in a spreadsheet to calculate the average yield for each farm, shrunk to a standard moisture content, and each landlord's share of the crop. She sends each crop-share landlord a letter after harvest, telling them the exact quantity of corn they own, stored in the farm's bins.

Some crop-share landlords market their own grain, and either hire a trucking company or John Doe to do the hauling. Others want John to market their grain at the same time as he markets his own. To make this arrangement fair—so the landlord receives the same corn price as John does—when John sells a load of corn for a landlord, the payment is split in proportion to their respective crop shares, such as 60/40.

Mary does most of the accounting for the operation, in QuickBooks. She tracks the farm's corn inventories using an Inventory Part Item named Corn. She also tracks landlord inventories, using subitems of Corn—one for each landlord.

At any time, Mary can get detailed inventory reports for any landlord —bushels sold, remaining inventory, number of bushels contracted for sale, and number of bushels available to sell (not contracted). She can get the same information for John Doe Farms too, of course, but the farm's reports also include financial amounts—things like the dollar amount of corn sales, asset value of the corn inventory, and so on.

>  **Author's note:** My wife proofread this chapter, and afterward pointed out that I should have described Mary Doe here as Superwoman: she does all of the accounting for a sizable farming operation after hours from her job at the local dentist's office, heads a number of school and church activities, runs a grain cart part time during harvest, raises a vegetable and flower garden that is the envy of many, and maintains a spotless home and farm office. I'm not going to jump into the middle of this discussion...just thought you ought to know her opinion.

# Setting up Accounts and Items

## Setting up Accounts

See: *Accounts for Raised Inventories* 59

When keeping inventories for someone outside of the farm business, avoiding financial ties to the farm's accounting records is important. Income and asset values related to landlord inventories *should not* appear in the farm business accounts, not even temporarily.

To make sure that happens, landlord inventory Items *must not* post income or asset value to the farm's accounts. The best approach is to use accounts reserved for landlord inventory income and asset value when setting up landlord inventory Items. Equity accounts are the recommended choice. Here are the ones Mary Doe uses, as they appear in the Chart of Accounts window (**Lists > Chart of Accounts**):

| | | |
|---|---|---:|
| ◆ Capitalized Inventory | Equity | 47,425.00 |
| ◆ Landlord Inventory Sales | Equity | 0.00 |
| ◆ Landlord Inventory Value | Equity | 0.00 |
| ◆ Opening Bal Equity | Equity | 0.00 |

And here are their setup details:

## Chapter 12 - Tracking Inventories for Others (Landlords, etc.)

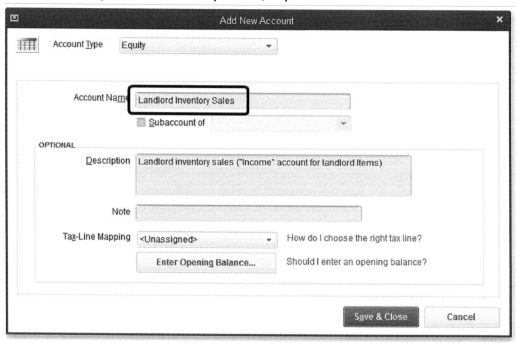

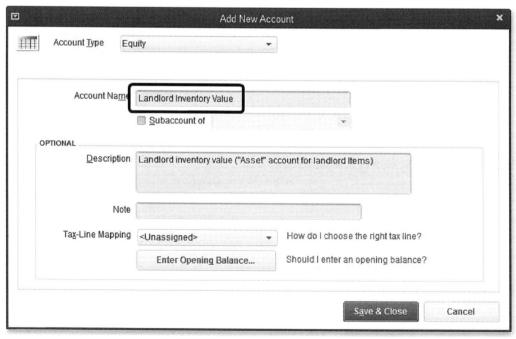

⭐ **If you enter sales as recommended later in the chapter,** only $0 amounts should be posted to these accounts. If you ever notice a non-

# Setting up Accounts and Items

zero balance in either account it signals the possibility that a transaction was entered incorrectly. Because both accounts should always have a $0 balance, *neither account should appear on the farm's balance sheet reports,* which is important for avoiding the appearance of a financial involvement with the landlords' inventories.

 **In balance sheet reports, if either account appears and has a $0 balance** you can remove it by selecting the *Except Zero Amounts* report option: click the Customize Report button at the top of the report window, then select *Except Zero Amounts* on the Fonts & Numbers tab:

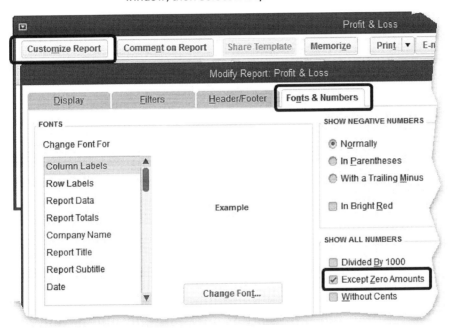

# Setting up Items

See: *Setting Up Raised Inventory Items* [80]

Here are the Items Mary has set up for corn inventories, as they appear in the Item List window (Lists > Item List):

## Chapter 12 - Tracking Inventories for Others (Landlords, etc.)

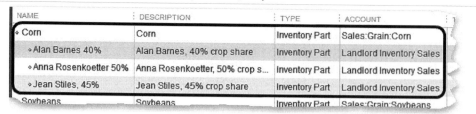

The Corn Item represent the farm's own inventory of corn, and is set up this way:

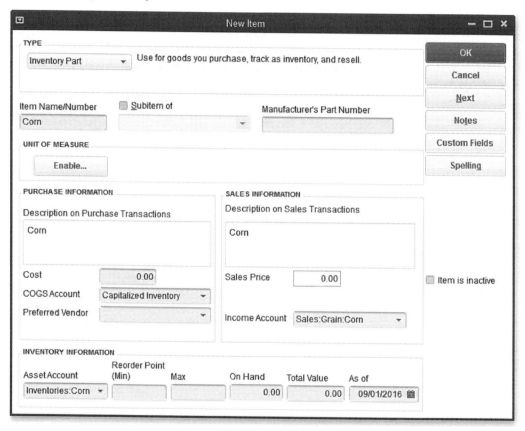

The subitems of Corn each represent a landlord's inventory. Here is the subitem for Alan Barnes, as an example:

# Setting up Accounts and Items

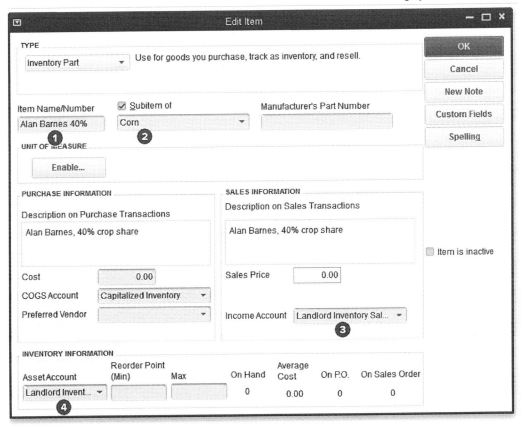

1. **Item Name/Number** should identify the landlord and *should describe the landlord's share* of the crop. This can be useful information when you need to do a quantity calculation for a landlord but only the Item name (and not the Description) is visible.

2. **Subitem of.** Each landlord Item must be a subitem of a parent Item which represents the kind of inventory involved—corn in this case.

3. **Income Account.** This *must not* be an actual income account of the farm business. Instead, select an equity account here, like the Landlord Inventory Sales account[288] described earlier. (You can use the same account for all landlord Items.)

291

# Chapter 12 - Tracking Inventories for Others (Landlords, etc.)

**④ Asset Account.** This *must not* be an actual asset account of the farm business. Instead, select an equity account here, like the Landlord Inventory Value account 288 described earlier. (You can use the same account for all landlord Items.)

# Adding Production to Inventory

See: *Adding Farm Production to Inventory* 123

After calculating a yield for a landlord's farm, Mary Doe makes an inventory adjustment like the one below to get inventories for that farm into QuickBooks. Dealing with only one farm's production per adjustment entry makes it easy to check for errors: a quick glance at the Quantity Difference column's figures lets Mary verify that they match the crop shares she has calculated.

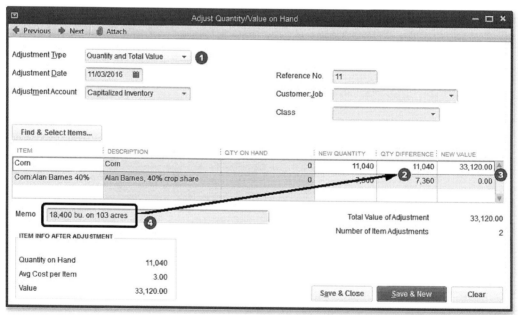

**① Adjustment Type.** Quantity and Total Value is selected here, to allow assigning an inventory value to the corn owned by John Doe Farms. However, if you prefer you can select the Quantity adjustment type and just enter inventory quantities, then assign a value later.

## Adding Production to Inventory

**❷ Qty Difference.** The inventory quantities in this column are for John Doe Farms' and Alan Barnes' shares of the 18,400 total bushels harvested on Alan's farm. (Alan gets a 40% share.)

**❸ New Value.** Mary assigned a value to the inventory owned by John Doe Farms but not to Alan Barnes' inventory, because landlord inventory values are not tracked.

**❹ Memo.** Adding details here may help explain the inventory adjustment's purpose, if you need to review it weeks or months later.

Mary doesn't always get the inventories updated in QuickBooks immediately after harvest is completed on each farm. In fact, sometimes she doesn't receive all of the truck weights and moisture information until the main rush of harvest is over. Then, some or all of the adjustments may be entered on the same day. But Mary still uses a separate adjustment entry for each farm's production, to make it easier to find and correct errors.

Here is another landlord's adjustment entry, for the Anna Rosenkoetter farm:

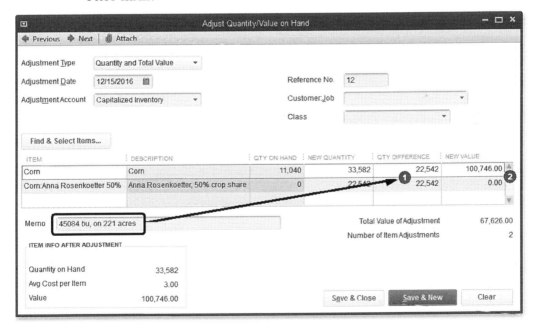

## Chapter 12 - Tracking Inventories for Others (Landlords, etc.)

**❶ Qty Difference.** The same quantity is entered on each line, because the rental arrangement with Anna Rosenkoetter is a 50/50 crop share.

**❷ New Value.** As with the inventory adjustment made earlier, Mary only assigned a value to the corn owned by John Doe Farms, and not to the landlord's corn, because she does not track landlord inventory values.

### What if sales were made during harvest?

Those sales are entered the same as other sales, as you will see later 292, but if no inventory has been established for a landlord at the time of a sale, the sale will cause the landlord's inventory to be negative in QuickBooks. That's OK, as long as you understand why. Later when you establish an inventory for the landlord, the negative inventory quantity can be replaced by the correct remaining inventory for that landlord.

For an example, see the discussion of sales made during harvest in *Raised Inventory Questions & Special Situations* 171.

Finally, here is an adjustment which adds John Doe Farms' corn to inventory. It represents corn harvested from owned and cash-rented land (no landlord inventories are involved):

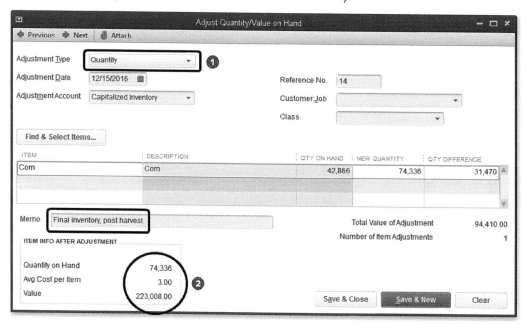

294

# Adding Production to Inventory

❶ **Adjustment Type.** This example shows that if you adjust only the inventory quantity, QuickBooks will automatically apply the inventory Item's current value (established by prior inventory adjustments) to the new quantity—you can see that at ❷, where the Corn Item's $3.00 per bushel value was applied to the new quantity, resulting in a new value of $223,008.00.

## Seeing current inventories

After Mary has finished updating all of the inventories, any time she wants to see current inventories she can simply look in the Item List window (Lists > Item List). The Total Quantity column lists corn inventories owned by John Doe Farms (74,336 bushels) and by each landlord:

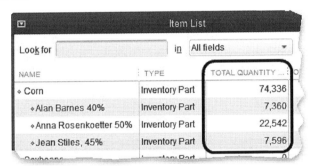

However, the Item List does not give her a *total* for the entire inventory of corn—all bushels in storage—for John Doe Farms and for the landlords, combined. A QuickReport 185 for the Corn Item would provide a total but would also list all of the transactions involved. When Mary just wants a total, without transactions, she opens an Inventory Stock Status by Item report (Reports > Inventory > Inventory Stock Status by Item):

295

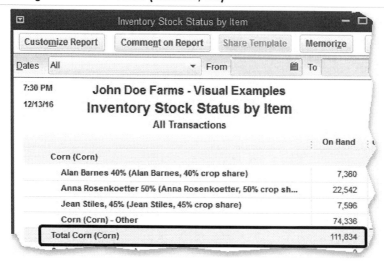

# Entering Sales of Landlord Inventories

## Landlord/Tenant Joint Sales

When a crop-share landlord puts John in charge of marketing their part of the corn crop, he considers each load sold to be partly owned by him and partly by the landlord. That way they each receive the same corn price—an assurance for the landlord that John is working hard to get a good price for the landlord's corn. When John makes a sale he has the buyer split the payment between the landlord and John Doe Farms according to their shares of the crop and mail a separate check to each party. Here is how Mary enters a sale in QuickBooks:

# Entering Sales of Landlord Inventories

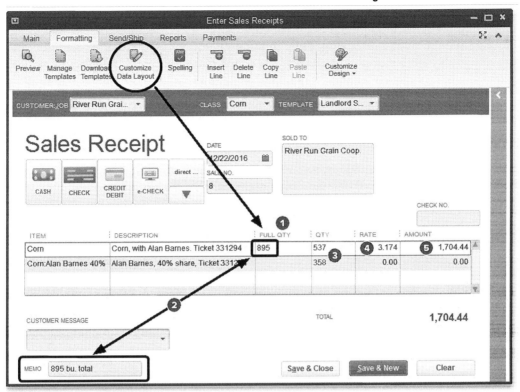

**1** **Full Qty** is an optional column added to the form—not a standard column of the Sales Receipts form. Mary added it by customizing the form (**Formatting > Customize Data Layout**). It provides a place in the form's detail area where she can enter the total bushels sold—which are split into 60/40 shares in the Qty (quantity) column.

**2** **Memo.** If a Full Qty column is not added to the form, the total quantity sold should be entered somewhere else, such as in the Memo field. (Having it in both places is not necessary.)

**3** **Qty.** These numbers in this column are shares of the 895 bushel total—60 percent for John Doe Farms, and 40 percent for Alan Barnes.

**4** **Rate (price).** Mary enters the quantity (Qty) and Amount and lets QuickBooks calculate the Rate, because after discounts and fees the net price received may not be an exact dollars-and-cents amount, as shown here. (The amount is not evenly divisible by the quantity.) Mary enters the Amount directly, to assure that it matches the payment amount.

**⑤ Amount.** *Only* the lines representing corn sold by John Doe Farms should have a non-zero Amount. Mary does not track the dollar amount of landlord sales (though she does track the quantities they sell).

## Landlord-Only Sales

Every load of grain hauled away from the farm is weighed before leaving, and that includes loads hauled out for landlords who market their own grain. Having weights lets Mary enter those loads in QuickBooks as if they were sales, to keep track of each landlord's inventory.

Landlord inventory changes like these can be recorded with an inventory adjustment 97, or with a sales receipt entered for a zero dollar amount. Some accountants would argue that sales receipts should only be used for recording sales made by the farm business, not sales made by others. But that concern is unwarranted. So long as they are entered for a $0 amount, sales receipts are a good way to enter sales made by landlords, partly because they make intuitive sense: the corn is hauled away and sold, so it makes sense to enter it as a sale. (However, the choice of whether to use an inventory adjustment or a sales receipt is yours.)

Here is a zero-dollar sales receipt (Customers > Enter Sales Receipts) Mary entered for corn sold by a landlord, Jean Stiles:

### Entering Sales of Landlord Inventories

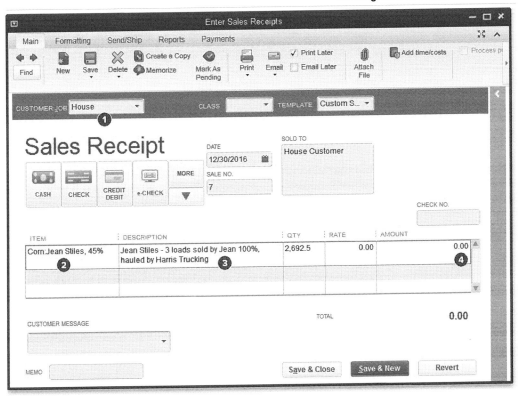

① **Customer:Job** should not be an actual customer, because this is not an actual sale. *House* is a bogus customer, set up to use for in-house transactions such as this.

② **Item** should be the landlord's inventory Item.

③ **Description.** One advantage of using sales receipts is that they let you document the reason for the inventory change, in the Description field on each line. This gives you more transaction detail in reports, without the need to "drill down" in a report to the originating transaction.

④ **Amount.** The Amount *must* be $0, to avoid any appearance of a financial tie between the farm business and the landlord.

🔧 **For safety, the subtems used for landlord inventories** 289 are set up to post income to an equity account. That prevents landlord sales from posting income for the farm business even if the Amount would happen to be non-zero. However, entering the sale of a landlord's corn for a non-zero amount would still cause problems: the sales receipt's total would post to Undeposited Funds 176, where it would be available to include (incorrectly!) in a bank deposit.

(In case you are wondering, yes, $0 sales receipts also post to Undeposited Funds. But QuickBooks does not make $0 amounts available to deposit, so it does not cause any problems.)

# "Settling up" with Landlords After Sales are Completed

Rarely do the total bushels of sales for a landlord exactly match the landlord's inventory quantity in QuickBooks. The last truckload sold for a particular landlord may have more or fewer bushels on it than the landlord is due. Usually, either John Doe Farms or the landlord writes a check to the other, to settle up for the difference.

There are two things to keep in mind when settling up with a landlord:

- ❖ **QuickBooks inventories** need to be updated properly to close out (zero out) the landlords' inventory. Usually that requires adjusting the farm's inventories too.

- ❖ **Corn sales income** for the farm business may be affected and may also have to be adjusted.

The following examples show how to handle both considerations, in different situations.

## Landlord was Overpaid, and Reimburses John Doe Farms

Often the last load of corn sold jointly [298] with a landlord is larger than would have been necessary to close out the landlord's inventory. When that is the case, and the buyer splits the payment based on crop shares, the landlord will be paid for more bushels than he or she was due (more bushels than he or she actually owned). When that happens, the landlord reimburses John Doe Farms for the extra bushels.

When Mary receives the payment for the load of corn she enters it on a sales receipt as shown before [298], with bushels divided between John Doe Farms and the landlord based on their shares of the crop (because that is how the buyer split the payment). However, this means more bushels will be removed from the landlord's inventory than he or she actually owned, making the landlord's inventory negative in QuickBooks. The sales receipt will have removed the correct *total* number of bushels from inventory, but in the wrong proportions for the landlord and for John Doe Farms. When the landlord's reimbursement is entered, it needs to correct the inventories for the landlord and for John Doe Farms.

Let's say the landlord's payment from the grain buyer was for 16 bushels more than the landlord was due, leaving her with a -16 (*negative* 16) bushel inventory in QuickBooks. When the landlord's check is entered, to reimburse for these bushels, the transaction needs to *increase* the landlord's inventory by 16 bushels (to make it 0), and *decrease* the inventory for John Doe Farms—so the total corn inventory will stay the same. All of this can be accomplished on the sales receipt (Customers > Enter Sales Receipts) which records the landlord's reimbursement:

# Chapter 12 - Tracking Inventories for Others (Landlords, etc.)

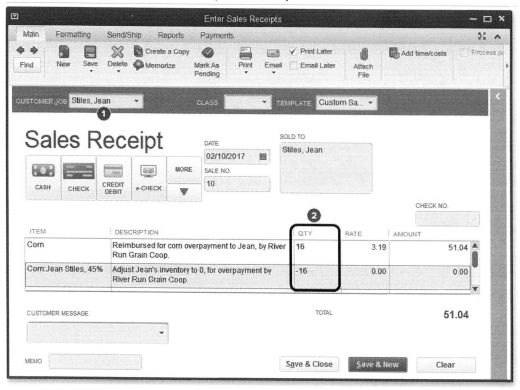

① **Customer:Job** should identify the landlord from whom the reimbursement was received.

② **Qty.** A sales receipt's effect on inventory quantities is opposite of the numbers you see in the Qty (quantity) column. The first Item line *decreases* Corn inventory by 16 bushels, and the second line *increases* the inventory for Corn:Jean Stiles, 45% by 16 bushels. This sales receipt will leave total corn inventories unchanged, but Jean Stiles' inventory will be zero, as it should be.

# Landlord was Underpaid, John Doe Farms Buys the Landlord's Remaining Inventory

After selling most of a landlord's crop, a small quantity—less than a truckload—may remain. When that is the case, Mary Doe usually just settles up with the the landlord by buying out his or her remaining inventory at the current market price. This simplifies things for Mary—she doesn't have to dabble with selling a small quantity for the landlord as part of a larger sale—and most landlords like having all of their corn sales completed for the year.

Buying out a landlord's corn is not as straightforward as you might expect. Raised inventory Items used for cash basis inventories are set up in a nonstandard way [80]. Because of this, *they cannot be used to record purchases!* (Actually they can be, but the job is convoluted and not at all intuitive.) A secondary reason is that, from a tax accounting standpoint, purchasing a landlord's corn is technically a purchase of corn for resale (assuming the corn will be sold later).

## Creating a resale corn Item

The simplest solution is to have an Item set up specifically for purchases of resale corn. Here is a the Inventory Part Item Mary has set up for purchases of landlords' corn inventories:

Chapter 12 - Tracking Inventories for Others (Landlords, etc.)

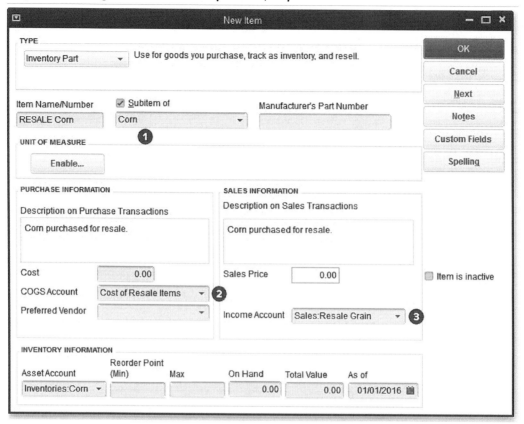

① **Subitem of.** *Optional,* but making the resale Item a subitem of Corn means resale corn inventories will be included in total corn inventories on reports.

② **COGS Account.** Unlike Items for raised inventories, the account you select here *actually should be a COGS-type account* (either that, or a contra-income account). That way, when you enter a sale of resale corn QuickBooks will automatically record its purchase cost as expense (normally reported on IRS Form 1040 Schedule F, line 1b: "Cost or other basis of livestock or other items...").

③ **Income Account.** Select an income account to use for recording income from the sale of resale items. It *should not* be the same income account you use for raised items, because sales of resale items are reported separately on income tax

## "Settling up" with Landlords After Sales are Completed

forms. (On IRS Form 1040 Schedule F they are reported on line 1a: "Sales of livestock and other resale items".)

Here is the resale Item as it appears in the Item List (Lists > Item List):

Chapter 12 - Tracking Inventories for Others (Landlords, etc.)

## Entering a check to purchase the landlord's corn

Near the end of the crop marketing year Anna Rosenkoetter had 104 bushels of corn left in inventory. Here is the check (Banking > Write Checks) Mary issued to Anna to buy out her inventory:

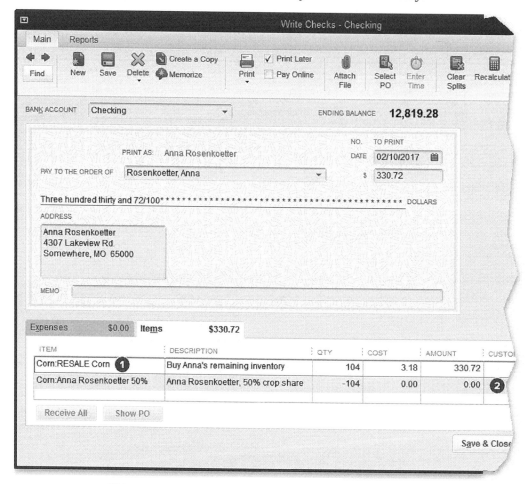

① **The first line** records the purchase of resale corn.

② **The second line** reduces Anna's inventory to zero, and has a $0 Amount so it does not affect the amount of the check. (The same thing could be be accomplished with an inventory adjustment. If you prefer, you can omit the second line of the

## "Settling up" with Landlords After Sales are Completed

check and make a separate inventory adjustment to reduce Anna's inventory to zero.)

Here is an Inventory Stock Status by Item report (**Reports > Inventory > Inventory Stock Status by Item**) which shows how the check affected inventories for Anna and for the RESALE Corn Item:

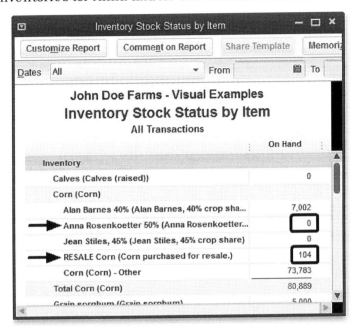

## Selling resale corn

Mary doesn't really buy much corn to resell; she does it mostly as a service to landlords. To avoid having small inventories of resale corn on the books she usually tries to get rid of them the next time she enters a corn sale. That is simple to do: she just sells the current inventory of resale corn as part of the sale. Here is a sales receipt (**Customers > Enter Sales Receipts**) showing how:

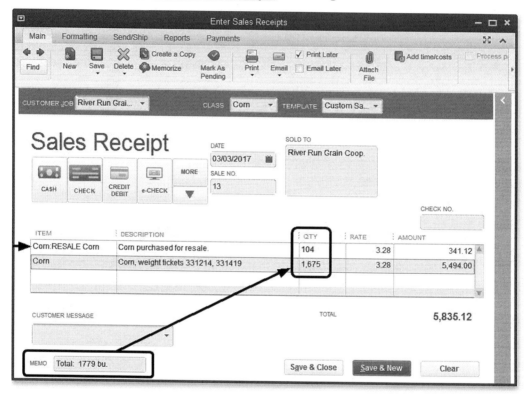

# Getting Inventory Reports and Information

The Item List window shows inventory quantities for all landlords, and for John Doe Farms:

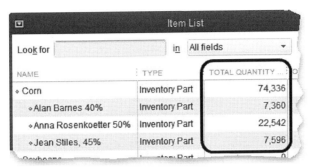

You can get a QuickReport to see transactions for any Item, for whatever date range you select. In the Item List (**Lists > Item List**), click on the Item to select it, then type *Ctrl-Q* to open a QuickReport. Here is one for Alan Barnes, for the month of December, 2016:

## Chapter 12 - Tracking Inventories for Others (Landlords, etc.)

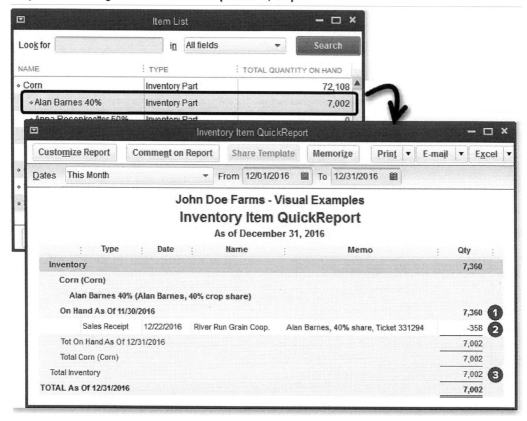

1. **On Hand.** This line shows inventories as of the beginning date of the report.

2. **The period's transactions** are listed in the center section of the report. This example has one transaction, a corn sale.

3. **Summary lines** show that Alan's corn inventory was 7,002 bushels at the end of December 2016.

A QuickReport is handy for mailing or emailing to a landlord, if you need to communicate about specific corn sales, transaction quantities, or current inventories.

**CHAPTER 13**

# Appendix

## Other Books from Flagship Technologies

Other titles in the QuickBooks Cookbook™ series are available from Flagship Technologies, Inc. Visit us on the Web at
 www.goflagship.com.

### The QuickBooks Farm Accounting Cookbook™, Volume I: QuickBooks Basics, Income & Expenses, and More...

***The QuickBooks Farm Accounting Cookbook™, Volume I***, by Mark Wilsdorf, is a 370-page book written for QuickBooks users in agriculture. This step-by-step guide and reference is written specifically for farmers and ranchers, and provides information about setting up QuickBooks for a farm business (Accounts, Classes, Lists, etc.) plus loads of transaction examples—all of them agricultural! It is called a "cookbook" because of its recipe-like approach to dealing with agricultural accounting topics and problems.

Volume I is a sister publication of the book you are reading right now.

***On the Web:***  www.goflagship.com/cbk.html

Chapter 13 - Appendix

# Online Banking, Transaction Downloading, and Online Bill Payment in QuickBooks

***Online Banking, Transaction Downloading, and Online Bill Payment in QuickBooks*** is a 105-page book about using online financial services in QuickBooks desktop editions. Written for people who use QuickBooks day-to-day in a small business, it guides readers through setting up and using online banking and other online financial services with step-by-step procedures and abundant screenshots.

***On the Web:*** www.goflagship.com/onl.html

# Software Products from Flagship Technologies

Here are QuickBooks add-on software products available from Flagship Technologies, Inc.

**ManagePLUS Gold for QuickBooks** is a QuickBooks add-on program for gleaning management information from any set of QuickBooks accounting records, especially where the Classes feature of QuickBooks is used.

ManagePLUS Gold gives you reports with per-unit revenue and cost information...things like fuel and maintenance costs per mile driven by trucks in a fleet, materials costs per unit of production in a fact-ory, herbicide and fertilizer cost per acre or per bushel of corn production, and so on. The expanded quantity handling and Class reporting it offers are not available in any other QuickBooks add-on.

ManagePLUS Gold's cost accounting and activity-based costing features give you an easy drag-and-drop way to allocate income and expenses to Classes identified as cost centers and profit centers of the business. It provides spreadsheet-based profit analysis reports for Classes, and can send allocation transactions directly to QuickBooks with a single mouse click.

ManagePLUS Gold works with these Microsoft Windows editions of QuickBooks:

   **U.S.:** Pro, Premier, and Enterprise editions.
   **UK:** Pro and Premier editions.
   **Canadian:** Pro and Premier editions.

A **30-day free trial** is a free download from our Web site.

**ManagePLUS Gold on the Web:** www.goflagship.com/mp.html

**ManagePLUS Gold is also listed** on Intuit's QuickBooks desktop add-ons site: desktop.apps.com.

# FormCalc SST
## for QuickBooks

**FormCalc SST for QuickBooks** is the "newer, stronger brother" of the older FormCalc product (described below). FormCalc SST is a QuickBooks add-on which gives you calculated columns, column totals and subtotals, statistical functions, text handling, IF logic, and a lot more on your QuickBooks forms: Invoices, Sales Receipts, Estimates, and others—any form where Items are used.

FormCalc SST lets you set up calculations in its internal Excel-compatible spreadsheet, then applies your calculations "on the fly" to your QuickBooks forms. Our customers use it for calculating shipping weights on invoices, box and pallet counts, area calculations on customer orders (yards of fabric, board-feet of lumber, etc.), quantity totals for alcohol taxation recordkeeping requirements, and much more.

FormCalc SST works with <u>nearly all</u> Microsoft Windows versions of QuickBooks desktop editions (Pro, Premier, Enterprise), *including most older versions and most non-U.S. versions:* **US, UK, Canadian, and Australian.** FormCalc SST also works in hosted QuickBooks environments, and in fact is certified to run on **Right Networks hosting**—one of the most popular QuickBooks hosting services.

A **30-day free trial** is a free download from our Web site.

**FormCalc SST on the Web:** www.goflagship.com/sst.html

**for QuickBooks**

**FormCalc for QuickBooks** is an add-on that gives you calculated columns, column totals and subtotals, unique-item counts, and much more on your QuickBooks forms, such as Invoices, Sales Receipts, Estimates, and others—any form where Items are used.

*FormCalc is an older product than FormCalc SST (described above). It does fewer calculations but is simpler to set up for basic needs.*

Our customers use it for calculating shipping weights on invoices, box and pallet counts, area calculations (yards of fabric, board-feet of lumber, etc.), quantity totals for meeting alcohol taxation recordkeeping requirements, and more.

FormCalc works with <u>nearly all</u> Microsoft Windows versions of QuickBooks desktop editions (Pro, Premier, Enterprise), *including most older versions and most non-U.S. versions:* **US, UK, Canadian, and Australian.**

A **30-day free trial** is a free download from our Web site.

**FormCalc on the Web:** www.goflagship.com/fc.html

Software Products from Flagship Technologies

# FULLSPEED
## The macro calculator

**FullSpeed** is an add-on for QuickBooks Online and the QuickBooks desktop editions. Like our FormCalc and FormCalc SST products, it can give you calculated columns, column totals and subtotals, and more...but it is designed to work in QuickBooks Online and other Web browser-based accounting products.

FullSpeed works with QuickBooks Online, Xero, and <u>nearly all</u> Microsoft Windows versions of the QuickBooks desktop editions (Pro, Premier, Enterprise). *It also works with older versions and most non-U.S. versions:* **US, UK, Canadian, and Australian.**

A **30-day free trial** is a free download from our Web site.

**FullSpeed on the Web:** www.goflagship.com/fsp.html

# Catch Weights™ for QuickBooks

**Catch Weights** is an add-on for QuickBooks users in the meat, seafood, and food wholesaling industries. It allows entering a list of catch weights—multiple individual weights—for any line of a QuickBooks Invoice or Sales Receipt, then writes the total weight in the Quantity column and adds the list of individual weights to the Description column.

Catch Weights works with <u>nearly all</u> Microsoft Windows versions of QuickBooks desktop editions (Pro, Premier, Enterprise), *including most older versions and most non-U.S. versions:* **US, UK, Canadian, and Australian!**

A **30-day free trial** is a free download from our Web site.

**Catch Weights on the Web:** www.goflagship.com/cwts.html

This page is intentionally blank.

# Index

## 1
**1099-PATR** . . . . . . . . . . . . . . . . . . . . . . . . 115

## A
**accounting**
  double-entry, and inventory adjustments . . . . . . . . . . . . . 128
  equation, the . . . . . . . . . . . . . . . . . . . . . . . . 128
**Accounting 101**
  Capitalized inventory . . . . . . . . . . . . . . . . . . . . . 18
  Cost of Goods Sold . . . . . . . . . . . . . . . . . . . . . . 21
  Double-entry accounting and inventory adjustments . . . . . . . 128
  Lower of Cost or Market rule . . . . . . . . . . . . . . . . . 151
  Perpetual vs. periodic inventories . . . . . . . . . . . . . . . 92
  Problem with the Inventory Part Item type . . . . . . . . . . . 155
  Using invoices for outstanding sales . . . . . . . . . . . . . . 122
  Why use multiple invoices? . . . . . . . . . . . . . . . . . . 232
**accounts**
  asset . . . . . . . . . . . . . . . . . . . . . . . . . . . . . 62
  asset (in Item setup) . . . . . . . . . . . . . . . . . . . . . 83
  Capitalized Inventory . . . . . . . . . . . . . . . . . . . . . 65
  chart of accounts . . . . . . . . . . . . . . . . . . . . . . . 67
  equity (Capitalized Inventory) . . . . . . . . . . . . . . . . . 65
  offsetting, described . . . . . . . . . . . . . . . . . . . . . 17
  register windows for . . . . . . . . . . . . . . . . . . . . . 128
  used in this book . . . . . . . . . . . . . . . . . . . . . . . 67
**advance payments**
  on sales contracts . . . . . . . . . . . . . . . . . . . . . . . 240

## B
**balance sheet**
  valuing raised inventories for . . . . . . . . . . . . . . . . . 153
**basis contracts** . . . . . . . . . . . . . . . . . . . . . 270, 271
**basis later contracts** . . . . . . . . . . . . . . . . . . . . 273

## C
**Capitalized Inventory**
  account . . . . . . . . . . . . . . . . . . . . . . . . . . . . 65
  Item . . . . . . . . . . . . . . . . . . . . . . . . . . . . . . 85
**cash advance**
  on basis contract . . . . . . . . . . . . . . . . . . . . . . . 271
**cash basis**
  income tax report, preparing an . . . . . . . . . . . . . . . . 196
  reports, how to prepare . . . . . . . . . . . . . . . . . . . . 22
**cash sale**
  defined . . . . . . . . . . . . . . . . . . . . . . . . . . . . 111
**cash sale contracts**
  using Jobs for . . . . . . . . . . . . . . . . . . . . . . . . . 218
**Catch Weights for QuickBooks** . . . . . . . . . . . . . . . 315
**charity**
  gifting inventory to . . . . . . . . . . . . . . . . . . . . . . 172
**chart of accounts reference** . . . . . . . . . . . . . . . . . 67
**checkoff**
  corn . . . . . . . . . . . . . . . . . . . . . . . . . . . . . 113
**Classes**
  enabling in QuickBooks . . . . . . . . . . . . . . . . . . . 139
  how to set up . . . . . . . . . . . . . . . . . . . . . . . . 138
**closeout**
  contract, defined . . . . . . . . . . . . . . . . . . . . . . . 250
  of a sales contract . . . . . . . . . . . . . . . . . . . . . . 262
**contracts**
  advance on . . . . . . . . . . . . . . . . . . . . . . . . . 240
  basis . . . . . . . . . . . . . . . . . . . . . . . . . . . . . 270
  basis later . . . . . . . . . . . . . . . . . . . . . . . . . . 273
  basis, cash advance on . . . . . . . . . . . . . . . . . . . . 271
  below the line charges . . . . . . . . . . . . . . . . . . . . 259
  closeout . . . . . . . . . . . . . . . . . . . . . . . . . . . 262
  closeout of . . . . . . . . . . . . . . . . . . . . . . . . . 250
  defined . . . . . . . . . . . . . . . . . . . . . . . . . . . 259
  delayed-payment . . . . . . . . . . . . . . . . . . . . . . 272
  final invoice . . . . . . . . . . . . . . . . . . . . . . . . . 256
  hedge-to-arrive . . . . . . . . . . . . . . . . . . . . . . . 273
  inactive, hiding . . . . . . . . . . . . . . . . . . . . . . . 266
  minimum-price . . . . . . . . . . . . . . . . . . . . . . . 273
  premium cost . . . . . . . . . . . . . . . . . . . . . . . . 273
  price-later . . . . . . . . . . . . . . . . . . . . . . . . . . 272
  progress payment on . . . . . . . . . . . . . . . . . . . . 240
  services fees, entering . . . . . . . . . . . . . . . . . . . . 272
  settlement of, defined . . . . . . . . . . . . . . . . . . . . 250

## Index

**contracts**
    shortage . . . . . . . . . . . . . . . . . . . . . . . . . . 267
    using subitems to represent . . . . . . . . . . . . . . . 274

**cooperatives**
    per-unit retains income . . . . . . . . . . . . . . . . . . 115

**Cost of Goods Sold (COGS)**
    COGS field, in Item setup . . . . . . . . . . . . . . . . . 83
    explained . . . . . . . . . . . . . . . . . . . . . . . . . . 21
    in Item setup . . . . . . . . . . . . . . . . . . . . . . . . 83

**credit sale**
    defined . . . . . . . . . . . . . . . . . . . . . . . . . . 111

**Customer:Jobs**
    in inventory adjustment entries . . . . . . . . . . . . . 144
    using for cash sale contracts . . . . . . . . . . . . . . 218

## D

**delayed-payment contracts**    272

**Deposit To field**
    Preference setting for. . . . . . . . . . . . . . . . . . . 176

**deposits**
    entering income directly on . . . . . . . . . . . . . . . 179
    of received payments . . . . . . . . . . . . . . . 175, 175
    online banking and . . . . . . . . . . . . . . . . . . . . 180
    Undeposited Funds. . . . . . . . . . . . . . . . . . . . 175
    vs. Sales Receipts . . . . . . . . . . . . . . . . . . . . . 179

**discounts**
    grain moisture . . . . . . . . . . . . . . . . . . . . . . . 236
    grain quality . . . . . . . . . . . . . . . . . . . . . . . . 236
    grain, weight-for-weight . . . . . . . . . . . . . . . . . 237

**Domestic Production Activities Deduction (DPAD)**    260

## E

**examples**
    corn feed usage report . . . . . . . . . . . . . . . . . 137
    corn used as feed, adjusting for . . . . . . . . . . . . 135
    grain sorghum value loss (spoilage). . . . . . . . . . 132
    livestock death loss (calves). . . . . . . . . . . . . . . 129
    simple inventory . . . . . . . . . . . . . . . . . . . . . . . 8

**expense-related inventories**    16

## F

**Finished Goods inventory**    152, 155

**Fixed Asset Item type**
    vs. other types . . . . . . . . . . . . . . . . . . . . . . 161

**fixed assets**
    economic valuation . . . . . . . . . . . . . . . . . . . 167
    income tax basis. . . . . . . . . . . . . . . . . . . . . . 167
    Inventory Part Items for . . . . . . . . . . . . . . . . . 167
    market value . . . . . . . . . . . . . . . . . . . . . . . 167

**FormCalc for QuickBooks**    314
**FormCalc SST for QuickBooks**    313
**FullSpeed**    315

## G

**gifting**
    inventory . . . . . . . . . . . . . . . . . . . . . . . . . 172
    inventory to a charity. . . . . . . . . . . . . . . . . . . 172

**grain**
    moisture discounts. . . . . . . . . . . . . . . . . . . . 236
    quality discounts. . . . . . . . . . . . . . . . . . . . . 236
    weight-for-weight discounts . . . . . . . . . . . . . . 237

**growing crop**
    valuing . . . . . . . . . . . . . . . . . . . . . . . . . . 152

## H

**hedge-to-arrive contracts**    273

## I

**income tax**
    basis of fixed assets . . . . . . . . . . . . . . . . . . . 167

**inventories**
    adjusting after sales were made. . . . . . . . . . . . 119
    adjusting for farm production. . . . . . . . . . . . . . 124
    adjusting for usage. . . . . . . . . . . . . . . . . . . . 135
    expense-related. . . . . . . . . . . . . . . . . . . . 16, 26
    insufficient quantity to sell. . . . . . . . . . . . . . . . 117
    insufficient quantity warning. . . . . . . . . . . . . . . 118
    moving among stages of production . . . . . . . . . 168
    negative, warnings about . . . . . . . . . . . . . . . . 117

# Index

**inventories**
- perpetual vs. periodic . . . . . . . . . . . . . . . . . . . 92
- raised . . . . . . . . . . . . . . . . . . . . . . . . . . . . . . 15
- resale . . . . . . . . . . . . . . . . . . . . . . . . . . . . . 15
- sales-related . . . . . . . . . . . . . . . . . . . . . . . . 15
- simple example . . . . . . . . . . . . . . . . . . . . . . . 8
- tracking by location . . . . . . . . . . . . . . . . . . 199
- usage records . . . . . . . . . . . . . . . . . . . . . . 137
- usage reports . . . . . . . . . . . . . . . . . . . . . . 137
- valuing for the balance sheet . . . . . . . . . . . 153

**inventory**
- Finished Goods . . . . . . . . . . . . . . . . . 152, 155
- gifting . . . . . . . . . . . . . . . . . . . . . . . . . . . 172
- growing crop . . . . . . . . . . . . . . . . . . . . . . 152
- losses, adjusting for . . . . . . . . . . . . . . . . . 129
- pre-harvest, adjusting . . . . . . . . . . . . . . . . . 38
- resale, defined . . . . . . . . . . . . . . . . . . . . . 23
- sale, effects of . . . . . . . . . . . . . . . . . . . . . 115
- shrinkage . . . . . . . . . . . . . . . . . . . . . . . . 129
- Work In Process (WIP) . . . . . . . . . . . . 152, 155

**inventory adjustments**
- after harvest . . . . . . . . . . . . . . . . . . . . . . . 40
- and double-entry accounting . . . . . . . . . . . 128
- deleting . . . . . . . . . . . . . . . . . . . . . . . . . 110
- effects of . . . . . . . . . . . . . . . . . . . . . . . . 127
- for livestock deaths . . . . . . . . . . . . . . . . . 129
- for loss . . . . . . . . . . . . . . . . . . . . . . . . . 132
- steps for making . . . . . . . . . . . . . . . . . . . . 98

**Inventory Part Items**
- resale inventories and . . . . . . . . . . . . . . . . 24
- vs. Non-inventory Part . . . . . . . . . . . . . . . . 72
- why use . . . . . . . . . . . . . . . . . . . . . . . . . 72

**invoices**
- in cash basis accounting . . . . . . . . . . . . . . 122
- multiple vs. single . . . . . . . . . . . . . . . . . . 232
- reasons for using . . . . . . . . . . . . . . . . . . 122
- reconciling to settlement sheet . . . . . . . . . . 261

**Item List** 183
- customizing columns in . . . . . . . . . . . . . . 183
- organizing . . . . . . . . . . . . . . . . . . . . . . . . 77

**Items**
- adding new . . . . . . . . . . . . . . . . . . . . . . 103
- asset account for . . . . . . . . . . . . . . . . . . . 83
- Capitalized Inventory . . . . . . . . . . . . . . . . . 85
- changing the type of . . . . . . . . . . . . . . . . . 74
- changing type of . . . . . . . . . . . . . . . . . . . . 73
- Corn Checkoff . . . . . . . . . . . . . . . . . . . . . 88
- DamageDiscount . . . . . . . . . . . . . . . . . . . . 87
- defined . . . . . . . . . . . . . . . . . . . . . . . . . . 68
- Feed Corn . . . . . . . . . . . . . . . . . . . . . . . 158
- Fixed Asset Item type . . . . . . . . . . . . . . . . 161
- for fixed assets . . . . . . . . . . . . . . . . . . . . 167
- Inventory Part (why use) . . . . . . . . . . . . . . . 72
- moving inventories among . . . . . . . . . . . . 168
- raised inventory, setting up . . . . . . . . . . . . . 81
- reusing . . . . . . . . . . . . . . . . . . . . . . . . . . 74
- selecting . . . . . . . . . . . . . . . . . . . . . . . . 101
- Storage Fees . . . . . . . . . . . . . . . . . . . . . . 89

# J

**Jobs**
- hiding . . . . . . . . . . . . . . . . . . . . . . . . . . 266
- making inactive . . . . . . . . . . . . . . . . . . . 266
- using for cash sale contracts . . . . . . . . . . . 218

# L

**livestock**
- death loss, adjusting for . . . . . . . . . . . . . . 129
- raised, for personal consumption . . . . . . . . 173

**locations**
- storage, contract delivery and . . . . . . . . . . 238
- tracking inventories for . . . . . . . . . . . . . . 199

**losses**
- from inventory, adjusting for . . . . . . . . . . . 129
- grain quality, adjusting for . . . . . . . . . . . . 132

**Lower of Cost or Market (LCM)**
- raised inventories and . . . . . . . . . . . . . . . 150

# M

**ManagePLUS Gold for QuickBooks**  312
**market value**

**319**

## Index

**market value**
    net market value defined . . . . . . . . . . . . . . . . . . . . . . 152
    of fixed assets . . . . . . . . . . . . . . . . . . . . . . . . . . . . . . 167
**minimum-price contract**    273
**moisture**
    discount for . . . . . . . . . . . . . . . . . . . . . . . . . . . . . . . 236

### N

**net market value**    152
**net realizable value**    151

### O

**offsetting account**
    described . . . . . . . . . . . . . . . . . . . . . . . . . . . . . . . . 17
**online banking**
    deposit entries and. . . . . . . . . . . . . . . . . . . . . . . . . . 180
**outstanding sales**
    tracking with invoices . . . . . . . . . . . . . . . . . . . . . . . . 122

### P

**paper records of inventory usage**    137
**payments**
    depositing. . . . . . . . . . . . . . . . . . . . . . . . . . . 175, 175
    receiving on invoices. . . . . . . . . . . . . . . . . . . . . . . . 263
**periodic inventories**    92
**perpetual inventories**    92
**per-unit retains**    115
**Preferences (QuickBooks)**
    Not enough inventory to sell. . . . . . . . . . . . . . . . . . . . 118
    Prompt to assign Classes. . . . . . . . . . . . . . . . . . . . . . 139
    Quantity on Sales Orders. . . . . . . . . . . . . . . . . 224, 248
    Undeposited Funds as default . . . . . . . . . . . . . . . . . . 116
    Undeposited Funds as default deposit account . . . . . . . . 176
    Use Class tracking . . . . . . . . . . . . . . . . . . . . . . . . . 139
    use Undeposited Funds as default. . . . . . . . . . . . . . . . 177
**price-later contracts**    272
**production**
    adjusting inventories for. . . . . . . . . . . . . . . . . . . . . . 124
    estimating from inventories. . . . . . . . . . . . . . . . . . . . . 41
    moving inventories of . . . . . . . . . . . . . . . . . . . . . . . 168
    multiple stages of . . . . . . . . . . . . . . . . . . . . . . . . . 168
**progress payment**
    contract . . . . . . . . . . . . . . . . . . . . . . . . . . . . . . 240

### Q

**quality loss**
    grain, adjusting for. . . . . . . . . . . . . . . . . . . . . . . . . 132
**quantities**
    "in limbo" for inventory adjustments . . . . . . . . . . . . . . 120
    delivered but not paid for . . . . . . . . . . . . . . . . . . . . 120
**QuickReport**
    corn, example . . . . . . . . . . . . . . . . . . . . . . . . . . . 185
    filtering by Class. . . . . . . . . . . . . . . . . . . . . . . . . . 141

### R

**Receive Payments form**
    Deposit To field . . . . . . . . . . . . . . . . . . . . . . . . . . 176
**receiving payment**
    on invoices . . . . . . . . . . . . . . . . . . . . . . . . . . . . 263
**Register window**
    how to open . . . . . . . . . . . . . . . . . . . . . . . . . . . 128
**reports**
    cash basis, how to prepare. . . . . . . . . . . . . . . . . . . . . 22
    filtering by Class. . . . . . . . . . . . . . . . . . . . . . . . . . 141
    filtering by name. . . . . . . . . . . . . . . . . . . . . . . . . . 246
    income tax, cash basis. . . . . . . . . . . . . . . . . . . . . . 196
    Inventory Stock Status by Item. . . . . . . . . . . . . . . . . . 189
    inventory usage (as feed) . . . . . . . . . . . . . . . . . . . . 137
    Inventory Valuation . . . . . . . . . . . . . . . . . . . . . . . . 190
    memorizing . . . . . . . . . . . . . . . . . . . . . . . . . . . . 191
    QuickReport, Item . . . . . . . . . . . . . . . . . . . . . . . . 185
    Sales by Customer. . . . . . . . . . . . . . . . . . . . . . . . . 193
    Sales by Customer Detail . . . . . . . . . . . . . . . . . . . . 253
    Sales by Item . . . . . . . . . . . . . . . . . . . . . . . . . . . 192
**resale inventory**
    accounting for . . . . . . . . . . . . . . . . . . . . . . . . . . . 24
    defined . . . . . . . . . . . . . . . . . . . . . . . . . . . . . . . 23
    examples . . . . . . . . . . . . . . . . . . . . . . . . . . . . . . 23

# Index

## S

**sales**
    cash, defined .......................... 111
    credit, defined ......................... 111
    entering before adjusting inventories .............. 119

**Sales by Customer Detail report**
    filtering ........................... 253

**sales contracts**
    entering deliveries on ...................... 227

**sales orders**
    converting to invoices ..................... 227

**Sales Receipts form**
    Deposit To field ........................ 176

**selling fees**
    entering separately. ...................... 114

**services fees**
    contract, entering. ....................... 272

**settlement sheet**
    example ........................... 250
    reconciling to invoices. .................... 261

**shortage**
    sales contract ......................... 267

**storage fees** 114
    entering separately. ...................... 114

**subitems** 77
    cash contracts and ....................... 274
    location, and contract delivery. ................ 238

## U

**Undeposited Funds account**
    depositing funds from ..................... 175
    deposits and ......................... 176
    Preference setting for. ..................... 176
    why you should use ...................... 176

## W

**Work In Process inventory**      152, 155

Made in the USA
San Bernardino, CA
28 January 2017